D1238067

KEEP YOUR GEAR RUNNING

ELECTRONICS FOR MUSICIANS

BY PATRICK L. McKEEN

New York / London / Paris / Sydney / Tokyo / Berlin / Copenhagen / Madrid

Schirmer Trade Books
A Division of Music Sales Corporation, New York

Exclusive Distributors:
Music Sales Corporation
257 Park Avenue South, New York, NY 10010 USA
Music Sales Limited
8/9 Frth Street, London W1D 3JB England
Music Sales Pty. Limited
120 Rothschild Street, Rosebery, Sydney, NSW 2018, Australia

Order No. SCH 10142
International Standard Book Number: 0-8256-7302.X

Printed in the United States of America
By Vicks Lithograph and Printing Corporation

Library of Congress Cataloging-in-Publication Data
McKeen, Patrick L.
  Keep your gear running : electronics for musicians / by Patrick L. McKeen.
     p. cm.
  Includes bibliographical references and index.
  ISBN 0-8256-7302-X (pbk. : alk. paper)
  1. Electronic musical instruments—Maintenance and repair. I. Title.
  ML1092.M4 2004
  786.7'192—dc22
                        2004002483

CONTENTS

ACKNOWLEDGMENTS

Thanks to Nick Robinson, my boss at my first electronics repair job, for checking my text for glaring errors and for teaching me more about electronics in my first two weeks on the job than I learned in two years at tech school; Gayle Adams, for technical assistance; friends and family, for encouragement; and the Internet, for supplying free advice and information at all hours of the day or night.

CREDITS

Managing Editor: Andrea M. Rotondo
Technical Editor: Leonard Hospidor
Copyeditor: Barbara Schultz
Cover Design: Mike Bell
Production Director: Dan Earley
Interior Design: Len Vogler
Publicity Coordinator: Alison M. Wofford

DEDICATION

Dedicated to my wife, Kathleen: my biggest fan and my best critic.

ABOUT THE AUTHOR
or, who does this guy think he is, anyway?

Patrick L. McKeen is a musician first, an electronics repair technician second, and a writer last. Pat began playing guitar at age seven and still plays in local bands. When he was twenty-two years old, because he was tired of cleaning up other people's messes for a living, he decided to go back to school to learn electronics. He chose this field of study mostly because he wanted to know how to fix his own stuff, and so he could make his own guitar effects and design his own amplifiers. (Plus, it was a way to make a living that didn't require a suit and tie.)

He left the local community college in 1978 with a degree under his belt and landed his first job at a stereo repair shop. He worked there for seven years, while still playing in jazz and rock bands. In 1986, he went to work for a local music store, and as of this writing, he's still there. Over the years, he has seen trends develop and fade off—tubes have come in and out of style several times—and he has learned how to communicate with musicians about their gear. He still cleans up other people's messes, but they are a different kind, and now he enjoys it.

INTRODUCTION
or, a little knowledge is a dangerous thing.

This book is for every guitarist, bassist, keyboardist, electronic drummer, recording engineer, and soundtech who has ever thought, "I wish I knew more about how this stuff works." I've always felt that there was a need for a book that didn't talk down to musicians, but didn't talk way above their heads, either. As a musician and repair technician dealing with musicians and their broken stuff for many years, I've learned how to explain technical things in layman's terms, without making them overly simple or too complex. The purpose of this book is to help non-technical people deal with a technical world, particularly where music and electronics merge. I have always been a musician first and foremost. I found electronics repair was a great way to make a living so I could support my musical "habit," and I've been lucky enough to be moderately successful at both. Working with musicians on a day-to-day basis and remembering back when things like "impedance," "joules," "ohms," and "anode" were mysterious terms found in crossword puzzles and magazine articles, I understand how the technical side of things can overwhelm musicians and other non-technical folks (and sometimes, even tech-heads!). I'm hoping that this book will clarify some of the murky waters.

The purpose of this book is not to teach advanced electronics; just to offer a basis of knowledge. If you find the electronic theory in Chapter Three overwhelming, feel free to skip ahead to the next section. It is also not to help musicians work on their own gear. There are lots of books that tell you how to hot-rod your tube amps, but this isn't one of them. (We in the business love those books because of the business they bring in, when we're hired to un-modify them back to original condition.) The goal of this book is to teach practices that will help you prevent your gear from needing repair work. I explain technical jargon in a way that reduces confusion and increases understanding. I dispel a bunch of commonly held erroneous ideas. There's a chapter on terminology, another on speakers, and yet another about batteries. I don't claim to know everything, but I've been a performing musician most of my life, and I've owned lots (and repaired thousands) of P.A. systems, guitars, amps, effects, keyboards, recorders, etc. The information in this book is accurate to the best of my knowledge, based on my personal experience. It's not everything there is to know about any particular subject, but it is as much as I think most musical-equipment users need to know.

This book is about using electronic gear. Everyone knows that there is a right way and a wrong way (usually several wrong ways) to do anything. Avoiding the wrong ways can save lots of time, money, and frustration when the gear performs as it was meant to, rather than going bye-bye in a puff of smoke during a performance. Knowing the right way is helpful, but knowing why the right way is right and the wrong way is wrong helps it all make sense. Electronics are complicated, but they are not nearly as complicated once you know a few basics. Some of the basics are covered in the chapters about general electronics, impedance, speakers, and amps.

When I started electronics classes, I was afraid I wouldn't be "smart" enough. I didn't like math, and I had heard that there was a lot of math involved. After a few classes, it became obvious that electronics were not as mystical and complicated as I had been led to believe. I even found out that, if you have a good teacher, math and electronics actually make sense. Don't get me wrong, there is an awful lot going on in there, but it's not as totally incomprehensible as you might think. Like anything else, half of knowing about something is knowing the terminology. If you have a computer, you remember how it felt the first time some techno-nerd started talking about "gigs" and "megs" and "bytes" and "skuzzy-ports" and "modems" and...Well, now you can talk tech with them because you know what the terminology means. You may not know what a "data bus" looks like or be able to open a computer and know where the power supply is located, but you don't need to know these things to use your computer. It's the same with electronic musical gear.

My hope is that this book will help clarify some of the less-understood aspects of using electronic music equipment. My goal is that when you finish this book, you'll know a lot more about how electronic music gear works, why it works the way it does, and how to keep it working properly.

Pat McKeen

PART 1

THE BUILDING BLOCKS

Chapter ONE

ELECTRONIC TERMS
or, just what are you trying to say?

To me, one of the hardest things about learning something new is getting the terminology down. You can't fix an automobile engine if you don't know what the parts are called: "Hello, Super-Duper Car Parts? Yeah, I've got a bad thingy on my car. What is it? Well, I got it right here...It's kinda cylindrical, and it's covered with grease. It hooks up to the thingamabob with the doohickies and gadgets and whatchmacallits in the front end under that flappy thing." Once the pertinent terms have been committed to memory, things get much easier and make much more sense. I usually have to hear new terms several times before I easily remember what they mean. That's why I put this chapter first. There are a whole bunch of technical terms in this book. Some are common enough that most people know what they mean. Others, only electronics geeks like me would know. Whenever one of these terms is used for the first time in the book, it will be **bold**. Any term that is bold will also be found, with its pronunciation and definition, in the glossary at the end of the book (except for the word "bold").

If you skip around the book, you may come across a term you don't recognize that isn't bold. Chances are it was used in a previous chapter and was highlighted there, and you should be able to find it in the glossary.

MISUSED TERMS

Some of the more universally recognized electronics terms are sometimes used incorrectly. An example of this is the word: **short.** If there is something causing one part of a circuit to connect to another part that isn't supposed to be connected, this is called a short circuit, or a short. If a part of the circuit that is supposed to be connected to another part becomes unconnected, this is called an **open** circuit, or an open. If you have a cable that only works part of the time, or it cuts in and out as it is moved, most people would say it "has a short in it." In reality, it has an intermittent open connection. The wire is broken and is interrupting the circuit. Most of the time when people use the term "short," they are actually describing an intermittent open. This is now so common that it has become an accepted generic term like Coke for cola, or Kleenex for facial tissue.

One term you will not find in this book except on this page, is the word "pod." Many people refer to the **controls** in an amp or guitar as "pods." There ain't no such thing, kids. The term that is being misused here is "pot," short for **potentiometer,** which is what those controls are really called. Pods have beans in them, or are the things that zombies hatch out of in old sci-fi movies. Just to make matters even more confusing, a prominent amplifier company has a line of effects processors called, you guessed it, PODs.

MATH

You won't find a lot of mathematics in this book, but there are a few math terms used. They are also explained in the glossary. Most simple electronic formulas are very basic **algebra**. Don't let that scare you. You use algebra any time you divide or multiply. The most basic algebraic function is shown by this little equation: $2 \times 3 = 6$. If we substitute letters for the numbers, it looks like this: $X \times Y = Z$. If X is 2 and Y is 3, then Z = 6. And if $X \times Y = Z$, then $Z \div X = Y$ ($6 \div 3 = 2$). It's that simple. The thing about this equation that makes it useful is the fact that, if you know any two of the variable numbers, you can find the third one. That is the extent of the math needed to understand the principles in this book. Some of the formulas in Appendix D require finding the square root of a number. Because many electronic calculators include this function, you don't need to know how to find square roots on paper or in your head.

METRIC SYSTEM

Scientists use the **metric system** of weights and measures so that any testing done and all conclusions that are reached can be duplicated by other scientists. Don't be scared off by metric measurements. We all use the metric system daily, whether we realize it or not. United States currency is metric. The metric system is easy because it makes sense. Unlike some systems of measurement—for instance, our English measurement where a mile is 5,280 feet, a yard is three feet, a foot is twelve inches, etc.—everything in the metric system is divided into groups of ten. The divisions have standard prefixes that remain constant, regardless of what is being measured. For example, the metric unit of length is the meter. A meter contains ten decimeters, a decimeter has ten centimeters in it, and ten millimeters make up one centimeter. Ten meters is one Decameter. A thousand meters equal one Kilometer.

The same relationships apply to any other type of measurement using metric. The basic unit of metric weight is the gram. A thousand grams is one Kilogram, etc. In this book, almost all values will be expressed in metric terms. Frequencies will be shown in Hertz: The basic unit for cycles per second. For example, 10,000 cycles per second might be written: 10kHz, or: ten kiloHertz. Component values will similarly be expressed in metric values: 330 microFarads, 3 Megaohms, etc.

The common prefixes used are shown below along with their values. Measurements of more than one unit are usually capitalized, and measurements that are fractional, or less than one whole unit are lower-case. This helps to differentiate between decimeters (tenths of a meter) and Decameters (ten meters), for example.

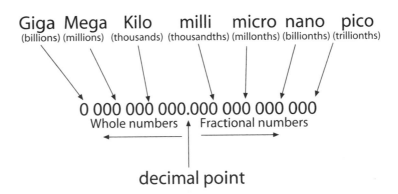

Figure 1-1: Decimals chart

Here are the prefixes that are commonly used in electronic measurements.

Less than one whole unit:

pico = one millionth (one million of these make up one whole unit)

nano = one one hundred-thousandth

micro = one ten-thousandth

milli = one thousandth

centi = one hundredth (not commonly used)

deci = one tenth

More than one whole unit:

Deca = ten units

Kilo = one thousand

Mega, or Meg = one million

Giga = one billion, or a thousand millions

Refer to this chart if you need to as you read the book. I still get pico- and nano- mixed up sometimes, and I've been doing this for more than twenty years! Most of the terms in the book are explained and defined when they are first mentioned. If you run into a term you don't understand, check the glossary. My aim is to make the information in this book as easy to understand as possible, and knowing what the various terms mean is the first step.

Chapter TWO

COMPONENTS
or, what are all those things that look like little firecrackers?

If you happened to look inside a typical piece of electronic music equipment, such as a guitar amp or a synthesizer, chances are you'd see a lot of small, colorful things that might resemble tiny firecrackers, or pills, or cough drops with little wires coming out of them. These are the **components** that make up the electronic circuitry. Some of them are **resistors**, some are **capacitors**, others might be **transistors**, **diodes**, or **integrated circuits.**

This chapter contains a lot more information than you really need to know, so unless you're interested in becoming a technician, it isn't important to memorize any of this. But you do need to *understand* it. If you'd like to learn what function these things perform, read on, and with luck, you'll glean enough knowledge to avoid saying things like, "A bunch of smoke came out of it. I think it's just a **fuse**." (An actual quote from one of my customers.)

PASSIVE COMPONENTS

There are two types of components: Passive and active. We'll start by discussing **passive** devices. Basically, this means that they only act in a subtractive fashion (i.e., removing, reducing, blocking, etc.). They passively change circuit characteristics, based on the nature of the materials they are made of and the way they are constructed.

Resistors

Resistors function as **current**- and/or **voltage**-dropping (reducing) devices. As electrons flow through a resistor, they produce heat and use up some of the energy in the **circuit.** This is desirable when a different voltage level is needed for a particular part of a circuit. For example, the voltage going into a resistor might be 24 volts, and the voltage coming out of the other side will have been dropped to 15 volts in order to operate a part of the circuit that needs only 15 volts. Resistors are measured in **ohms**, and vary in value from zero ohms (no resistance, such as a piece of wire) to hundredths of ohms ($^1/_{100}$ of an ohm), to hundreds, thousands, and millions of ohms. The value being used is determined by the requirements of the rest of the circuitry. The Greek letter omega is often used to designate ohms and looks like this: Ω.

Resistors are often cylindrical in shape with a wire lead coming out of each end. They vary in size from tiny little surface-mount "chip resistors"— about $^1/_8$ inch by $^1/_{16}$ inch—to huge wire-wound power resistors several inches long and one to two inches in diameter. They will normally be coded in some way to show the value, either color-coded or the value might be written directly on the component. Color-coded resistors have a series of painted stripes; the color of each stripe represents a number. By knowing the code, one can easily determine the value of the component. Non-technical folks really don't need to know the color code, but if you're interested, the resistor color code is shown and explained in Appendix D, Formulas and Miscellaneous Information.

When resistors fail, they will often smoke or even ignite. If a resistor burns, it will sometimes be charred to the point where the value is no longer readable. A **schematic** (a diagram showing all of the components of a circuit and all of the **connections** between them) is then necessary to determine the value before the resistor can be replaced. The schematic symbol for a resistor is shown here in *figure 2-1*.

Figure 2-1: Resistor schematic symbol

There are also variable resistors. The resistive material in a variable resistor has a connection at each end, with the addition of a movable **contact,** called a **wiper** (because it "wipes" the resistive material as it is moved). This allows the **resistance** to be changed, or "dialed in," as the wiper moves from one end to the other. These devices are called potentiometers or **rheostats**. They are used for level and tone controls in many amplifiers and are often just referred to as pots or controls. As they are turned, some pots change resistance at different rates. This is called the **taper** of the control. The make-up of the resistive **element** in a potentiometer determines the taper of the pot. Linear pots change in a linear fashion: That is, if the total resistance of the pot is 100k ohms, and the wiper is set to the mechanical center of the pot, the resistance from the wiper to each of the other two terminals will be half of the total, or 50K ohms. Other controls are **logarithmic**, or "audio taper." The resistance of the element varies logarithmically as you turn the control. This effects a smaller change in the first half-turn, and a much larger change in the second half. This is advantageous because of the way our ears detect variations in sound levels. The louder a sound is, the more the volume must increase for our ears to detect a change. A gradual increase at low volume sounds more natural to humans. Then, as the volume increases further, the change must take place at a faster rate in order to seem "smooth" or continuous.

Variable resistors are available in many different taper configurations, including special tapers for specific functions, like reverse log taper and special mirror-image ganged (joined) pots for stereo balance and pan controls.

Capacitors

Capacitors are used for several purposes including filtering (reducing hum in power supplies), **tone-shaping** (tone controls in audio circuits use resistor-capacitor networks to change the tonal quality of sound), and **bypassing** (removing certain frequencies from other components in circuits). Capacitors are **frequency**-sensitive, and the way they work is detailed in the next chapter, Electronic Basics. Like resistors, capacitors come in a wide range of sizes, depending upon their function. Capacitors are rated in **Farads**, named after Dr. Michael Faraday, the scientist who discovered and developed some of the properties of capacitance. Because one Farad is an extremely large capacitance value, capacitors, or caps, are usually rated in microFarads (thousandths of a Farad) or even picoFarads (millionths of a farad).

Some schematic symbols of capacitors are shown here *(figure 2-2)*.

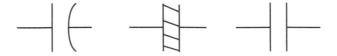

Figure 2-2: Capacitor schematic symbols

Some capacitors are **polarity** sensitive, which means they have a positive terminal and a negative terminal, similar to a battery. It is very important to place this type of capacitor correctly in the circuit, or it might fail. When capacitors malfunction, they often simply stop working. However, sometimes they will explode.

Coils

Coils, also called **inductors** or **chokes**, are just what the name implies: coils of wire. In audio electronics, they are used mostly in **crossover networks**, although some tone circuits and many wah-wah pedals utilize them. They are found in almost all **radio frequency transmitters** and **receivers**. Inductors are also frequency-sensitive. They tend to pass lower frequencies and block higher frequencies, so they are useful in tone filtering and frequency-selection circuits. An air-core inductor may be wrapped around a nonconductive plastic or cardboard **coil form**, or **bobbin**, or may have no core at all. A ferrous-core coil uses a metal core. The metal core changes the inductance value of the coil, depending on how much of the core is actually inside of the coil. These metal coils are often magnetic, and some are threaded like a bolt in order to facilitate adjusting the value, or **tuning**. Inductors, like most other electronic components, vary in size from very, very small—like the tuning coils in a tiny portable radio—to large, high-power chokes measuring several inches in diameter used in speaker crossover networks. The unit of inductance is the **Henry** (yep, another scientist). As with capacitance, one Henry is a very large amount of inductance, so inductors are usually measured in milliHenries or microHenries.

The schematic symbol of an inductor is shown in *figure 2-3*.

Figure 2-3: Inductor schematic symbol

ACTIVE COMPONENTS

The next bunch of components we'll discuss are called **active** devices. They change characteristics of circuits by amplifying or changing the form of electronic current.

Diodes

Diodes are the simplest type of active devices. They are called diodes (from the Latin prefix di-, meaning two) because they have only two terminals: The **anode** and the **cathode**. The first diodes were **vacuum tubes**, and are described in detail in Chapter Ten, How Tubes Work. Early **solid-state** diodes were made of two small pieces of **germanium** material, but **silicon** was later found to work better, so most diodes are now made of silicon. Without going into too much detail, a diode is useful in electronic circuits because it will only pass current in one direction. This allows a **direct current** (DC) to be directed, or "steered," and can allow an **alternating current** (AC) to be converted to direct current. This is explained in greater detail in Chapter Ten, How Tubes Work.

The schematic symbol for a solid-state diode is shown in *figure 2-4*.

Figure 2-4: Solid state diode schematic symbol

Other types of diodes include **zener** diodes, which conduct only at specific voltages and are useful in power-supply regulation, among other things. IR diodes produce **infrared** light waves that are invisible to the human eye, but are useful for things like **wireless data** transmission. (That's how night-vision equipment and most remote-control units for home entertainment equipment work.) **Laser** diodes produce very low-power laser beams, which are used for scanning items at check-out counters and for data pick-up in compact disc and DVD players.

Transistors

Transistors are devices that can perform a variety of functions. They can be used to amplify AC signals, switch things off and on, and regulate DC voltages. There are two basic types of transistors: **Bipolar** and **field-effect** transistors (FETs), which are both made from the same semiconductive materials, but which operate in different ways.

Some of the schematic symbols for transistors are shown in *figure 2-5*.

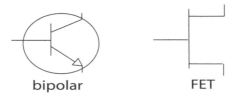

bipolar   FET

Figure 2-5: Transistor schematic symbols

Transistors also vary in size quite a bit and have numerous **case** styles, from little metal cans to molded plastic in a variety of shapes. Some of them are shown in *figure 2-6.*

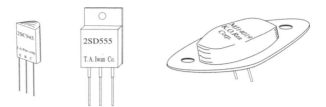

Figure 2-6: Shapes of transistors

Integrated Circuits

If we take all of the previously mentioned components and wire them together correctly, we can make electronic devices that perform a wide variety of functions. Radios, televisions, microwave ovens, computers, tape recorders, CD players...you name it, they all consist of these components. One major advancement that has made these things cheaper, easier to produce, and smaller is the integrated circuit, or I.C. Some bright engineer somewhere noticed that there were a few small circuits that were being used over and over in a lot of different products and thought it would save a lot of time if these commonly used circuits were made in advance. That way, they can just be plugged in where needed. This is the concept behind the integrated circuit.

The first I.C.s were just small circuit boards with standard-size components that were "encapsulated." That is, they were built, tested, and dipped in epoxy or enamel with only the essential leads coming out of them. That saved a lot of time in manufacturing, but didn't save much space. With the development of lasers, the manufacturers discovered they could take a small chunk of silicon and use a laser beam to etch areas of different thickness and produce super-small transistors, diodes, and other components. Soon they were making complete circuits on tiny squares of silicon, and encasing them in plastic. A circuit that had previously taken several square inches of circuit board space now fit on a single silicon "chip," just a few millimeters square. These second-generation I.C.s were relatively simple, but saved a lot of time and space in the manufacturing process. As with every-thing, repetition brings improvement. Now there are computer circuits that would have taken up entire buildings forty years ago, that fit on one tiny chip of silicon. These I.C.s are called **Large Scale Integrated Circuits**, or LSIs. There are also VLSIs (**Very Large Scale Integrated**). As this is being written, there are scientists and engineers all over the world working on new tech-nologies that will make these seem large and bulky in time.

MISCELLANEOUS PIECES AND PARTS

There are many other parts that may be found in a piece of audio gear or an electric musical instrument. Let's discuss switches, relays, fuses, circuit breakers, photo resistors, opto-couplers, photo transistors, and indicators.

Switches

There are many other devices used in electronics. **Switches** are used to direct current from one place to another. The schematic symbol for a simple single **pole**, single **throw** (SPST) switch is shown in *figure 2-7*.

Figure 2-7: SPST switch schematic symbol: common; n/o: normally open

It has just two positions: Open or no connection, and closed or connect-ed. The input only connects to the output when the switch is "on." A switch like this might be used to apply power to a piece of electronic equipment, or it might just turn on a light. Another type of switch is shown in *figure 2-8*. This is called a single-pole, double-throw (SPDT) switch.

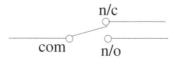

Figure 2-8: SPDT switch schematic symbol n/c: normally close

The **common** contact (C) is connected to either the **normally** closed (N/C) contact or the normally open (N/O) contact. These switches are used to select from two signal sources, like two guitar pickups, or they can be used to send a current to one of two places. Some switches have more than one pole, and can be used to switch two or more circuits simultaneously. A double pole, three-throw (DP3T) switch is shown in *figure 2-9*. Other switches might have more than one or two positions or throws, like the rotary switch that selects inputs on a stereo receiver. There are hundreds of config-

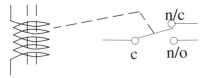

urations used, and I'm not going to try to show all of them.

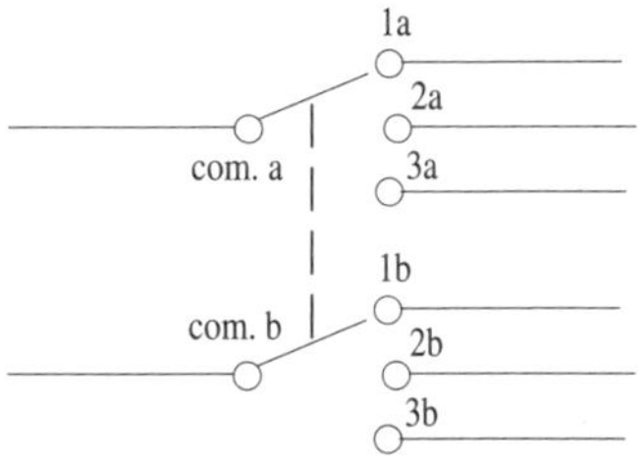

Figure 2-9: DP3T switch schematic symbol

Relays

Relays are electrically activated switches. A switch assembly is connected to a coil of wire called a **solenoid**, which causes the switch to close when it is **energized**; that is, when current is run through the coil. The schematic

symbol for a relay is shown in *figure 2-10*.

Figure 2-10: Relay schematic symbol

Fuses

Fuses are pieces of resistive wire that are designed to burn up if more than a certain amount of current flows through them. They range in value from tenths of an amp to hundreds of amps, depending on where they are to be used. Fuses vary greatly in style, size, and design. One schematic sym-

bol for a fuse is shown in *figure 2-11*.

Figure 2-11: Fuse schematic symbol

There are two basic types of fuses. Fast-blowing fuses **blow** the instant their rated current is exceeded. Slow-blowing (or time-delay) fuses will tolerate short-term current surges above their rating, but will blow if the current exceeds their rating, stays there for a few moments, and then drops back to a safe level, such as during power-up of an amplifier. Fuses are sometimes used to prevent damage to components due to excessive current (such as a fuse on a stereo amplifier's output to prevent overpowering the speaker), but the main purpose of most fuses is to prevent fire in case excessive current draw occurs due to a defective component. One of the most common things I hear from my customers is, "How can it be blown up? Isn't the fuse supposed to protect it?" The fact is, most of the time, the fuse is only there to shut down power after the unit already has a problem, so the components don't ignite and burn down the building. This is why it is so important never to use a higher value fuse than the one the equipment manufacturer specifies. Also, never use a slow-blow-type fuse if the unit calls for a fast-blow fuse.

Circuit Breakers

Circuit breakers are like fuses, but they can be reset after they are "tripped." Like fuses, they are designed to interrupt current if the current exceeds their rating. Circuit breakers use special heat-sensitive metal elements. When the element is at normal temperature, it touches a contact point and current is passed through to the output. If the current through the element exceeds the rated level, the metal heats up and bends until it no longer touches the contact point. Once this happens, it can be pushed back into place, or "reset" manually. These devices are also available in fast- or slow-blowing types. Some circuit breakers automatically reset themselves after they cool down. They are called **thermal** breakers, or **thermocouplers**. Many audio power amplifiers use thermal breakers to prevent damage in high-temperature situations.

Photo Resistors

Light-sensitive devices are used in some electronic gear. **Photo resistors** are used for a variety of things. A photo resistor has the property of changing its resistance, depending upon the amount of light to which it is exposed. This makes light-operated switching, and no-moving-parts level controlling possible. Many foot-operated volume controls use a light bulb and a photo resistor to control the output. Because there are no sliding contacts, like those in a conventional potentiometer, there is no unwanted noise generated by this type of control.

Opto-coupler

Some guitar amplifiers use opto-couplers to switch things like reverb on and off, or to switch between channels. An opto-coupler is a photo resistor encapsulated in a tiny, sealed box with a light source—usually an LED (**Light Emitting Diode**). Opto-couplers are desirable for this type of switching because they do not generate audible clicks or pops. The main drawback to using these devices in audio circuits is the short delay between the triggering of the device and the full effect. The light source in the opto-coupler doesn't come on or go off instantaneously, so the photo resistor takes a little while to start or stop conducting. This results in a short "drop out" of the signal from one function to the next. Some amp-makers see this as a small price to pay in order to avoid excess noise when functions are switched.

Photo Transistors

Photo transistors work in a similar fashion to photo resistors; they only conduct when exposed to a light source. Some photo transistors are made only to respond to invisible infrared (IR) light. These are the devices that allow wireless IR remote-control units to work. The handheld remote unit produces pulses of infrared light, and the photo-transistor inside of the pickup unit in the receiver senses them.

Indicators

Electronic equipment also uses some other little gadgets. LEDs and **lamps** are used to indicate if something is on, or to illuminate something in dark conditions. Motors make things turn or move. Digital **displays** tell the status of digital equipment. SCRs (silicon controlled rectifiers), diacs, and tri-acs are all devices that are used as switches to control voltage flow and are found in light dimmers. They are also used to turn high-current equipment on and off. Meters, both **analog** needle indicators and LED ladder-type displays, are used to indicate levels on amps and mixers; as indicators on guitar tuners, etc.

SUMMING UP

As you can see, there are many types of devices used in electronic equipment. The way they work is not as important as the functions they perform. For example, it's nice to know that if a power amplifier is being used in a hot place, and it shuts off for a few minutes and then comes back on, it's a fair assumption that there's a thermocoupler in there telling us the amp's getting too hot. Knowing what we do about thermocouplers, it would then become apparent that we need to find out what is causing it to over-heat and remedy the problem. The following chapters will show how many of these electronic devices are utilized in electronic music equipment.

Chapter THREE

ELECTRONIC BASICS
or, how much light would a flashlight flash if a flashlight could flash light?

This is the nuts-and-bolts chapter. The heaviest and most technical information in the entire book is here. Don't let that scare you. I understood it well enough to write it, and believe me, I'm no rocket scientist. It's as simplified and user-friendly as I can make it, without sounding like an episode of Mr. Whutsits Neighborhood. If you get confused, slow down, take a break, play your musical instrument of choice, or read one of the other chapters for a while. Come back to it when you're fresh. Reread the tricky parts (if there are any). Take your time. This book isn't going anywhere. Remember, the key to learning new things is familiarizing yourself with the concepts, and repetition, repetition, repetition...

ABOUT ELECTRICITY

We begin our tale with the building block of all things, the lowly **atom**. Atoms make up everything in our known universe, as you should remember from basic science class (unless you slept through it, like I did). The elements that make up an atom are called neutrons, protons, and **electrons**. The ones we are concerned with regarding electronics are...you guessed it!... electrons! These are the little particles that spin around the middle part, or **nucleus**, of the atom. They also tend to fly from one atom to the next, to the next, and on and on...kind of like a girl I knew in high school. There are zillions of them doing this all the time (the electrons, I mean). This is the force that holds everything together. If atoms all of a sudden stopped sharing electrons like a bunch of greedy little Scrooges, everything in the universe would fall apart. Fortunately, that cannot happen. At least I don't think it can...

So, atoms share electrons. Some atoms tend to share them much more than others. These atoms are the ones found in materials such as iron, zinc, steel, etc. Because they share atoms so well, these materials are called conductors. The atoms that don't share well with others are in materials that are less conductive, or not conductive at all. These materials are called insulators. Atoms that share only some electrons are in semiconductive materials, such as germanium and silicon.

The fact that atoms share electrons is what makes electricity and electronics something that we humans are learning to control. That's right, we're still learning about it. When I was in school, they taught us that the elements of the atoms were the smallest particles in the universe. They were just sure of it! Now, atomic science has found sub-atomic particles and given them cute names like "Quarks." Just goes to show you that, no matter how certain anyone is about something, there's always more to learn. We know enough about electricity to be able to use its properties to our advantage, but it's called electronic theory, because there is still so much we don't know. Well, on to the main plot of the story!

THE CIRCUIT

Let's make an electronic circuit. What do we need to start? Well, in electronic circuits you have three basic elements: Voltage, current, and **load**. The technical term for voltage is **electromotive force**, or EMF. EMF is a potential, but as yet unused, source of electrons that we measure in volts. Picture an imaginary 9-volt **battery** sitting on a table in front of you. It's a nice, fresh, new, and as-yet-unused battery *(figure 3-1)*. It's got 9 volts "in it," but it isn't connected to anything, so it isn't doing anything. It has the **potential** to run anything that can be run with a good 9-volt battery, but it's not connected. Inside the battery are atoms just waiting to give up some of their electrons in order to accomplish some work, but the electrons can't leave yet. They aren't connected. Even in the life of an electron, to get anywhere you've gotta be connected.

Figure 3-1: 9-volt imaginary battery

The technical term for current is...current. Current is the rate at which electrons flow through an electronic circuit. When we measure current, we call it **Amperes**, or amps, for short. If we take our imaginary 9-volt battery, connect an imaginary wire to the positive (+) terminal, and connect the other end to the negative (-) terminal, current will flow through the wire *(see figure 3-2).*

Figure 3-2: 9-volt imaginary battery with wire from + to - terminals

The positive terminal now has a path to the negative terminal. This is the simplest form of an electronic circuit. Do not do this with a real battery and wire. I'll tell you why later in this chapter. Back in the early days of experimenting with electricity, it was mistakenly thought that the flow was from the positive battery terminal to the negative terminal. Later, scientists discovered that this is incorrect. The actual flow of electrons is from the negative end of the battery to the positive end. Because the current flows at about the speed of light (300,000,000 meters per second), you really can't blame them for guessing wrong.

The technical term for a load is resistance. This is called **impedance** in AC circuits; I'll explain the difference in a minute. A load is anything placed in the path of the electrons that changes their rate of flow through a circuit. Load resistances are measured in ohms. A load can be in the form of a light bulb, a speaker, a heating element, or any one of a whole mess of electronic components that use current and make up part of an electronic circuit. Let's take our imaginary 9-volt battery again and connect a wire to the positive (+) terminal. This time, we'll connect the other end of the wire to one lead of a little imaginary 9-volt lamp (light bulb). We'll connect the other lead of the lamp to the negative (-) terminal of the battery *(figure 3-3).*

Figure 3-3: 9-volt imaginary battery with lamp

Voila! Let there be imaginary light! The voltage (EMF) from the battery is being transferred in the form of current through the load resistance (lamp) via the wiring. The current heats the filament in the lamp, and it lights. Work is being performed, light and heat are being produced, and we have built a simple circuit. Hooray for us! Now that we have voltage, current, and resistance figured out, I'm going to toss in another factor: **Power**. Power is the heat generated by the lamps or other loads in a circuit. Power is measured in watts. Whenever you have an electrical circuit, there will be some power produced in the form of heat. Household light bulbs are categorized by the amount of heat they produce. A 60-watt bulb produces 60 watts of heat. Fortunately for us consumers, this also tells us the approximate brightness of the light produced (**lumens**), so we know what size light bulbs to buy.

Volts, amps, resistance, and watts are all related to each other. If our imaginary 9-volt battery and 9-volt lamp circuit suddenly had an imaginary 12-volt lamp added, the amount of current flowing through the circuit would change. The amount of power in watts being produced would also change, and the resistance measurement in ohms would change, too. The imaginary 12-volt lamp would not be as bright, and might not even light at all. Any time you change the value of any one of these circuit parameters, at least one of the other parameter values must also change.

The smart fellow who discovered this fact many moons ago was named Ohm. His fellow scientists named the resistance measurement in his honor. (Many electronic terms are named for scientists. Ampere is one. Volts were named for a guy named Volta.)

Professor Ohm assigned values to the components of electronic circuits so that if you knew the values of any two of the factors, you could figure out the other two mathematically. Most importantly, his formulas enabled circuit designers to predict exactly what would happen in circuits as these values changed. These formulas are called **Ohm's laws**. They are amazingly simple. Resistance (R) times current (I) equals voltage (E). Voltage divided by resistance equals current. Current times voltage equals power. You may investigate these formulas in greater detail in Appendix D, Formulas and Miscellaneous Information. If we go back to our imaginary battery and light circuit, we can plug in some numbers to show how these things relate to each other, and we'll see why you shouldn't connect the positive and negative terminals of a battery together. For the sake of simplicity, we'll use nice round numbers for the component values in our circuit. First, let's make our imaginary battery be 10 volts instead of 9, since 10 is easier to work with mathematically. So, we'll say we have a 10-volt battery connected to a load resistor (in place of the lamp) that measures 100 ohms *(figure 3-4)*. By using Ohm's Law, we can find the current (amps) and the power (watts). Given the fact that voltage divided by resistance is current, 10 divided by 100 is .1, or one tenth of an amp. Because current times voltage equals power, we can figure the amount of power being produced by multiplying .1 (one tenth) times 10. That equals 1, and seeing as power is measured in watts, our circuit is producing 1 watt of power.

Figure 3-4: 10-volt theoretical battery with 100-Ohm resistor

If the resistor is changed to 1,000 ohms, the voltage of the battery will stay the same, but the current and power will change. Volts divided by resistance equals current, so 10 divided by 1,000 equals .01, or one one-hundredth of an amp. The power (current times voltage) or, .01 times 10 equals .1 watts, or one tenth of a watt. The main thing I'm trying to get across here is that these circuit values are all interrelated.

Now, what happens if you connect the positive terminal directly to the negative terminal of our imaginary battery *(figure 3-2,* again)? Because the imaginary wire has no resistance, or zero ohms, the theoretical, imaginary current would be 10 volts divided by 0 ohms equals... Error! Our calculator knows you can't divide a number by 0. The fact is, the wire does have some, although not much, resistance. So, let's plug in a number—say, a millionth of an ohm, or .000001 ohms—for the wire's resistance. Ten volts divided by .000001 ohms equals a million amps. How is this possible? Well, it isn't possible. Every component in an electronic circuit has limits, and the imaginary battery we're using "jest cahn't dew it, cap'n!" In the real world, if you tried this, the real-life battery would produce as much current as it possibly could, and one or more of several things might happen. A) The wire would get hot and burn your fingers, thereby causing you to toss the whole thing in the air and break the circuit; B) The battery would get hot and explode; C) The wire might burn itself into two pieces, breaking the circuit; or D) The battery would rapidly discharge, the wire would get hot, and the battery would get hot and eventually go dead without causing harm to life and limb. But why take the chance? Do not try this at home! Light fuse, get away! Do not hold in hand!

In a simple theoretical circuit like this one, the voltage from the battery will never change. In real life, however, battery and power supply voltages can and do vary somewhat. Also in this theoretical example, we haven't taken into account the resistance of the wiring. Usually with short runs of wire, the resistance they add is so low, it's not considered. However, in extremely long runs of wire, such as some speaker and power wiring, the resistance of the wire itself can be enough to affect the performance of a circuit.

You don't have to memorize Ohm's Law to play music, but it is important to have this knowledge if you are wiring speaker cabinets, or connecting a sound and lighting system to a 220-volt AC **power-distribution system**. We'll get into speaker wiring in Chapter Five, Speaker Impedance, and I'll discuss power wiring in Chapter Twenty-One, Bits and Pieces Worth Noting. We're almost through the tough stuff!

There are just a couple of other important things you should know about. Earlier in this chapter, I called the circuit load a resistance/impedance. There are two forms of electricity that we use. One is DC, or direct current. That is what you get from a battery, or DC power supply, and loads in a DC circuit are usually called resistance. The other is AC, or alternating current. That is what you get from the wall sockets in your house, and that is the form audio frequency signals take in electronic circuits. The loads in an AC circuit are called impedance. AC impedances can vary greatly with frequency. For instance, a large-value capacitor will have a very high impedance at low frequencies, and very low impedance at high frequencies. DC, by its very nature, has no frequency (0 Hertz), so DC resistance is said to be constant, or **continuous**. Both DC resistance and AC impedance are measured in ohms.

Alternating current is constantly changing its voltage. The voltage starts at zero, rises to its maximum positive voltage **peak**, drops past zero to its maximum negative voltage peak, and rises again to zero *(see figure 3-5)*. In the case of the AC from your wall socket, it rises to +117 volts (RMS), drops to -117 volts (RMS), and repeats this cycle 60 times every second.

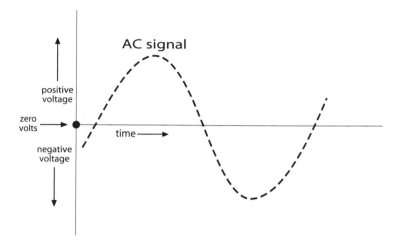

Figure 3-5: Graph of an AC signal: 117v RMS

The notation RMS above refers to a method of measuring AC signals. RMS stands for **Root-Mean-Square**, which is sort of shorthand for the formula used to determine this level. The RMS level of an AC signal is the relative DC level. This means, if all of the factors of the circuit remain the same, and a DC current was substituted for the AC current, the DC level would be this number. Using RMS levels for AC current allows us to use standard formulas to determine electronic values, rather than having an entirely different set of formulas for use with AC currents.

WHY AC?

Why use AC voltage instead of DC? Good question! The answer is, it is much more **efficient** to send AC current from the generating station to your house this way. Remember awhile back when I was talking about long runs of wire having enough resistance to cause performance problems? Of course you do! It was only a few paragraphs ago!

Back in the early 1900s, the power to homes was direct current, but it was very inefficient to transfer from the power company to the houses because a lot of the current would be wasted as heat (power) being generated by the resistance of the wiring. Well, along came a couple of scientists named George Westinghouse and Nicola Tesla (a very interesting guy, check out his biography if you have a chance). Tesla and Westinghouse envisioned alternating current as a way to transfer huge amounts of current without huge losses. As a result of their experiments, we know that if you run a current through a wire, it will generate a **magnetic field** around the wire.

The reverse is also true. If you move a magnetic field past a wire, it will generate a current in the wire. So, if you have two wires really close to each other, and run current through one, it will generate enough magnetism to induce a current into the other one. This is the principle behind every transformer in the world today. The problem Tesla ran into was that this effect only occurred while the voltage was either rising or falling. DC didn't have the effect at all. His solution was to have the voltage constantly rising or falling, going from zero volts up to a certain point, then dropping to zero again, continuing to drop below zero to a point, and then rising back to zero to make one complete cycle. The concept of alternating current was born.

By using special **transformers**, your power company is able to increase the voltage at a relatively low current level and transfer power great distances without large power losses. The relatively low current flowing through the (resistive) wires (current squared times resistance equals power) decreases the power losses, but the extremely high voltages maintain the potential for high power at the other end of the line after the voltage is dropped back down.

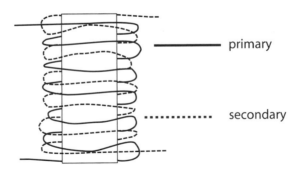

Figure 3-6: Basic transformer

Transformers are basically two coils of wire wrapped around each other *(figure 3-6)*. Often, both coils are wrapped around an iron core to help focus the magnetic fields and make the transformer more efficient. The input coil is called the **primary**, and the output coil is called the **secondary**. By winding more turns of wire in the secondary than in the primary, the secondary's voltage will be higher than the primary's. We might, for example, put 100 volts AC into the primary and get 500 volts out of the secondary (but only one-fifth the current, see below). This is called a **step-up** transformer, and it is what allows the power company to send electricity at high voltages (10,000 to 150,000 volts AC) across long runs of wire. The opposite type, or **step-down** transformer, is what makes it possible for the power company to take the high voltage and knock it down to a lower voltage for use in homes and businesses. Another trait of transformers that makes this possible is the fact that the voltage-to-current relationship on one side of the transformer is **inverse** (backward) on the other side. In other words, a high-voltage, low-current signal on the input side (primary) of the knock-down (or step-down) transformer produces a low-voltage, high-current signal on the output (secondary) side.

Smaller transformers inside of appliances and other electronic equipment reduce the voltage even more, so the devices can operate at the most efficient level possible. The bulky, boxy, **wall-wart** thing on the end of the power cord for a calculator or answering machine is a transformer. Transformers are our friends.

Household AC almost everywhere in the world is alternating at a rate of either 50 or 60 cycles per second. Sixty cycles is standard in the U.S.A. That is called the line frequency, and is measured in **Hertz**, abbreviated Hz. As mentioned before, the frequency of an AC circuit has an effect on the impedance of some load components, specifically inductors and capacitors. Capacitors have more impedance at lower frequencies than they do at higher frequencies and inductors are just the opposite. There are many advantages to this action, such as the ability to tune circuits, making tone controls, crossovers, **equalizers,** and other frequency-specific functions possible in audio circuits, as well as allowing single channels of television and radio to be received without interference from adjacent channels. All of the electronic appliances, toys, gadgets, etc. that we use today would not work without alternating current. Thank you, Professor Tesla.

As I mentioned previously, electronics is still considered a theory. That means that one day, out of nowhere, some young upstart scientist could come along and discover some new factor that would make everything that we now assume to be correct, completely wrong. The concepts that I've been discussing have been tested enough times, that we know they are accurate in so far as they relate to each other, so electrical functions wouldn't change, but the way we think about them and use them in the future could be drastically different. The theory of electronics as we now understand it is very precise, in that if you know the values with which you are working, you can predict on paper, using electronic formulas, exactly how things should work. That's for design engineers. Those of us in the real world have a unique set of problems. Nothing in real life is as exact as it is in theory. Everything in the real world has **tolerances**. A theoretical 9-volt battery is exactly 9 volts. A real-life 9-volt battery may be 9.2 volts or 8.7 volts, and it just might go from 8.7 volts to 8.8 volts if the room's temperature changes a dozen degrees.

A 10-ohm resistor (on paper) is 10 ohms. A 10-ohm resistor in real-life might be rated at 10 ohms plus or minus 1%, 2%, 5%, 10%, or 20% (and then you'll find one every now and then that tests way out of range). This is true of almost every electronic component made. I have a friend who once worked for a famous microphone-maker. He told me that in one line of mics, varying in price (at the time) from around $75 for the bottom-of-the-line unit to more than $250 for the top-of-the-line, they all used the same mic element! They'd make a batch of them, send them off to quality control, and test them. The ones that met the published specifications became the top-of-the-line mics; the ones that didn't quite cut it became the next-from-the-top-of-the-line, on down to the bottom-line mics; and the remaining 25% to 30% were so bad, they were thrown out. The point is, if you put any two production guitar amps side by side, they will each sound a little bit different at exactly the same settings, because of the tolerances in the parts used to make them.

Well, you made it! The big trick with all of this electronics stuff is to understand the relationship between voltage, resistance, and current. They are different properties of electricity that relate closely to each other. You can't have one without the others. Reread this chapter a time or two in order to get this concept down if you need to. The rest is relatively simple. There's more basic information in the next chapters.

Chapter FOUR

ABOUT SOUND
or, catching the perfect wave.

Sound wave physics is an area of study that some people spend their entire lives pursuing. I am *not* one of them. The purpose of this chapter is merely to provide basic information about the properties of sound, so you can get an idea of how it is manipulated electronically.

First, we need to know a couple of things about sound and audio signals in general. Audio signals are waves, no matter what form they take (electrical, electromagnetic, or mechanical). To visualize an audio sound wave, picture a pond on a calm day. The surface of the water is unrippled, smooth as glass. Some kid comes along and grabs a handful of small pebbles from the shore and tosses one into the exact center of this pond. The resulting ripple forms a perfect circle (wave) that expands slowly to the outside edge of the pond. If he tosses another pebble in the exact same spot, another wave forms. The faster this kid tosses pebbles (the more frequent his tosses), the closer together these waves become (the higher the frequency of the waves).

HEARING

The following is an extremely simplified explanation of how hearing works. The human ear detects differences of pressure in the air that comes into contact with the eardrum. These pressure fluctuations are very small, and the hearing organs must be highly sensitive in order to detect them. The movement of the eardrum sends messages to the brain via nerves, and the brain then decides what type of sound is being detected by the ears. The amount of air being moved by anything that produces sound can be measured. This measurement is called **sound pressure level** or SPL, and is measured in **decibels** or dB. The human ear is capable of hearing a wide range of frequencies and SPLs. The "normal" range of human hearing is from about 25 cycles per second (25Hz) to 16,000 cycles per second (16kHz). Some folks don't hear this well, and some can hear lower and/or higher than this. Audiophiles hope to achieve the "ideal" of 20Hz to 20kHz. Sound is subjective, meaning that how something sounds to you might not be exactly how it sounds to someone else (keep this in mind the next time somebody calls your favorite music "noise").

Sound Pressure Level

The human ear also detects SPL differently, depending upon the frequency of the sound. For example, a sound pressure level of 103dB is usually considered fairly loud, but at 100Hz, it's really pretty bearable. The same 103dB at 1kHz can be quite annoying, and a 10kHz tone at 103dB is downright painful to some people. This helps explain why woofers are larger than tweeters in a speaker system. Quite a bit of air must be moved around to produce low-frequency sounds at normal SPLs, so a larger cone or diaphragm is used. Not as much air needs to be moved to produce comfortable listening levels at higher frequencies; consequently, smaller-diaphragm surfaces are used. There is more about how speakers move air in Chapter Eight, How Speakers and Microphones Work.

Time Alignment, Phase, and Doppler Effect

Different frequencies of sound waves move through the air at different rates. This is why some speaker systems are **time-aligned**, meaning the woofers may be placed closer to the listener than the midrange and treble speakers. That way, the sound from all of the drivers (hopefully) will converge at the listener's position at the same time. These sound waves are then **phase-coherent** and will sound more like the original sound being reproduced. If both of our ears are working properly, we hear things in stereo, which allows us to tell where sounds are coming from. Human hearing detects higher frequencies more accurately than it detects low frequencies. If you step outside on a calm spring day and hear a bird chirp, you can pretty much pinpoint the location of the bird, but if you hear the low rumble of a jet flying over, it takes awhile to find its location in the sky, because the sound seems to be all around you. This is characteristic of human hearing and the way we perceive sound; it is not a characteristic of the sound itself. Lower frequencies seem less **directional** than higher frequencies. The midrange and high-frequency speakers in a stereo system are usually placed very precisely, exactly the same distance from the listener on opposite sides of the room, in order to maintain correct stereo separation. Speakers that produce only very low frequencies (100Hz to 250Hz and below) are called **subwoofers** and can be placed almost anywhere in the listening field. By manipulating the time alignment (phasing) of frequencies, audio recording engineers can fool our ears into thinking things are in very specific places in our hearing field: In front of us, or behind us, or off to the side. That's a part of how surround sound works.

Sound waves move relatively slowly (about 755 miles per hour, compared to light, which travels at 300,000,000 meters per second), and when sound waves reflect off of hard surfaces back to our ears, the time difference can be noticeable. This is called echo, reflection, or reverberation.

Another property of sound and other waves is the **Doppler effect**. If you've ever been standing on the side of the road when a car blows its horn as it approaches and passes you, you've probably noticed that the horn sounds like it drops in pitch. This is the Doppler effect. Here's how the Doppler effect works: Say there's a ladybug on the surface of our smooth, calm imaginary pond. If the bug just floats in one spot, it won't make any ripples. If it wiggles its legs, it will produce ripples (waves) that will emanate from it out to the edges of the pond. If it swims in a constant direction, the ripples will continue to form, but the ones in front of the bug will be closer together, while the ones behind the bug will be farther apart. The close-together, front-side ripples appear to be a higher frequency than those not as close together behind the bug. Actually, the frequency is the same, but since the bug is moving, the waves are **compressing** in front and expanding behind. Waves from any moving source will act this way. The cop hiding behind the road sign uses this knowledge to catch speeders. His radar gun produces an extremely high-frequency, very directional wave that is sent out to your car and reflected back to the radar gun's detector. The difference in time between the original signal and the reflected signal is calculated, and your speed is displayed. The frequency at which radar operates is in the Gigahertz (GHz) range. The extremely high frequency of this wave causes it to move at a very high rate of speed through the air, so the reflection is almost instantaneous. This is about the same frequency at which microwave ovens operate. The first microwaves were actually called "radar ranges" because of this. The reason the cop's radar gun doesn't cook you is the power level is very low compared to a microwave oven.

Chapter FIVE

SPEAKER IMPEDANCE

or, what are all these ohms doing in my speaker cabinet?

This chapter will explain how the impedance of speakers is determined, and what happens when multiple speakers are connected together. The mechanics of how speakers work is discussed in Chapter Eight, How Speakers and Microphones Work.

Speaker impedance is rated by speaker manufacturers in ohms. Most speakers (also called **drivers**) are rated at either 4, 8, 16, or 32 ohms. Headphone drivers will often have impedances as high as 600 ohms. Impedance ratings can be very confusing and even downright misleading until one understands how they are determined. A standard speaker is actually rated in **nominal** impedance. Nominal impedance is kind of like an average impedance over the entire frequency spectrum. When a manufacturer first builds a speaker, the speaker is taken into a testing laboratory. This testing covers a whole range of parameters, such as sensitivity, frequency response, and free-air resonance. Those values do not concern us much, unless we are going to design a cabinet for a particular speaker, but they determine the nominal impedance of the speaker. Here is the (very simplified) explanation of the way this is done. Testing engineers run an AC audio signal at a specific level into one of these speakers and vary the frequency of the signal from low to high, while monitoring the current through the **voice coil**. The point at which the current is highest will correspond to the lowest impedance of the voice coil. The speaker impedance will vary considerably across the frequency range. Many speakers at low frequencies will have impedances below 1 ohm, even as low as .25 ohms. At higher frequencies, the impedance will become much higher. Remember, this is a coil of wire we're talking about (an inductor), and as we learned in Chapter Two, Components, the impedance of an inductor varies with frequency. The nominal impedance rating is an average of these values, based upon the frequency range the speaker is expected to reproduce.

An 18-inch subwoofer speaker will be tested at relatively low frequencies, from 20Hz (or less) to up around 1kHz or 2kHz. The speaker isn't designed to produce frequencies higher than that, and due to the diameter and wire gauge of the voice coil, it won't. A 2-inch tweeter will be tested at much higher frequencies.

TOTAL IMPEDANCE

One thing musicians and soundtechs should be able to determine is how many speakers can safely be connected to one amplifier.

Series and Parallel Speaker Wiring

Why can't you connect as many as you want? An amplifier connected to a speaker is an electronic circuit, similar to the 9-volt battery and load resistor in our example from earlier in the book. In this case, the amp is the AC source taking the place of the battery, and the speaker—not a resistor—is the load impedance. Time for a little more theory and a couple of formulas. Check out *figure 5-1*. This shows two speakers wired in **parallel**.

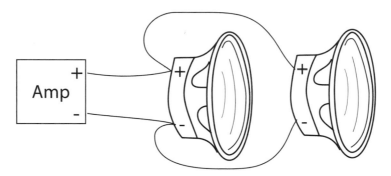

Figure 5-1: Two speakers wired in parallel

This is called parallel wiring, because both positive terminals are connected to the amp's positive output, and both negative terminals are connected to the amp's negative output. The circuit splits into two parallel circuits. Should one speaker's voice coil fail (open), the other speaker will continue to play. But the circuit's impedance will change.

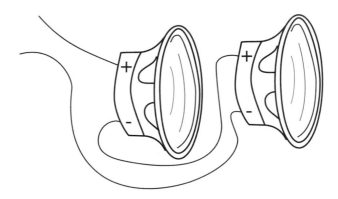

Figure 5-2: Two speakers wired in series

Figure 5-2 shows two speakers connected in **series**. It's like a chain: The positive terminal of the first speaker connects to the amp's positive output; the negative terminal of speaker one connects to the positive terminal of the second speaker, and its negative terminal connects back to the negative speaker terminal of the amp. The total circuit current must pass through the first speaker before getting to the second speaker. If one speaker's voice coil opens, it interrupts the path from positive to negative, and both speakers stop working.

Series and Parallel Electronic Theory
Let's take a minute to examine electronically what is happening in each of these circuits.

Here we have our theoretical 10-volt battery back again *(figure 5-3)*.

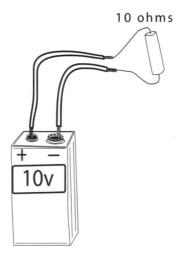

Figure 5-3: Diagram of theoretical 10-volt battery, with one 10-ohm resistor

The impedance of the speaker is being represented by a resistor. Once again, we'll use nice round numbers to make the math easy. We'll say the resistor is 10 ohms. With only one resistor (speaker) connected to the battery (amp), Ohm's law (volts divided by resistance equals amps) tells us the current through the resistor must be (10 volts divided by 10 ohms equals) 1 amp. The voltage at the positive battery terminal will stay the same, no matter how many resistors are connected.

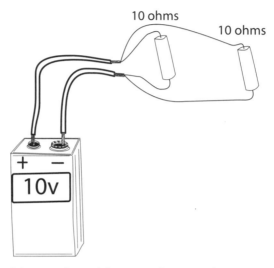

Figure 5-4: Diagram of theoretical 10-volt battery, with two 10-ohm resistors in parallel

Now, when we add in the second resistor (speaker) in parallel *(figure 5-4);* since the voltage doesn't change, each resistor must have 1 amp going through it, meaning the total current in the circuit is now 2 amps. Because the battery voltage doesn't change, the voltage in each leg of this (or any) parallel circuit is the same, regardless of the resistance of the legs, however many there may be. The currents in the legs of the circuit add together to make the total circuit current. In this example, the two resistors are the same value, so the current is the same. If they were different values, say, 10 ohms and 20 ohms, the current in each leg would be different.

Seeing as we've calculated the total circuit current in our example and found it to be 2 amps, we can now figure the total load resistance. Ten volts divided by 2 amps equals 5 ohms. Yep, that's right. Two identical loads in parallel divide in half. Two 8-ohm speakers connected to an amp equal a 4-ohm load. The power produced by this circuit would be: Voltage times current equals power, or 2 amps times 10 volts equals 20 watts.

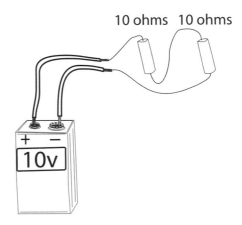

Figure 5-5: Diagram of theoretical 10-volt battery, with two 10-ohm resistors in series

Now, let's see what happens when we place our second load resistor in series instead of parallel *(figure 5-5)*. The voltage at the battery terminals remains at 10 volts. The resistor values in a series circuit add together, so the resistance is 10 plus 10 or 20 ohms. Ten volts divided by 20 ohms equals .5 amps (half an amp, or 500 milliamps). The power of this series circuit would be: .5 amps times 10 volts equals 5 watts. So, adding resistors in series reduces the total output current and power, and adding resistors in parallel increases total circuit current and power.

Let's try putting four 10-ohm resistors in parallel *(figure 5-6)*.

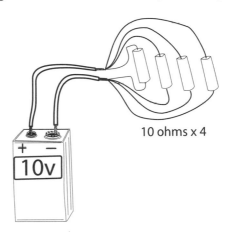

Figure 5-6: Diagram of theoretical 10-volt battery, with four 10-ohm resistors in parallel

Again, the voltage stays the same. Each resistor has 1 amp going through it. The currents in the legs add together. That's a total of 4 amps, or 10 divided by 4 equals 2.5 ohms total load, and 4 times 10 equals 40 watts total power. So, as you see, you can't keep adding speakers in parallel to an amp's output, because you'll eventually drop the load impedance of the amplifier too low, and the amp will attempt to output more current than it can safely provide (remember the battery and the piece of wire we discussed in Chapter Three, Electronic Basics). This will cause the poor overworked amp to shut down, blow a fuse, or cook one or more of its output devices. Remember that voltage stays constant, and if the speaker impedance (load) drops, the current must increase proportionately. The amp can only provide so much current before meltdown occurs. Many amps are designed to run into loads no lower than 4 ohms, although some are 2-ohm **stable**. Better quality amplifiers usually have their minimum impedance rating listed near the speaker terminals, but when in doubt, go high rather than low, to be safe. Here's a handy rule to memorize: The total impedance of a parallel circuit will always be less than any one leg of the circuit. One 8-ohm speaker: 8 ohms; two 8-ohm speakers: 4 ohms; three 8-ohm speakers: 2.7 ohms, etc. So, how can speaker cabinet manufacturers put four, six, or eight speakers in one cabinet? They combine series and parallel circuits to keep the total impedance correct. If we place two resistors in series, place two more in series, and then wire these two series-connected legs in parallel *(figure 5-7)*, what happens?

10 Ohms x 4

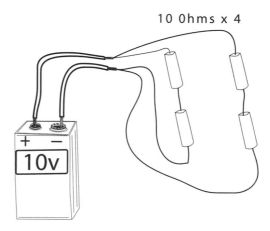

Figure 5-7: Diagram of theoretical 10-volt battery, with four 10-ohm resistors in series-parallel configuration

We already know the resistance of two 10-ohm resistors in series is 20, and we know that two identical resistances in parallel divide in half. So, the total must be half of 20, or 10 ohms. Same as what we had with just one resistor. So, with four identical 8-ohm speakers connected in series/parallel *(figure 5-8)*, the amp will run safely into an 8-ohm load, but with four times the speaker cone area and four times the power-handling capability of just one speaker.

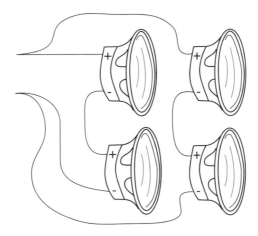

Figure 5-8: Four speakers wired in series-parallel configuration

So far, we've only considered identical impedance loads. What if you want to connect a 16-ohm speaker in parallel with an 8-ohm speaker? That's when you whip out your handy-dandy calculator and use your impedance formulas. You can figure the total impedance of any number of loads in series by simply adding them together. (R1+R2+R3+R... = R total) Conversely, you can figure the total impedance of any number of parallel loads by using the following impedance formula:

$$\frac{1}{\dfrac{1}{R1} + \dfrac{1}{R1} + \dfrac{1}{R1} + \dfrac{1}{R1}} = R\ total$$

figure 5-9: Parallel resistor formula

SEVENTY-VOLT LINE SYSTEMS

Maybe you've gone into a department store, dentist's office, or grocery store and seen a bunch of speakers mounted in the ceiling, and now you're wondering: How do they connect all of them to one amp? Or do they use several amps? Do they figure the series-parallel wiring out so the impedance is right? Most multiple-speaker systems like this use a transformer coupling system called a 70.7-volt constant-voltage line, usually referred to as a "**70-volt line**." The term 70-volt line refers to the output voltage (not power) of the amplifier, whose output is designed to run into a relatively high-impedance load. Most electrical codes say that any voltage over 100 volts peak must run through conduit, so the maximum voltage in this constant voltage system is 100 volts peak, or (peak times .707) 70.7 volts RMS. The speaker line voltage will never exceed 70.7 volts at full power output of the amp. Each speaker on the line has a special transformer attached to it. The primary impedance of these transformers is high enough that many of them can be connected in parallel without overloading the drive transformer in the amp. These small transformers step this higher voltage back down to a lower voltage, match the speaker's impedance, and allow the speaker to play normally. Many transformers have various output tap points: ½-watt, 1-watt, 2-watt, 5-watt, 10-watt, etc. This allows the output level (volume) of each speaker to be selected individually. One speaker in a high background-noise situation, for example, might be set to play louder than the others. Variable **attenuators**, or level controls, can also be connected to the speaker line to control the volume of a particular speaker or set of speakers.

There is, of course, much more to know about speakers and impedance. If you're interested in these theories and formulas, check out the suggested reading list and formulas in the appendices at the end of the book.

Chapter SIX

MICROPHONE IMPEDANCE
or, you take the high-Z and I'll take the low-Z.

There's a lot to learn about microphones. While they may all look very similar, there are several different types that excel at different tasks in the audio world.

MICROPHONE TYPES

Just about everyone involved in music, bands, stage productions, or public speaking has heard the terms high impedance and low impedance used with regard to **microphones**. This chapter will attempt to explain the hows, whys, and wherefores of this sometimes confusing subject, and will discuss **balanced** and unbalanced systems. Microphones are used for an amazing number of things. There's the clip-on lavalier (tie-tac) mic worn by a television newscaster or a preacher in church, the mic the person at the fast-food counter uses to tell the kitchen your order, the one your favorite singer uses, the mic used to record the birds chirping in the background of the PBS special on endangered snail darter mating rituals, mics used in state-of-the-art recording studios, mics used in not-so-state-of-the-art recording studios (like mine), mics used by the FBI to listen to your house from a quarter of a mile away, and countless others. Microphones are generally divided into two categories: High impedance (hi-Z) and low impedance (lo-Z). Like many electronic terms, impedance is represented by a letter so it can be placed into electronic formulas. Scientists assigned the capital letter Z to impedance. "I" was already taken (I = current).

Impedance

The inputs and outputs of all audio electronic circuits—whether they are guitar-amp inputs or speaker outputs, mixer mic inputs or line outputs, amplifier line inputs or speaker outputs—have an impedance rated in ohms. Exactly what the ohm value is for these is only important if you are a design engineer. For our purposes, the only thing we need to know is whether the input/output is high-impedance or low-impedance. Audio circuits work most efficiently and offer the best sound quality and **frequency response** when the devices plugged into and out of them match impedance fairly closely. A low-impedance microphone sounds best if plugged into a lo-Z mic input on a mixer or P.A. (**Public Address** Amp). A hi-Z mic will work, but the output will be reduced, and the frequency response will suffer. It just will not sound as good as a lo-Z mic. Likewise, a hi-Z mic's output will work better running into a hi-Z input.

The impedance we're talking about with a microphone is output impedance. Lo-Z mics have output impedances in the range of around 50 to 600 ohms. These will sound best if plugged into similarly low-impedance microphone inputs. It is generally accepted that lo-Z mics tend to be higher-quality mics than hi-Z mics. That isn't to say that there aren't good-quality hi-Z microphones or poor-quality lo-Z mics; it's just a generalization, based on the early days of radio and recording when hi-Z mics were "consumer" mics, and lo-Z mics were "professional" mics. In the old days, lo-Z mics were only found in recording studios and radio stations.

Hi-Z microphones have impedance ratings around 10k (ten-thousand) to 40k ohms. Of course, these work best when plugged into hi-Z microphone inputs. Hi-Z mics plugged into lo-Z inputs will work, but they tend to sound "thin" and "tinny." If a person has no choice but to use a mic that does not match the inputs available, there are devices called matching transformers that may be used to convert hi-Z to lo-Z, and vice versa. These are fairly inexpensive **adaptors**.

Balanced Mic Lines

One thing you'll notice when working with microphones is that most hi-Z mics use ¼-inch phone plugs, while lo-Z mics use three-pin connectors called XLR or Cannon connectors. (More on connectors can be found in Chapter Twenty-One, General Info.). This is because most lo-Z mics use a balanced output. This balancing performs the unique function of protecting the mic signal from being degraded by outside sources of hum and noise over long runs of cabling. It is a **noise**-canceling configuration. Here's how it works.

Audio wave signals are AC (alternating current) signals, which means they alternately rise positive and fall negative with respect to signal "ground" or common *(figure 6-1)*. Because the wave starts at zero volts and ends at zero volts, we can represent the relation of the wave to time in degrees, 0° to 360° like a circle. This is referred to as one **cycle**. The rate at which this happens (cycles per second) determines the frequency of the signal. A **steady-state** (not changing in frequency or **amplitude**), 10-volt AC, 1kHz audio signal wave is represented by the graph in *figure 6-1*.

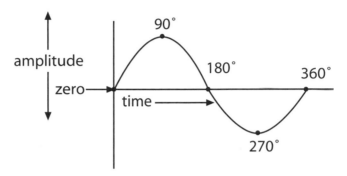

Figure 6-1: Graph of AC signal—one complete wave

The vertical line is the voltage level of the signal or amplitude. The horizontal line represents time. The wavy line is the audio signal, with the zero, 90, 180, 270, and 360-degree points marked. The chart shows one complete wave or cycle. This 1kHz (1,000 cycles per second) wave will repeat itself along the "time" line, 1,000 times every second. Now, if we were to add a second identical signal to the first signal, starting at the same point in time, the two signals would be said to be coherent, or **in phase**. The amplitude of the new signal would be added to the original signal, and the amplitude would therefore double *(see figure 6-2)*.

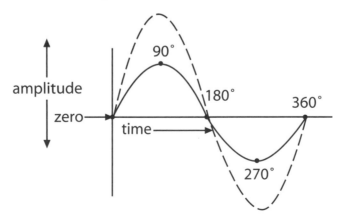

Figure 6-2: Same graph with second identical sine wave equalling twice the amplitude sine wave

What do you suppose would happen if we were to take our original signal and add one that is exactly the opposite, or 180° **out of phase**, with the first one *(figure 6-3)?*

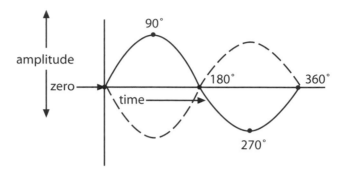

Figure 6-3: Two identical sine waves, 180 degrees out of phase

Any number plus its negative counterpart equals zero. For example, ten plus negative ten equals zero. Because the amplitudes of our two signals add together, and the signals are exactly opposite, any point along the "time" line will always add to zero. The result is the two signals will completely cancel each other out, and the output will be nothing *(figure 6-4)*. This is why balanced systems can cancel hum and make noise, as explained below.

Balanced Mic Cables

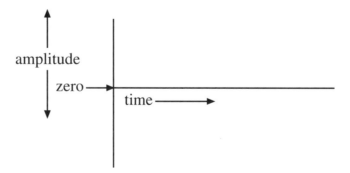

Figure 6-4: The resulting wave—no signal

A balanced mic cable uses three wires *(figure 6-5)*.

Figure 6-5: Balanced mic cable, two conductors with shield.

One is wrapped around the other two and is called a shield. The shield is connected to **ground**, or zero volts, and acts as a barrier against electromagnetic signals. This helps to further reduce the hum and noise induced into the wires. The other two carry the audio signal. One wire has the signal in normal phase (+ phase, or hot), the other is 180° out-of-phase (- phase, or cold). If you were to tie these together at their destination, you would get no signal, because they would cancel as in our preceding example. However, the folks that designed the balanced input circuitry of the mixer or other equipment have taken this into account. They take the out-of-phase signal and electronically reverse its phase, thus making the two signals coherent, or in-phase again. That way, they add together instead of canceling.

Hum and Noise Cancellation

Why go to all of this trouble? When transferring audio signals, especially relatively low-level ones like microphone signals, the wires tend to pick up interference and noise. These can be from strong radio signals, magnetic fields, lightning storms, or dozens of other sources. Where they come from doesn't matter as much as that they add unwanted noises to the audio. In a balanced line *(figure 6-6a),* these noises are picked up just like in any other wires, but at the next audio input stage, they are eliminated.

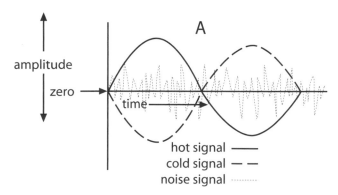

Figure 6-6a: Microphone hot, cold, and noise signals

The noises will be induced equally into both of the signal carrying wires, but they will be in-phase with each other, unlike the audio, which at this point is out-of-phase. Are you with me so far? At the mixer input, the negative phase signal is inverted, or placed in-phase.

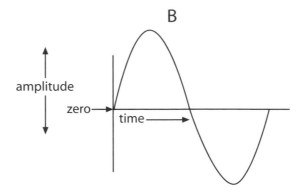

Figure 6-6b: Resultant wave after noise cancellation

The noise at this time is also inverted, which places it out-of-phase with the identical noise in the other wire, canceling and eliminating the noise. An ingenious concept, no? Hi-Z mics usually use an unbalanced two-wire cable and, although they also use shielded cabling, if they are run for long distances, they can pick up unwanted hum and noise. Unbalanced cabling is usually undesirable if cable runs are to be more than 15 or 20 feet. However, this will vary depending on the location and the level of the signal. Speaker cables do not need to be balanced because of the higher signal levels. Speaker wiring will still pick up noises, but because the noise is at such a low level compared to the audio, it goes unnoticed.

Balancing is generally used with microphones and in pro-audio signal processing gear, such as equalizers, compressors, crossovers, and pro-line amplifier inputs. Many of these units give you the option of running balanced or unbalanced. The way they are used and the distances between them will determine the best way to configure them.

How Speakers and Microphones Work (Chapter Eight) and How P.A.s Work (Chapter Fifteen) in the next part of this book provide more information about the various types of microphones available and how they are used.

PART 2

HOW THINGS WORK

Chapter **SEVEN**

HOW BATTERIES WORK
or, more than you ever wanted to know about batteries.

We take batteries for granted, and, indeed, they have been with us since the first scientists began experimenting with electricity. In truth, many of the things we call batteries are not batteries at all, but people have been calling them batteries for so long, the term has come to mean any voltage-producing unit. The most basic voltage-producing device is called a **cell**. A true battery is made up of two or more cells. Each cell of a lead-zinc or alkaline battery produces about 1.5 volts, so a 9-volt battery contains 6 cells. A 6-volt battery has four cells. AAA, AA, C, and D cells are not technically batteries, because each only contains one cell.

To most people, a battery is a battery is a battery. However, there are several different kinds of batteries, all serving different purposes. The least expensive of these—and the least long-lasting—are lead-zinc batteries. These are generally called "heavy-duty" batteries, which is a very misleading moniker because in the world of batteries, they are about the lightest-duty of the bunch. These little gadgets will also leak battery acid if they are left unused for too long.

Next up the battery food chain are the alkaline batteries. These moderately expensive fellows generally last up to three times as long as the cheaper "heavy-duty" batteries. They are also less likely to leak if left idle for too long. Alkaline batteries will leak, but they leak a slightly less volatile alkaloid substance than "heavy duty" batteries. *Hint:* If you can find a source for them, buy industrial alkaline batteries. They can last twice as long as standard alkalines.

Lead-acid batteries are used mostly in things like cars and trucks, wheelchairs, golf carts, and forklifts, and will not fit in your average portable CD player, wah wah pedal, or wireless microphone. Therefore, we won't say much about them except, where would we be without golf carts and forklifts and trucks and cars?

Less often seen are lithium and mercury batteries. These are more expensive and are commonly used where batteries are required to last a very long time at relatively low current drain, such as in hearing aids, commercial smoke detectors, and heart pacemakers. All of the previously mentioned batteries may explode(!) if exposed to high temperatures. Don't toss them into your fireplace or campfire.

SHELF LIFE

Batteries have a "shelf-life." That means if a battery is manufactured and stored, even if it is never used, it will go dead eventually. An alkaline battery will hold its full charge for about four years if it is stored in perfect conditions. Unfortunately, perfect conditions rarely occur. Several factors affect shelf-life, most notably humidity and temperature. A battery stored at optimum humidity and temperature, say, in a NASA warehouse, will last about the full four years, maybe even longer. A battery stored at 85% humidity at 85° will probably be close to dead in a year (or less). Most alkaline batteries are now dated by the manufacturer. Unfortunately, they are labeled, "Best if used by..." instead of with the actual date of manufacture. This "use by" date is based upon the assumption that the batteries will be stored under optimum conditions and sold relatively soon after being made. In reality, this rarely occurs. Batteries with no date codes may be years old before you buy them, so you are better off buying the batteries with the latest "use by" date that you can find. Battery distributors want to move the older stock quickly, so they drop the price on the old stuff. Buyers for chain stores often get paid bonuses based upon the amount of money they save their employers, so they buy these older, reduced-price batteries. Avoid buying batteries from large chains, especially discount stores. One notable exception to this is the Radio Shack chain. They have a high turnover of batteries, plus they specialize in electronic products and are aware of the shelf-life problem. Their batteries are usually pretty fresh. Remember: New batteries are not necessarily fresh batteries!

WHICH BATTERY SHOULD YOU USE?

The kind of battery to buy depends on how it is going to be used. If you want your kid's toy to last a couple of weeks until the toy breaks or the kid gets tired of it, buy "heavy-duty" lead-zinc batteries. They're cheap, and there is no sense buying a long-life battery for a short-life item. If you've got a portable music keyboard that you usually run from an AC adaptor, but you want to take it camping for a week or two, "heavy-duty" batteries will probably suffice. Just be sure you remember to remove them when you get back home so they don't leak and ruin the keyboard. If you normally run your favorite gadget on batteries all of the time, use alkaline or rechargeable batteries. They cost more, but the extra life will more than make up the difference in price. If you have a portable tape recorder and you record college lectures or business seminars, you won't want to miss a thing, so it's a good idea to use alkaline batteries. You may even want to use extremely long-lasting lithium or mercury batteries for these crucial applications.

ADAPTORS

DC power adaptors are usually available for most non-portable applications. Be certain, however that you use the correct adaptor for the piece of equipment you want to run. The voltage, current, and polarity must be correct, or the adaptor, the unit, or both may be damaged.

RECHARGEABLE BATTERIES

Nickel-cadmium or "NiCad" batteries, are a great thing for people who use large quantities of batteries. You can buy two sets of batteries so that one set is always charging while the other is being used. Ni-cads have a slightly lower voltage (1.2V) than standard batteries (1.5V) and will usually not last as long on a charge as a standard alkaline in low-current drain applications. NiCads tend to develop a "charging memory," where each time the battery is recharged, it charges to a slightly lower level, thus lasting a shorter length of time. Nickel Metal Hydride (NiMH) batteries work like NiCads with the additional advantage of no charging memory. Both NiCad and NiMH batteries actually work better at supplying higher current than alkaline batteries, which is why they are often used in things like cellular phones and digital cameras.

PREMIUM BATTERIES

Industrial alkaline batteries and mercury batteries will outlast traditional alkalines in most cases, but they cost considerably more to buy.

SOME QUESTIONS AND ANSWERS

Q: What's the difference between a "battery" and a "cell"?

A: A cell is a unit that produces a voltage. A battery is more than one of these cells connected together to give a higher voltage. One cell of a lead-zinc battery produces 1.5 volts. Put six of these together and you get 9 volts. D, C, AA, and AAA "batteries" only have one cell each, so they aren't really batteries; they are cells. The word "battery" has been used to identify any combination of cells for so long that the meaning has been convoluted to mean any voltage-producing unit.

Q: Many wireless manufacturers recommend Duracell-brand batteries for use with their equipment. Does this mean that Duracell is better than other brands?

A: No. The fact is, Duracell 9-volt batteries are shorter than most other brands of 9-volt batteries, by about 3/32 of an inch. If you use a longer battery, it may compress the spring battery terminals enough that a Duracell-size battery used later may not make good contact. The fact that the manufacturer recommends these batteries is based only upon the physical size of the battery (and maybe a promotional fee or two).

Q: Can I recharge alkaline batteries?

A: The answer to this question used to be no, but recently battery manufacturers have made a special type of alkaline battery that is rechargeable. Note the word "special." These are not standard alkaline batteries. They must be recharged in a special charging unit and can only be recharged a limited number of times. Standard alkalines are not rechargeable. There are several companies that sell battery "rechargers," or "rejuvenators" that claim their products can recharge alkaline batteries. They can't. What they actually do is put a voltage on the battery that disturbs the battery elements enough that they may produce a little more current before finally going completely dead (kind of like shaking a wind-up-type watch after it has run down—it might run for a few minutes before it stops again). The reason this is not a good idea is the batteries will sometimes explode if you try to charge them.

Q: Why do batteries leak?

A: Batteries work by breaking down the atoms in the metal parts inside the battery to release electrons. In order for them to do this, there must be some corrosive material in contact with the metal. In lead-zinc batteries, it's usually a paste of sulfuric acid and other chemicals. In alkaline batteries, it is an alkaloid (saline-based) mixture. Sometimes these corrosive agents will break through the protective layers and get to the outside. This is not only messy, but it can do damage to whatever the corrosive material touches, like circuit boards and components.

Q: So, what do I do with them when batteries go dead?

A: Many batteries (not only mercury batteries) contain mercury and should not just be thrown in the trash. Most stores that sell a lot of batteries will recycle them for you.

See, I told you it was more than you wanted to know! Here is a famous battery-related tongue twister: She sells "C" cells down by the sea shore...

Chapter EIGHT

HOW SPEAKERS AND MICROPHONES WORK

or, air, magnets, and little coils of wire.

Any device that changes energy from one form to another is called a **transducer**. Most microphones, speakers, and guitar pickups are electromagnetic **dynamic** transducers. Microphones change sound waves in the air into small electrical currents. Speakers change electric current to sound waves, and guitar pickups change string vibrations into electrical current. This chapter will explain how they work, and what can go wrong with them.

SPEAKERS

Speakers come in hundreds of different sizes, from those little tiny things inside of hearing aids—speakers so small they are measured in millimeters and microns—to the half-inchers in your walkman-style headphones; from the 1- to 3½-inch tweeters in car and home-audio sound systems; to 10-, 12-, and 15-inch woofers, and up to the 18-, 21-, and even 30-inch woofers used in movie theaters and in some pro touring sound systems.

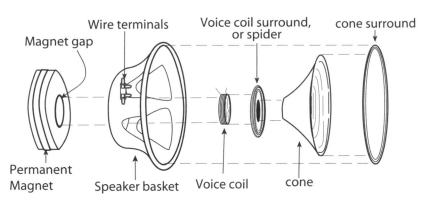

Figure 8-1: Exploded view of a speaker

This is how dynamic speakers work *(see figure 8-1):* A relatively high level AC (audio) current is sent by the audio amplifier to the speaker, via the speaker cables. This current goes through a coil of wire, called a voice coil, inside the speaker. This coil of wire is cylindrical and is situated inside what is called the **gap** of a permanent **magnet**. As we learned in a previous chapter, when you send current through a wire, the wire generates a magnetic field. The magnetic field generated by the speaker's voice coil interacts with the stationary magnetic field of the speaker's permanent magnet, pushing away from or pulling toward the permanent magnet, causing the voice coil to move. The movement of the voice coil is limited by the speaker's **cone**, or **diaphragm**, which is attached to the voice coil and at the top and bottom of the speaker **basket** (the metal or plastic outside frame part of the speaker). The cone moves forward and backward as the signal from the amp changes, pushing air around and creating sound. The baskets, or frames, on most speakers are pressed from a piece of sheet metal. This is called a stamped frame. Others are cast (molded) using aluminum, steel, or another lightweight alloy. These are called cast frames. Small speakers like tweeters often have plastic frames. Speaker failures are discussed in Chapter Nineteen, Blowing Speakers.

All sound waves have a frequency or frequencies. The note A in concert pitch is about 440 Hertz (or cycles per second). All notes (and indeed all tones, noises, thumps, thuds, anything we can hear) are made up of one or more (usually many) frequencies. When speakers move, they move rapidly front to back. The rate at which they move determines the frequencies of the sounds they reproduce. In general, a smaller speaker cone can move faster than a larger one because it takes more energy to move the larger, heavier-weight cone than it does to move a smaller, lighter one. There is less inertia with a small cone, allowing it to change directions faster, so small cones tend to reproduce high frequencies more efficiently. Conversely, large cones are better at reproducing lower frequencies, which is why you won't see a speaker system with 2-inch woofers and 15-inch tweeters.

DYNAMIC MICROPHONES

Dynamic microphones work in much the same way speakers do, only backwards. In fact, a speaker can be used as a low-quality microphone. Many fast-food drive-through windows use a cruddy speaker as an even more cruddy microphone (which may be why I always find strange and wonderful things in my order when I get home). Here is how it's done in higher-quality mics. The microphone's diaphragm is suspended in much the same way a speaker's cone is. The diaphragm is extremely light-weight, and when sound waves travel through the air, they cause it to move very slightly. This diaphragm is attached to a small coil of wire (the **pickup coil**), which is sitting in the gap of a small permanent magnet, similar to the voice coil in a speaker. When the coil moves in the permanent magnetic field due to changes in air pressure (sound), it induces a current in the coil, which varies at the same frequency as the sounds that caused it to move. This signal is very small, however, and requires quite a lot of amplification before it can be heard.

CONDENSER MICROPHONES

Another type of microphone is the condenser mic. **Condenser** is another word for capacitor, and these mics work differently from dynamic mics. Condenser mics require a current source to function. This might take the form of an internal battery or an external power supply, called a **phantom-power** supply. Phantom supplies for microphones are often built into mixing consoles, or they can be stand-alone units. Higher-quality condenser mics will usually sound better if the voltage of the phantom power is the recommended voltage. The diaphragm that senses the presence of sound waves in a condenser mic is actually a plate of a capacitor, which changes capacitance as the diaphragm moves. These changes are amplified inside the microphone by a transistor or a tube, and so condenser mics can be quite sensitive. I'll get into more detail of how, when, and why different mics are used in Chapter Fifteen, How P.A.s Work.

Microphones and guitar pickups are most frequently damaged by being dropped. Do not tap on a microphone to test it, and don't blow into it. Talk or sing into it; that's what it was meant for. It doesn't look cool onstage for a performer to be careful with a microphone, and most are built to take some abuse, but the less you swing a mic by its cord, drop it, spit into it, rain on it, hit it, and generally beat it up, the longer it will last and sound good.

GUITAR PICKUPS

Guitar pickups work similarly to a dynamic microphone in that they change sound waves into electrical current. But they do it in a different way *(see figure 8-2a).*

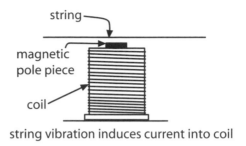

string vibration induces current into coil

Figure 8-2a: Guitar pickup

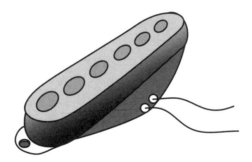

Figure 8-2b: Single coil pickup with individual pole pieces

The coil of wire in a guitar pickup doesn't move. It is wrapped around one or more pieces of magnetized metal called **pole pieces**. Some pickups have just one or two pole pieces that run under all of the guitar's strings. These are called bar, or blade-type pickups, but most pickups have individual pole pieces for each string. The advantage to this is the pole pieces can be adjusted, either at the factory or by the end-user (or a repair shop) to match the output of the individual strings. The waves picked up by the guitar's transducer are not sound waves in the air, but are the actual vibrations of the ferrous metal strings (a magnetic pickup will not work on a nylon or gut-stringed instrument). The string's proximity to the pole piece causes the magnetic field of the pole piece to vary at the same rate that the string is vibrating. This changing magnetic field is induced into the pickup coil as electrical current. As with a microphone, the output is fairly small—although slightly higher-output than most mics—and must be amplified to be heard. Pickup design has come a long way since the first guitar pickups were made. These days, you can buy after-market pickups that have been optimized for output, frequency response, tonal quality, etc.

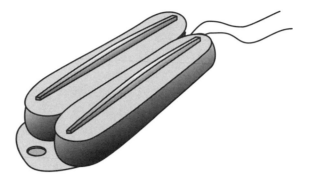

Figure 8-2c: Double-coil bar magnet pickup

Pickups can sometimes become **microphonic**, meaning that they respond to mechanical vibration, as well as magnetic (string) vibration. This is caused by the coils of wire in the pickup becoming loose enough to move next to each other. This movement causes unwanted currents to be produced within the pickup as these loose coils move. Most high-quality pickups are potted, meaning they have been dipped in a molten, heavy wax and then allowed to cool. This helps to prevent pickups from becoming microphonic, and can sometimes repair older pickups that have developed this problem.

OTHER TRANSDUCERS

So far, we've discussed only dynamic, (electromagnetic) transducers. There are many other kinds, one of the most common being piezo-electric transducers. They are sometimes used as tweeters in medium- to low-quality home-stereo speakers, car speakers, keyboard amps, monitors, and even P.A. cabinets. Piezo-electric tweeters possess both advantages and disadvantages when compared to dynamic tweeters. They are very lightweight and can often be used without a crossover due to their frequency response and impedance characteristics. However, they usually have lower power-handling capabilities than dynamic tweeters, and they tend to produce higher levels of **distortion** and poor overall sound quality. Distortion is more difficult to hear at higher frequencies, so it is not very noticeable in some applications. Piezo-type drivers work on a completely different principle from dynamic transducers. The driver element of a piezo-electric transducer is made of a special type of ceramic that produces a small electrical current when pressure is placed upon it. This is the same material used to make drum triggers. When you hit a drum trigger, the piezo-element produces an AC voltage similar to that produced by a microphone, but with much less low-frequency content and higher output. When a piezo-element is used as a tweeter, the process is reversed. Audio signals in the form of AC electrical current are sent to the element, which flexes slightly, vibrating an attached diaphragm at the audio frequencies. These types of elements have widely varying impedance, depending on what frequencies are being sent to them. Most dynamic tweeters are 4 ohms to 16 ohms nominal impedance. The impedance of a piezo-tweeter increases as frequency decreases, so at 1kHz or lower, they are often higher than 10k ohms impedance. This causes them to virtually ignore lower frequencies, often meaning a crossover is not necessary. Because crossover components are expensive, this saves speaker manufacturers big bucks, so it's no wonder they use them when they can.

PICKUP FAILURES

Guitar pickups will sometimes fail for no apparent reason, but rough handling is often a contributing factor. There's not much to go wrong with a pickup; it's just one continuous piece of wire wrapped around a magnetic pole piece or two (or six, or twelve, or...). If it fails, it's because the wire became loose or broke. Not much can cause these things to happen, other than being banged around, or possibly by being exposed to weather extremes. Always treat your musical equipment as well as you treat yourself. If it's too hot, cold, or wet someplace for you to be comfortable, your guitar, keyboard, microphone, bass, snare drum, trumpet, or harmonica probably won't like it any better than you do.

Chapter NINE

How Wireless Works
or, "Look, Ma, no cables!"

By golly, when I was a kid, you had your guitar, you had your amp, and you had your guitar cord. There weren't any wireless gadgets for your guitar, you used a guitar cord, and that was that. I also had to walk uphill both ways through three feet of snow to get to school, even in summer, but that's another story. Today, wireless units are as common as, well, old guys like me whining about the good ol' days. Guitar players use them, vocalists use them, and there are even wireless **MIDI** units for keyboard players. They are handy and convenient gadgets, and they have made tripping over cords onstage a thing of the past. Seems like everybody's using them.

Along with the advantages, of course, comes a whole new set of problems. Wireless units use batteries. If you don't carry spare batteries, you might lose your signal half way through a performance and have to switch over to a cable. You may find that you're picking up CB radio signals from the truckers on the nearest highway. Your signal may be weak, or distorted, or full of static. There is no way to avoid occasional problems like this, but if you know how these units work, it might help you to deal with these inconveniences.

RADIO WAVES

First we need to know a little bit about radios, and what makes them tick. **Radio waves** are just like sound waves, except they are considerably faster and higher in frequency. (If you need to, refer back to Chapter Four, About Sound, to refresh your memory about waves.) Sound waves travel through the air at the speed of sound (duh!): About 755 miles per hour, also known as Mach 1. Radio-frequency waves move at about the **speed of**

light: 186,000 miles per second, a whole lot faster than sound waves. Audio frequencies are typically 20 Hertz (cycles per second) to 20,000 Hertz. Radio frequencies are considered to be anything above about 100,000 Hertz.

When radio **transmission** was invented, there were no regulations, so anyone could broadcast anything they wanted at any frequency. This was fine, as long as the people you were trying to broadcast to knew what frequency to tune in. But soon, the airwaves became crowded with dozens of signals interfering with each other. The folks using radios decided they needed to set up some rules, and several countries set up governing boards to determine frequency allocation. In the United States, the Federal Communications Commission was formed. The FCC decided what types of signals would be broadcast at which frequencies, so that the average radio listener wouldn't have so many interference problems. Today, there are so many different things being broadcast, that without regulating the allocation of frequencies, radios would be virtually useless due to the huge number of different signals competing with each other.

AMPLITUDE MODULATION

There are two basic types of radio frequency (RF) transmission: AM (**amplitude modulation**) and FM (**frequency modulation**). With AM transmission, the broadcaster sends a high-powered RF signal into a tall **antenna**, which **radiates** the signal out into the atmosphere. This signal is a constant wave, usually in the range of 500,000Hz (500kHz) to 2,000,000Hz (2MHz), and is called a **carrier** wave. This carrier wave is extremely constant in frequency and level (amplitude). The carrier wave is then **modulated**. That means another signal is added to it. This additional signal is any audio frequency signal (voice, music, etc.) that the broadcaster wants to transmit. When the radio receiver picks up this signal, the radio frequency carrier signal is removed, leaving only the audio signal that was modulating it. This music or voice information can then be heard. AM transmission has some drawbacks. Any noise added to the carrier signal, such as lightning in the air, will be treated by the receiving unit as audio noise, and will be heard as a loud, unpleasant crackle by the person listening. Also, when the FCC allotted frequencies in the early 1930s, audio equipment was not capable of reproducing **high-fidelity** audio. The wider the frequency range of audio being broadcast, the more **bandwidth** is required, so the FCC only allows AM stations to broadcast an audio frequency range of 500Hz to 5kHz. This is fine for human speech, but very limiting for music. Another undesirable trait of this particular band of the RF **spectrum** is that the length of antenna required to transmit and receive these relatively low frequencies is quite long. There's more information about frequencies, **wavelengths**, and antennas in Appendix D, Formulas and Miscellaneous Information.

Frequency Modulation

FM is a slightly newer technology. It works in a similar way as AM but normally transmits at a higher frequency, typically 100MHz and above. Many wireless units operate in the VHF (**Very High Frequency**) range and require much shorter antennas than AM transmitters and receivers. The audio signal that is added to the carrier frequency is added in such a way that it varies the frequency of the carrier signal rather than changing the amplitude. An FM carrier at 87MHz being modulated at 1,000Hz will vary higher and lower in frequency than the 87MHz carrier. It will do this 1,000 times per second (the frequency of the audio signal modulating it). How high and how low this variation is depends on the level, or amplitude, of the modulating audio signal being added. The receiving unit's decoding or demodulating circuitry responds only to these changes in frequency, not to any change in level or amplitude. This arrangement of being non-amplitude-sensitive enables the carrier to be broadcast and received without being affected as much by airborne noises, lightning, or other external interference. Also, since the carrier is at such a high frequency, the bandwidth allowed can be greater, enabling higher-quality audio signals to be sent and received. The audio frequency bandwidth allowed for standard broadcast FM is 50Hz to 15kHz. Still not super hi-fi, but good enough for most human ears.

WIRELESS SYSTEMS

Okay, now that we've gotten that out of the way, we'll talk about wireless units for microphones and guitars. A wireless system is made up of two components: The transmitter and the receiver. The transmitter produces a carrier wave and modulates it with the audio signal from the mic or instrument. It then transmits this composite signal via the transmitter antenna. The transmitting antenna on some wireless units is incorporated into the signal cable, which plugs into the guitar or connects to the microphone. The transmitter antenna can be concealed inside a handheld microphone's case, or it might be a short, thin, single wire coming out of the transmitter case. The first wireless units were AM, which meant they were prone to noise problems, as well as the long antenna we discussed previously. Fortunately, there weren't very many of these made before VHF FM transmitters and receivers were introduced. Most of the wireless units currently in use are VHF or UHF (**Ultra High Frequency**) FM. They are much better at rejecting unwanted noises. Many of them use a "true diversity" antenna system. True diversity wireless units have two antennas on the receiver unit, and the receiver selects the one with the strongest signal. This helps prevent signal drop-outs and noise.

Problems

Wireless problems can be divided into two major categories: Those you have some control over, and those you don't.

Interference

In the "no control" category, we find: Interference from illegally transmitted signals, such as CB (citizen's band), SSB (single side-band), and "ham" radio operators that boost their power and/or modulation higher than allowed by FCC rules. Or, they may be operating legally but just happen to be really close by. So, your location can also be a problem that you cannot control. Some other location problems include being inside metal buildings that inhibit or reflect the wireless signal, bars with dozens of neon beer signs generating large electromagnetic fields, and buildings situated too close to outside RF sources, such as radio stations or people using other wireless units close to your location. My band used to play at a bar that was across the street from another bar that also had live music. One night, our guitar player placed his amp on standby as we went on break, but noticed the "transmit" light on his wireless receiver was still on, even though his transmitter was turned off. He turned his amp back on and the wireless signal of the guitarist for the band across the street came through loud and clear. We could even tell which song they were playing.

Problems like these can only be solved by waiting for the offending external interference to stop, or by leaving the location. There are, however, a lot of wireless-related problems that can be remedied or prevented. These include battery problems, connection problems, and maintenance-related problems.

Bad Batteries

Regarding wireless units, most of the problems I run into on a daily basis are battery-related. Everything you really need to know about batteries (and then some) is in Chapter Seven, How Batteries Work, at the beginning of this section. I will add one thing specific to wireless units: Wireless transmitters consume more current than most other musical gadgets that use batteries, such as guitar pedals and active instrument electronics, so the quality of the battery you use will have a more direct effect on how well the wireless transmitter performs. Here is one area where it is very important to stick to well-known brands. Also, try to be sure the batteries you buy are fresh. Old batteries are weak batteries, and it's difficult to know how old a battery is when you purchase it.

Broken Wires

The second most common failure in wireless transmitters is broken wires. The best way to prevent this is to try never to let the transmitter dangle from the cable. Don't wrap the cords up the same way every time you put them away. Bending any wire in the same place repeatedly will eventually break it. Also, don't transport the receiver with the power cord plugged in if it has a removable cord or a wall transformer-type supply. This can cause the connections inside the receiver unit to break.

Maintenance

Maintenance problems include dirty battery terminals. If the unit has been idle for a while, it is a good idea to clean the battery contacts with a rubber pencil eraser. This removes some of the **oxidation** and improves connections, which in turn will increase battery life. If you've noticed the signal cutting out but haven't taken it in to be checked, do so. It's not going to get better, and it will get worse. If you snapped off one of your antennas and stuffed it back together, and it seems to be working alright, take it in and get it fixed anyway. The range of reception can be seriously limited by a bad antenna, and you might not notice it now, but at your most important opening-for-a-national-act-in-front-of-a-dozen-record-executives gig, it will fail. I repeat: It's not going to get better, and it will get worse.

Wireless Quality

A couple of final thoughts I'd like to pass on to you about wireless units: You get what you pay for, particularly with signal-handling equipment. Don't cheap-out on your wireless. Buy the best one you can possibly afford. It will pay you back in consistent, quality operation. Don't buy a wireless system without checking to see what frequencies the other guys in the band are using. I've seen many a player get a "heck of a deal" on a used wireless just to find out it was the same frequency as another one already in use by someone else in the band. Having the bass and guitar coming out of both the bass amp and guitar amp simultaneously is not a nice noise. Several of the better quality-units on the market prevent this problem by allowing you to select from several frequencies.

In-Ear Monitors

Another development in recent years has been the wireless in-ear monitoring system. These can work very well, but again, you definitely get what you pay for. In-ear monitors work much like a traditional wireless system, except the receiver (rather than the transmitter) is worn by the user. Some of these units are designed to transmit and receive in stereo. Unlike a traditional wireless unit, these systems are not maintenance-free. Regular cleaning of the earpieces is necessary to keep them functioning properly. The earpieces in the better units are custom-made to fit your ears, so they cannot be traded around or used by several different people. Many folks I know who use them say they are great, and they wouldn't ever want to go back to regular speaker-type monitors.

Wireless is a technology that is becoming increasingly common. Wireless systems are now found in garage bands and little country churches. As with all electronic gear, if you use good batteries and take good care of them, good quality-wireless systems will perform well for a long time.

Chapter **TEN**

HOW TUBES WORK
or, why do they get so stinkin' hot?

Tubes are strange and wonderful devices. They get their name from the glass or metal tube-shaped enclosure (called an **envelope**) that surrounds the internal elements. There are a lot of different types of tubes. The simplest are two-element tubes, called diodes. Tubes with three elements are called **triodes**, and five-element tubes are known as **pentodes**. Some tubes have more than one stage inside; the dual-triode configuration (two separate tube stages in one envelope) is used in many audio preamplifiers.

TUBE CONSTRUCTION

Before we get into how they work, let's take a look at how tubes are constructed. *Figure 10-1* below shows the innards of a basic triode tube.

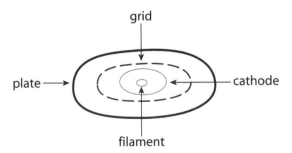

Figure 10-1: Triode tube element layout (top view)

A triode consists of three basic elements, a **plate** (P), a cathode (K), and a **grid** (G), plus a **filament** or "**heater**." All tubes have a heater of some sort, so they are not counted as a tube element. The filament in a tube is made of a special material, similar to the wires in a toaster, that get very hot when current flows through them. A red-orange glow produced by the hot filament is often, but not always, visible in a normally operating tube. Because the filament is supposed to heat the cathode, the filament and the cathode are placed physically close together. The plate wraps around the filament and cathode. The distance between the elements is very critical. Tubes operate at relatively high voltages, so if the elements are placed too close together, arcing may occur. This is highly undesirable. Putting them too far apart results in poor **emission** (transfer of electrons), so the tolerances must be very precise for the tube to function properly. After the elements are welded and soldered in their correct positions, the envelope is placed around the elements. The envelope is an airtight container usually made of blown glass or metal. Then, the air in the envelope is removed, creating a vacuum. Hence the term "vacuum tube." A perfect vacuum—an envelope with no air or gas molecules left inside—is impossible to achieve, even with the best modern equipment, so some residual gasses remain inside the envelope. The life span of tubes, the way they function and the way they sound in circuits is affected by these gasses. Tube manufacturing is a slow one-at-a-time process, and is very labor intensive. The skill required to assemble them makes it difficult to produce consistently high-quality tubes. In every batch of tubes manufactured, many are defective. Tubes are not being made at this time in the U.S.A. The American labor force demands too much money for this kind of precision work, making the cost of manufacturing tubes too high. As technology evolved in the mid-20th century, it was discovered that solid-state components could perform the same functions as tubes, but with better efficiency, lower production costs, and higher reliability. So, the last U.S. tube makers ceased production in the late 1980s.

Many people believe that tube-type audio amplifiers sound better than transistorized ones. This is a matter of personal opinion, of course, and some people prefer the sound of solid-state devices. But most guitarists and many recording engineers think tube circuitry sounds smoother and more musical, at least in some applications. There is enough demand for tubes worldwide that several Asian and European countries still have factories cranking out tubes (or **valves** as they are called in Europe).

HOW TUBES WORK

There you have the basics of the tube manufacturing process. Now let's find out what tubes do and how they do it.

The Diode

Figure 10-2 shows the schematic representation of a tube diode.

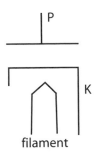

Figure 10-2: Schematic diagram of a tube diode

It has just two elements, the cathode (K) and the plate (P). Some diodes have a separate filament to heat the cathode, some have a self-heating cathode. In our example above, the filament and the cathode are separate. The metal material of the cathode is an alloy formulated to have an excess of electrons. They're just waiting for some outside force to knock them off and send them flying into space. The heat from the filament stimulates them to separate from the metal, and the vacuum inside the envelope allows them to disengage without bumping into a bunch of oxygen or hydrogen atoms. This process is called emission. What good are a bunch of loose electrons flying off in all directions, you ask? Absolutely none. This is where the plate comes in and saves the day. Electrons flow from negative to positive, so by placing a high positive voltage on the plate, the electrons are attracted to the plate and we get electrons flowing from the cathode to the plate.

"So what?" I hear you ask. Here is the useful thing about all of this. The electron flow, or current, only happens in one direction. This means we can use a diode as a **rectifier** to turn alternating current into direct current. Because the tube will only conduct when the plate is positive with respect to the cathode, and it will not conduct when the cathode is positive to the plate, only the positive half of an AC voltage will pass in the form of current through the diode. The negative portion of the AC signal is ignored.

Rectifying AC

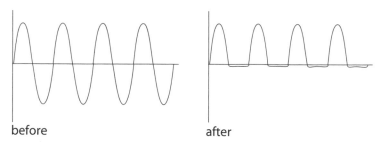

before   after

Figure 10-3: High-voltage AC signal

Figure 10-3 shows a high-voltage AC signal before and after being sent to our diode. The converted, or rectified AC voltage looks like a bunch of positive-going bumps. This is called unfiltered, or **pulsating DC.** By adding a **filter** capacitor to reduce the ripple effect, we have relatively **"clean"** (ripple-free) DC voltage. Most electronic equipment uses one or more DC power supplies, and this is how the AC from the wall socket is converted to DC in most of this equipment.

Adding Control: The Triode

Now, take a look at *figure 10-4*. This is the schematic symbol for a triode tube. The elements are the cathode (K) and plate (P), like our diode from before, with the addition of a grid (G). This type of tube is mostly used for amplifying audio or radio frequency signals. A separate filament is used in most multiple element tubes like this.

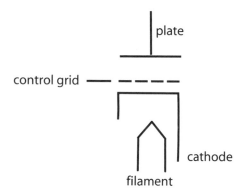

plate

control grid

cathode

filament

Figure 10-4: Schematic diagram of a triode tube

A triode works a lot like a diode, with current flow from the cathode to the plate. The grid is used to control the current flow. In fact, its full name is the **control grid**. Picture a garden hose, connected to a water spigot, with a sprinkler on the other end. If you turn on the water, you get water (current) flow, but it is uncontrolled. All of the water from the spigot is running out of the sprinkler. But if you bend the hose somewhere between the spigot and the sprinkler, you can cause the volume of water coming out of the sprinkler to decrease. If you fold the hose completely in half, you can stop the flow entirely. This is the effect the control grid has on the flow of electrons through the triode tube.

Now, let's say you're folding the hose, and unfolding it part way, and then folding it again. The "current" through the hose is getting less, then more, then less. The water coming out of the sprinkler squirts lower, spraying only a couple of feet in the air. Then as you unfold the hose, it squirts higher, maybe up to ten or twelve feet in the air. Then you fold the hose again, and it sprays lower, back to two or three feet. You're only moving the hose a few inches, but you're controlling the output of the hose by several feet—a factor of many times more. This is called **amplification**, or **gain**: A small control affecting a large change. If we add a small varying voltage such as a 1kHz audio frequency signal on the control grid of our tube, we can vary the current on the plate at this same frequency. The change at the plate will be much larger than the original 1kHz signal on the grid. Amplification, again! Take the output from a microphone, keyboard, or guitar, add in a few of these gain stages and pretty soon you can have enough signal to cause a speaker to produce sound.

More Control: The Pentode

Another type of tube often seen in musical instrument amplifiers is the five-element tube, or pentode. *Figure 10-5* shows the schematic symbol for a pentode tube.

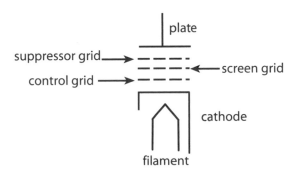

Figure 10-5: Schematic diagram of a pentode tube

The pentode looks and operates much like a triode, but it has a couple of extra grids. These extra grids allow the tube to carry much more current without burning up the tube. This makes them more appropriate for driving loads like speakers, which need larger amounts of current to produce sound. These extra grids are called the **screen grid** and the **suppressor grid**. They both function to increase the efficiency of the tube and improve its operation by focusing the electrons transmitted from the cathode to the plate. There are also **tetrodes** (four-element tubes with a screen grid, but no suppressor grid) and **heptodes** (six-element tubes), but they are rarely seen in audio equipment or guitar amps.

TUBE DESIGNATIONS

Tubes are assigned numbers according to their type and function, as well as their electrical ratings. For example, let's examine an extremely common dual-triode tube, the 12AX7a. The first numbers indicate the filament voltage of the tube. The letters and numbers that follow indicate the type of tube. The first number, in this case 12, is the filament voltage. The next part, AX7, is the actual tube type, and the small letter "a" after the rest indicates an improvement has been made to the tube since the number was first assigned. The original version of this tube was simply a 12AX7. Sometimes, tubes will also have a European number or an industrial or military number. Our 12AX7a might also be called an ECC83 (European) or 7025 (industrial U.S. number). European numbers were assigned by a standardizing organization in Europe in the early 1900s, just as American tube numbers were by an American standardizing organization. An industrial-type tube with the numbers 7025 is identical to a 12AX7 in form and function, but was built to higher specifications of temperature range and/or thickness of the envelope, metal used for the pins, and other minor variations. These tubes were often used in industrial or military applications.

Nowadays, there is no difference between a currently manufactured 12AX7a, a 7025, or an ECC83. Many companies sell NOS (**new old stock**) tubes, and they are often better-quality than new tubes, but they are expensive and will continue to get more expensive as supplies dwindle.

ABOUT TUBE-TESTERS

Tube-testers are helpful tools when you are matching output tubes or selecting preamp tubes for a specific purpose. For example, if you have a tube guitar amplifier that gets the majority of its distortion (or "overdrive") from the second-stage preamp tube, as many of them do, you can tailor the amp's gain characteristics to your personal taste by selecting preamp tubes with higher or lower gain factors. They also work well for matching output tube sets. Chapter Eleven, How Amplifiers Work, explains more about matched output tubes.

A tube-tester is good for letting you know if a tube is totally dead. However, most tube-testers are worthless for determining if tubes are intermittently or "kind-of" working. Many perfectly good tubes have been discarded because they tested "bad" in a tube-tester. Here is one reason this happens. The plate voltage on a typical preamp tube in a guitar amplifier runs in the 200- to 300-volt range, and output tubes run anywhere from 250 volts to 700 volts, depending on the tubes being used. Most tube-testers test them all at 120 volts. To my way of thinking, this is like driving a racecar twenty-five miles per hour and deciding it's ready for the Indy 500. Some tubes that test well at this voltage will fail under actual-use conditions. Tube-testers also tend to show some tubes as being "gassy" (having too much air left inside the envelope) when they either aren't or it doesn't matter. The 6L6GC tube is one of the most commonly used types of tubes for amplifier output, and they almost always test gassy in a tube-tester. Hundreds of perfectly good 6L6GC tubes were thrown away for being gassy back in the fifties and sixties when every corner drug store had a tube-tester in the back of the store.

Speaking of gassy 6L6GC tubes, a 6L6GC tube in a guitar amplifier will often glow a deep blueish-purple color. This is normal for this tube and does not indicate a defect. Tube-sellers will try to get you to replace them if they do this. Don't. It's perfectly normal. The best way to determine whether a tube needs to be replaced is to replace it, and if it sounds better, leave the new tube in. If it doesn't change, put the old tube back in. Tube-testers are like any other tool. They work really well for what they were designed to do, but they have limitations. Knowing their limitations allows us to use them to our best advantage.

TUBE PROBLEMS

Tubes sometimes become "microphonic." That means they produce audible noises when they are moved, thumped, or vibrated. Preamp tubes will usually produce a high-pitched ringing noise when they get microphonic. Output tubes, especially 6L6GC or EL34 tubes will "grumble" or "growl" a lower pitched sound when they are jarred. When they get very bad, preamp tubes may actually oscillate: A ringing, whistling, or howling sound. Output tubes may produce enough noise to compete with and distort the signal. To test for microphonic preamp tubes, first remove the tube shields or covers, then turn the amp on and let it warm up normally. Set the volume to normal operating levels and tap lightly on the preamp tubes with your fingernail. A normal tube will make a small amount of noise as you tap on it. But, a microphonic tube will "ping," and the ringing noise will sustain for a while.

If output tubes are microphonic, you can usually tell by running the amp normally and thumping the cabinet firmly with your hand. If your amp produces a low-frequency rumble when you do this, the output tubes are probably microphonic. Microphonic output tubes really don't present much of a problem unless they get so noisy that they interfere with the audio signal at normal volumes. Most tubes are microphonic to a small extent. This is perfectly normal. You only need to replace them if the tones they produce interfere with the normal operation of the amp.

TUBE BRANDS

Here's my opinion about companies that sell their own "brands" of tubes. None of the new tubes—even those being sold by U.S. companies— are made in the United States, and they are not comparable to the quality tubes that used to be manufactured in the U.S . As far as I know, unless the companies are selling new-old-stock (NOS) tubes, at this point in time they all import them from the same few factories in Russia, China, Germany, or one of the formerly communist Slavic countries. I've heard of a couple of companies trying to influence a factory or two in China to make the tubes to their specifications, and I applaud any effort to improve the quality of currently manufactured tubes. But to my knowledge, the quality has not improved yet. One American tube importer bought a factory in Eastern Europe and was tooling up to make primo-quality 12AX7a's when U.S./NATO forces bombed the factory while liberating the Kosovo Albanians. This company now hopes to try the same thing in China and may be up and running by the time you read this. I sincerely hope manufacturers succeed in getting the quality level up, but I still doubt that they'll match the quality of a 1960s Sylvania, RCA, or Raytheon tube.

I'm not naming names but one company in particular wants you to think that their tubes are superior to all others. They are not. The company imports the tubes, tests them with their super-duper tube-tester, screen-prints their logo on them, and sells them. So do all of the other companies. They all use the same tubes. They all have really good tube-testers. They all have cool logos and colorful paint. And they all have about the same failure rate. It doesn't matter how you dress a pig, he's still a pig.

TUBE LIFE

I often hear of companies recommending that you change all of the tubes, or at least the output tubes, every six months. Baloney. If you play loud for long periods of time, many hours a week, it's a good idea to change your output tubes as soon as you detect any change in output or quality. But there is nothing to keep you from using the same tubes for years with no adverse effects.

Preamp tubes are mainly amplifying voltage, so they are not under a lot of stress to provide current. Consequently, they can last a very long time. It is not uncommon to find 12AX7s that are 30 or 35 years old in an amplifier and working just fine. In fact, due to the inconsistent quality of currently available tubes, sometimes replacing them actually degrades the operation of the amp. I'd rather have a perfectly functional 30-year-old American 12AX7 than a brand-new Chinese or Russian 12AX7a. Preamp tubes do fail sometimes. They can lose gain or become noisy or microphonic and, of course, they should be replaced when this happens. Still, I don't believe in replacing preamp tubes unless there is something actually wrong with them. The only folks you'll hear promoting changing tubes frequently are the folks that want to sell them to you. Ignore the man behind the curtain, folks! It's just the dollars talkin'!

Chapter ELEVEN

HOW AMPLIFIERS WORK
or, what goes in must come out...louder!

In this chapter, we'll go through a typical guitar amplifier to see how it does what it does. You may wish to refer to the second chapter on components to refresh your memory about some of the devices discussed here. The first thing to understand about any complex piece of electronic equipment is that it is made up of many different stages, all linked together to form the complete unit. If we analyze each of these stages separately, the entire unit becomes simpler and easier to understand. Our example amplifier will be a two-channel amp featuring a clean, undistorted channel and an **overdrive** channel that adds distortion to the guitar's signal. Keep in mind, there are many different amplifier configurations and this is an example of only one.

BLOCK DIAGRAM

Figure 11-1 shows the many stages of this guitar amp as separate blocks. This type of layout is referred to as a **block diagram**. The triangle symbol indicates an amplifier stage. The "clean" signal path is shown as a longer dashed line, and the "overdrive" signal follows the path shown as a shorter dashed line.

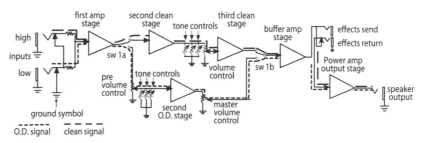

Figure 11-1: Block diagram of a two-channel guitar amp

THE PREAMP: CLEAN CHANNEL

The signal from the guitar enters the amp at the input jacks. The input section on many amps will allow you to select either high- or low-gain input level. This is handy if you have a guitar with high-output active electronics, or if you wish to plug in a line-level signal source. Using the low-gain input jack prevents ugly input overdrive distortion (more on overdriving later).

From the input, the signal goes to the first preamplifier stage. Often, this stage is common to both the nondistorting "clean channel" and the distorting "overdrive channel" of the amp. The first stage increases the signal level in order for the subsequent stages to process the signal without inducing excessive noise. All electronic circuits add a small amount of noise, and the higher the signal level is, the less noticeable the noise will be. This stage might be solid-state, in the form of transistors and discrete (individual) components; a single stage of an operational amplifier integrated circuit (op-amp I.C.); or it could be a tube stage in the form of half of a typical dual-triode tube such as a 12AX7a.

After the first stage, the signal is routed to either the clean or the overdrive preamp channel via some method of **switching**. Switching is accomplished many different ways: A simple mechanical push switch on the front panel of the amp, an external foot-operated switch that plugs into the amp, or an electronic switch such as a relay or opto-coupler. In our example amplifier, we're using the first half of a mechanical DPDT switch *(figure 11-2)*.

Figure 11-2: DPDT toggle switch

We're going to describe the operation of the "clean" channel first. The signal from the first stage, after being routed by the switch to the clean channel, goes to the second preamplifier stage. This stage brings the signal level higher still and sends it into the tone-control section. Some amps skip this stage and go directly to the tone circuit from the first stage.

Tone Controls

The tone controls are audio filters that allow the tonal quality of the guitar's signal to be manipulated. There are two basic types of tone controls. Passive controls use no amplifying components and are subtractive in nature. This means they cannot boost a frequency. They can only remove (cut) frequencies from the signal. Active tone controls use amplifier stages and may either lower (cut) or raise (boost) frequency levels. Potentiometers, fixed resistors, and capacitors are used to determine what frequencies will be affected and to what degree in both types of tone controls. Some tone circuits also use audio inductors. Tone controls can be designed to function in a variety of ways. A **low-shelving** tone control varies the level of everything below a certain frequency. A **high-shelving** control adjusts the level of all frequencies above a certain frequency. High- and low-shelving controls are typical of the treble and bass controls found on many guitar amps. Band-pass-type tone controls are also found on a lot of amps. A band-pass control varies a set frequency range only. For example, 800Hz to 2kHz. This enables the user to boost or cut a certain frequency. **Graphic equalizers** are simply collections of several (or many) band-pass-tone controls. A **parametric equalizer** includes a control or switch to allow you to choose the frequency to be adjusted, and may have a third control, called Q (for quality) or width (or whatever the particular amp maker decided to call it that day), which allows you to determine how many frequencies above and below the center frequency will be effected.

Volume Control

From the tone circuits, the signal then goes to the first volume control. A volume or level control is a mechanical voltage-dividing network, which uses a variable resistor called a potentiometer. As you can see in *figure 11-3*, the signal is inserted into the top terminal and comes out of the movable wiper terminal (with the arrow). The bottom terminal is connected to ground.

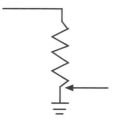

Figure 11-3: Volume control schematic diagram, wiper at ground

When the wiper is at the bottom of the control, there is maximum resistance from the input to the wiper, and zero resistance from the wiper to ground. So, no signal can pass from the control to the next stage. As we turn the control, the wiper moves up from the bottom. At this point, *(figure 11-4)*, there is now less resistance from the top to the wiper and more resistance from the wiper to ground, so some signal is allowed to pass on to the next stage. At the halfway point, *(figure 11-5)* there is even less resistance from top to wiper, and more from wiper to ground, so more signal comes from the wiper and on to the next stage of the amp.

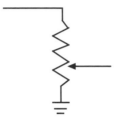

Figure 11-4: Volume control schematic diagram, wiper at ¼ way up.

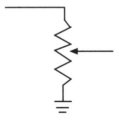

Figure 11-5: Volume control schematic diagram, wiper at ½ way up.

In *figure 11-6*, the control is all the way up. There is now almost zero resistance between the wiper and the input and maximum resistance from the wiper to ground. Maximum signal transfer to the next stage will occur.

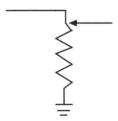

Figure 11-6: Volume control schematic diagram, wiper at full up

Level controls in audio gear can also be active, meaning that the control adjusts the gain of an amplifier stage, rather than simply removing all or part of the signal. These are actually gain controls, not level or volume controls. However, the terms are often used interchangeably.

The signal progresses from the volume control to yet another amplifier stage. This stage is referred to as a **buffer** and is designed to have very little or no gain. The buffer stage prevents the volume and tone controls from interacting adversely with the next section of the amp. The second half of the channel selector switch determines which preamp output, clean or overdrive, will be sent on to the next stage.

THE PREAMP: OVERDRIVE CHANNEL

Before we trace the signal out to the effects send and return, let's see what happens to the signal if we select the overdrive channel. If we switch the channel selector to overdrive, the signal from the input stage is now being sent to the first volume control of the overdrive preamp. This control works in the same way as the volume control in the clean preamp, but its purpose is slightly different. The clean preamp volume control was used to set the overall level of the clean preamp. Whereas, this control's purpose is to determine how much signal will be sent to another high-gain preamp stage. This will determine the amount of distortion or "overdrive" the preamp will induce into the instrument signal.

About Overdriving

Overdriving is the process of sending too much signal into a stage of an amplifier or other electronic signal-carrying device. The result is distortion of the original signal. This can be a good thing or a bad thing. Some distortion sounds pleasing, while other distortion does not. The reason for this is the **harmonic** content of the distorted signal. There is more about harmonics later in this chapter in the section on power amps. Here's how distortion is produced. The preamp stages are limited in how much signal they can reproduce cleanly by the power-supply voltage. An amp stage with a plus and minus 15-volt power supply cannot reproduce a waveform any larger than 30 volts peak-to-peak.

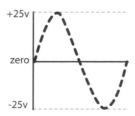

Figure 11-7a: Clean 50-volt peak-to-peak signal

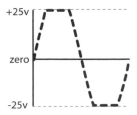

Figure 11-7b: Clipped 50-volt peak-to-peak signal

Figure 11-7 shows what happens if the signal level exceeds the power supply limits. The undistorted signal in *figure 11-7a* is exactly 50 volts peak-to-peak. The distorted signal shown in *figure 11-7b* has flat spots on the top and bottom. This is called **clipping** and is what the output signal looks like if an amp stage is driven by too large a signal. Solid-state circuits sometimes use clipping diodes *(figure 11-8)* to get more distortion than can be induced by overdriving alone.

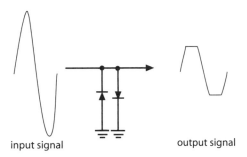

input signal   output signal

Figure 11-8: Clipping diodes

Remember, diodes will only conduct in one direction. If two diodes are placed in opposite directions as in the figure above, together they will pass signal in both directions. One diode will pass the positive wave to ground, and the other will pass the negative wave to ground. Diodes pass almost all of their voltage (in one direction), but a small voltage will remain. The remaining portion is called the **junction** voltage. A silicon diode has a junction voltage of about six-tenths of a volt, so the remaining clipped signal will be about 1.2 volts peak-to-peak. The distortion caused by clipping diodes is generally brighter and raspier sounding due to the faster response time of solid-state components, Additional tone-shaping components (resistors and capacitors) are required to "smooth-out" the tonal quality so it becomes pleasing to the ear. Overdriving the preamp stages doesn't hurt the amp's components, because very little current is present in these stages, and current is what produces the heat that burns up components.

The amount of overdrive is controlled by a level control, called volume, gain, pre-gain, or drive. The higher this control is set, the more distortion is produced. The overdriven signal now proceeds to the overdrive channel's tone controls (which are the same as the ones we looked at in the clean channel). After the tone controls, the signal goes to yet another amplifier stage and then to a second volume control. This control sets the overall level of the channel and is called main, post, or master volume on most amps. The output of this control connects to the second half of our channel-select switch and rejoins the signal path of the clean channel.

From here, the selected channel's output connects to another buffer amp stage, which feeds an **effects loop**. The purpose of this effects loop is to enable the user to connect external signal-processing devices to the amplifier. These might be reverb units, delays, equalizers, exciters, or any of a plethora of signal-processing units currently available. In this particular example, the effects loop is designed specifically for **line-level** effects. Instrument-level devices like guitar "stomp boxes" will not work properly in this circuit. The input signal would be much too high, and the output from the device would be too low. Unwanted distortion and loss of signal level would result from connecting an instrument-level device to this effects loop. It wouldn't damage the amp or the effects. It just wouldn't sound very good. Some amps have variable gain effects loops, which may be adjusted to use either type of signal processor which reduce the effects **send** level and boost the **return** signal to compensate for the difference in levels of pedal-type effects.

The effects send (output) jack is wired directly to the effects return (input) jack through a switch contact that connects to the return jack's tip contact, as long as nothing is plugged into the return jack. (Refer back to the block diagram in *figure 11-1*.) This is called a "normally closed" contact because it makes contact when the jack is in its "normal" state: Nothing plugged in.

This arrangement allows the signal to pass through from send to return when no effect is being used, yet interrupts the signal which "loops" out to the effects and back to the amp when effects are connected. The signal from the return jack then goes on to the power amp section.

THE POWER AMP: TUBE TYPE

There are many different types of power amps. A tube power amp differs greatly from a solid-state power amp, so I'll describe the way each works separately. In a tube power amp, the signal is first routed to another buffer stage, which also has quite a bit of gain. Tubes operate at very high power-supply voltages (typically 250 volts to 700 volts), and the signal levels are correspondingly higher than those in a solid-state amp. The signal then goes to what is called the phase-inverter stage. The phase inverter consists of one or two tube stages with two outputs. One output is 180° out of phase with the other output *(see figure 11-9)*.

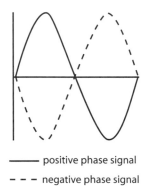

——— positive phase signal

– – – negative phase signal

Figure 11-9: Phase invertor outputs

These identical but opposite-phase signals are sent to the output stages. In a mid- to high-power tube power amp, the most common configuration is called "**class AB**." In a class AB amplifier, the positive half (plus a small amount of the negative half) of the signal is amplified by one stage, and the negative half (plus a little bit of the positive half) is amplified by another stage. The outputs are then sent to the primary, or input side, of the output transformer, where they again become phase coherent (in phase) and add together *(figure 11-10)*.

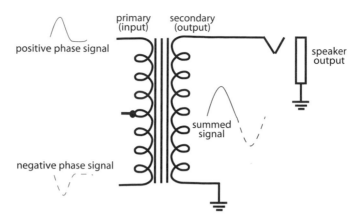

Figure 11-10: The positive and negative signals from the phase invertor become coherent at the output transformer, and add together.

This is a balanced circuit, similar to the ones used in microphone-input circuits. The secondary of the output transformer connects to the speaker or speakers. Another type of tube amp is called "**class A**." In a class A amp, the entire signal is amplified by the output stages. This type of amplifier has less distortion, but tends to run hotter and less efficiently, compared to one using class AB operation. Class AB amps have higher output power than class A amps, with similar power supplies and transformers.

Output tubes are often sold in matched sets. An amp will run cooler and quieter if the output tubes are matched. As mentioned earlier, many tube output circuits are balanced. It is therefore important that the positive and negative current be matched as closely as possible. All tubes have slightly different gain characteristics. Some will conduct better than others with the same **bias** voltage applied. Two tubes with very different gain characteristics will not balance properly, causing hum and noise to occur at the output. The lower-gain tube(s) will also get hotter and work harder than the higher-gain tube(s), shortening the useful life of the weaker tubes. Matched tubes will last longer, sound better, and produce more power than non-matched tubes in these types of balanced-output circuits.

If you remember the last chapter, How Tubes Work, I explained how a tube's cathode emits electrons to the plate, and how a small voltage change on the grid can result in a large voltage change on the plate. In addition to the signal on the grid, there is a negative voltage called a bias voltage. A tube with no negative voltage on the grid is effectively a diode, and it will conduct maximum current and burn itself up very quickly. A bias voltage is therefore placed on the control grid to regulate the flow of electrons at idle (when no signal is present). The bias voltage also determines what part of a signal the tube will amplify. If the bias is correct, the amp will amplify properly without getting too hot. If the bias is set incorrectly, the entire signal may not be amplified, and unwanted distortion, called crossover distortion, may occur. Or, the tubes might conduct excessive current and possibly damage the tubes and/or surrounding components. Most tube amps are factory-set for a particular type of tube and generally never need adjustment. Some amps have adjustable bias **trimmer** potentiometers, which can be used to optimize the circuit for the tubes being used. This procedure should only be done by a qualified tech: Somebody who knows what not to touch and how not to get zapped by the extremely high voltages inside the amp. (Please read the section on safety in Chapter Twenty, Making a Repair.)

Tube output amps do not like to be run with no speakers connected, or open-load. Sometimes, it might seem like a good idea to unplug the speakers from an amp for recording purposes or to practice quietly if using some other output from the amp, but tube amps will overheat and melt down if you try this. The reason is that the tubes in the output circuitry are designed to operate into relatively high-impedance loads. Speakers are generally pretty low in impedance, so the tubes cannot be connected directly to the speaker. That is why a tube amp uses a transformer on its output. This output transformer has a high-impedance input, or primary side; and a low-impedance output, or secondary. This matches the tube impedance to the speaker. In doing so, it also reduces the voltage level from the primary to the secondary, which is why the power supplies in a tube amp are so high. A change in the impedance on the secondary side of the transformer results in a proportionate but opposite change on the primary side. With no speakers connected, the secondary impedance increases, thus decreasing the primary side impedance. This, in turn, causes the current through the output tubes to increase and will damage the tubes and/or output transformer if it is played this way for very long.

Standby Switches

Many tube-amp manufacturers include a standby switch on their amps. The purpose of a standby switch is to allow the amp to warm up before high voltage is applied to the tubes. It is also supposed to extend the life of the output tubes if the amp is going to be sitting idle for long periods of time. That's the theory, anyway. In my personal experience, I've never seen the use of a standby switch prevent any sort of problem with a tube amp. I've seen no evidence that it extends tube life. The one advantage I can see is that it allows you to mute the amp while tuning, or to shut it down so it doesn't hum while you're on break, without having to wait for the amp to warm up when it's time to play again. Most components, including tubes, seem to fail most frequently during power-up. The sudden change of voltage will sometimes take a borderline component over the edge. As far as the tubes are concerned, the less often you switch the standby on and off, the better.

THE POWER AMP: SOLID STATE

Most solid-state output stages use either bipolar transistors or field-effect transistors (FETs). These can also be configured as either class A or class AB, but they go about things quite differently from tube amps.

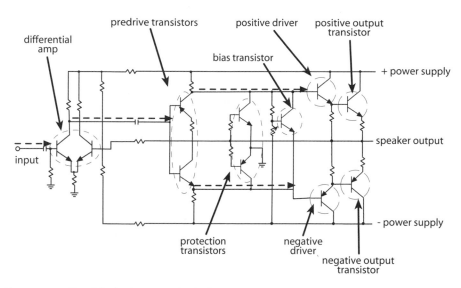

Figure 11-11: Simplified schematic of a typical bipolar transistor power amp.

Figure 11-11 is a simplified schematic of a bipolar solid-state output power amp. The signal from the effects return goes to an amplifier stage called a differential amp. This stage amplifies the signal and is connected (through a resistor or two) to the speaker output line. The differential amp compares the DC voltage level on the output line, which should always be 0 volts DC, to ground: A constant 0 volt DC reference. If the output line should vary in voltage, either above or below 0 volts DC, the differential amp senses the voltage and puts out either more or less current to compensate. This way, the voltage on the output line always remains 0 volts DC, and no output transformer is needed. This reduces both the cost and the weight of the amp. The signal then goes to a predrive transistor, which amplifies the signal to the proper level for the output stages.

The output section is where the signal's current is increased enough to be able to drive a speaker. The signal from the predrive transistors is sent to the driver transistors. The drivers amplify the signal one more time and send it along to the output transistors. This final stage is designed to produce current without much, if any, voltage gain. The amplitude of the signal doesn't get any higher; only the availability of current increases. High current is necessary to operate a low-impedance load, such as a speaker. Only some of the current generated by the amp gets passed on to the speaker load. The rest of this current is dissipated by the transistors as heat. Consequently, the output transistors are usually mounted on a large piece of metal called a heat sink to help dissipate the heat. Many power amps also have cooling fans mounted inside of them. The more of the current that gets transferred to the speaker load, the better. The ratio of heat generated (power used) by the amp to the power sent to the speaker load is called the efficiency of the amplifier.

Bipolar Transistors Versus FETs

The output transistors in a solid-state amp may be bipolar transistors or FETs. FETs operate differently from tubes or bipolar transistors, but they perform the same function. FET amps are sometimes preferred by musicians because of the way they sound when they are driven into distortion. When an amplifier is driven to the clipping point, the resulting distortion is rich in harmonics or overtones. These harmonics are weak tones that are multiples of the original signal's frequency. For example, a 1kHz tone's first harmonic would be twice as much, or 2kHz. The second harmonic would be twice 2kHz, or 4kHz, and so on. The first, third, fifth, seventh, etc. overtones are called odd-order harmonics. The second, fourth, sixth, eighth, etc. are the even-order harmonics. The overtones generated by a bipolar transistor amp are predominately odd-order harmonics. Odd-order harmonics are generally thought to sound harsher and less musical than even-order harmonics. Tube power amps and FET output amps generate more even-order harmonics and are thought by many to be more pleasant and smooth-sounding. Again, it's a matter of personal opinion.

So, Which is Better?

The question of which is better, tubes or transistors, can only be answered on a case-by-case basis. Like everything else in life, each has some advantages and some drawbacks. Tube amps are heavier than equivalent power solid-state amps. They run hotter. They require periodic replacement of tubes. But they sound really good for some things, like blues and rock guitar amps and studio microphone preamps. Many musicians find that the great sound of tubes well outweighs the disadvantages. Other players prefer the clean tone of a good solid-state amp. Recent advances in computer modeling have brought the sound of solid-state amps much closer to the smooth tube-amp sound, so that even some die-hard tube fans are being converted. Some people perceive enough difference that only tubes will do. Once more, it's a matter of individual preference and taste.

THE POWER SUPPLY

The section of the amp that provides voltage and current to the entire unit so the circuits can function is called the power supply. Power supplies use transformers to change the AC voltage from one value to another. Rectifier diodes are used to change the AC voltage to DC. Filter capacitors remove the AC ripple from the DC voltage to eliminate hum. Resistors change the levels of the DC voltages for use in the different sections of the amp, and regulators keep those DC voltages at a constant level, regardless of minor changes in AC line voltage or the loudness of the amp.

DC-to-DC Conversion Power Supplies

A standard power supply, such as the one described above, uses a big, heavy transformer and large filter capacitors. These add considerable size and weight to an amplifier. All amplifiers take current from the wall socket, convert it to DC, and end up powering speakers. The amount of power used by the amp versus the amount of power it puts out determines the amp's efficiency. Amps will always take in more total power than they put out into the speakers, due to the power used by the amp in the amplifying process. No amp is 100% efficient, but some get pretty close. Many high-efficiency amps use what is called a switching or **pulse power supply**. There are other names, too, but they are all basically similar in how they go about getting the DC voltages needed by the amp.

A pulse power supply uses a very different approach, called DC-to-DC conversion. AC voltage from the wall socket is directly rectified to DC voltage, bypassing the standard, heavy-power transformer. The resulting DC voltage is then used to power a high-frequency oscillator. The oscillator generates an ultrasonic wave—frequency higher than the human ear can hear—usually between 85kHz and 250kHz. This signal is then rectified and filtered, much like a conventional power supply. Why go to all of this trouble? The reasons are three-fold: At higher frequencies: A) The transformers do not have to be as large or heavy as with lower frequencies; B) The filter capacitors can also be much lower values, making them smaller and lighter, and C) The remaining ripple in the power-supply is ultrasonic. That is, it's too high for our ears to detect, so there is no audible power-supply hum. If we replace the large, heavy components in the power supply with smaller lighter ones, the amp's weight and size can be drastically reduced. This type of supply is used in some musical-instrument amps and is found in many professional P.A. amplifiers.

Switching Power Supplies

Another variation in power-supply design you'll find in some amplifiers is also called a switching power supply, but it operates much differently from the one described above. This type of supply is also called "**class G**," or "**class H**" by some amp makers. The maximum output from an amp is determined by the power supply voltage (refer to *figure 11-7*). An amp with plus and minus 45-volt power supplies can never put out more than 90 volts of signal, peak-to-peak (45 volts plus 45 volts), which works out to about 125 watts RMS, into an 8-ohm load. Music signal levels vary in **dynamics,** meaning that some sounds, such as a sustaining guitar note, will stay at roughly one level, whereas other transient signals (like a drum) go from no sound to very loud and back to no sound quite quickly. An amp playing loudly might handle the sustaining notes of the guitar just fine, but will run out of power and "clip" when a strong kick drum signal comes along. One way to handle these signals without running out of power is to build a bigger, heavier, more powerful amp.

Another way is to switch the power-supply voltage to a higher level only when the extra power is needed. In our 125-watt amp mentioned previously, the power supplies are plus and minus 45 volts. If we were to build in an additional power supply to provide plus and minus 60 volts, the amp could put out about 225 watts into 8 ohms. The rest of the amp's components would not be able to handle this much power on sustained notes, but for short transient bursts, they could handle it just fine. If the manufacturer builds in circuits to detect transient signals and switch the higher power-supply voltage in only when it is needed, the amp will be able to put out considerably more power than before, but only for short transient signals. The continuous power rating is still only about 125 watts, and the weight of the amp increases only a little, but the amp now performs like a 225-watt amp.

SUMMING UP

The examples given in this chapter are just the tip of the iceberg. There are dozens of other variations in design of audio amps, and every amp is different in some way. Sometimes, features might be called different names: One manufacturer's "switching power supply" might be called "class G" by another manufacturer, and a pulse power supply might be called a switching power supply by some other amp maker. Some amps will have more or fewer channels or controls, but most of the amps you will encounter in the real world use the basic principles outlined in this chapter.

Chapter TWELVE

How Digital Electronics Work

or, ones and zeros, bits and bytes.

Ones and zeros, zeros and ones. This is the language of **digital** electronics and is called **binary,** or **base two.** To understand how base two works, let's first take a look at the number system we're all familiar with: Base ten. We know that the number "2,415,389" in base ten represents two million, four hundred fifteen thousand, three hundred and eighty-nine just by looking at it.

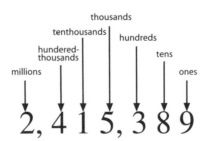

Figure 12-1: A number in base ten

In base ten *(see figure 12-1),* the first column of numbers is the ones, the next column is the tens (ten times one), the next is the hundreds (ten times ten), the next column is thousands (ten times 100), and so on. The reason we must use columns like this is that we only have ten digits. I don't mean fingers or toes. I mean we have only ten symbols that represent numbers: 0, 1, 2, 3... on up to 9 (notice that there is no single symbol for ten in base ten). If we want to represent twenty-one of something, we have to reuse a couple of our digits: Two and one, or 21. The base ten number twenty-one is actually a little addition problem: Two from the tens column is twenty, plus one from the ones column, equals twenty-one. It's so simple we don't even think about it; we just know it's twenty-one.

In base two, we only have two symbols that represent values: Zero and one, so you can see where our columns will have to have different values *(see figure 12-2).*

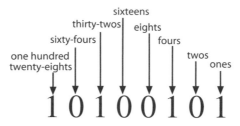

Figure12-2: Base two column values

The first column is still the ones column, but the second column is the twos column. Each digit in the two's column will have a value of two. The next column will be the fours column (two times two), and the next will be the eights column (two times four), and so on.

Let's try counting to ten in base two, starting at zero. Zero would be 0000. That's easy enough. And one would be 0001. Again, easy. And two would be... Remember, we don't have a digit "2," so we have to use a one in the two's column, and a zero in the one's column, or 0010. Sure looks like a ten, but there is no ten in base two. In fact, there's no two in base two, so we call this number: zero, zero, one, zero. Three in base ten would be 0011 (zero, zero, one, one) in base two. Let's do the math. We have one from the "two's" column. That equals two, plus one from the ones column, that makes three. Base two "four" is: 0100. Five is 0101. Six is 0110. Seven is 0111. Eight is1000. Nine is 1001. And finally, ten is 1010.

This all seems pretty complicated. The reason is, we're actually converting each number to base ten because that's what we're used to dealing with. Computers are happy to deal with base two and don't need to convert the numbers unless some lowly human comes along and wants something displayed on the screen. Computers like to deal with binary because there are only two possible digits, representing two possible conditions. Electrically, the concepts of "off or on" and "yes or no" are easily transferred to:"Current present or no current present." The circuitry doesn't have to mess around with trying to figure out if the number is a 3 or a 4, or if a 7 might be almost an 8. In digital electronics, each binary value is represented by an electrical state: Either on (current present) or off (no current present). There is much less room for ambiguity if there are only two possibilities.

You can see that large numbers would require an awful lot of columns. Fifteen is the largest number in base ten that we can represent in base two with only four columns. Eight columns give us a maximum equivalent in base ten of 255. Computers group columns together in sets, called **words.** The number (one or zero) representing the value of each column is called a data bit. A group of columns **(bits)** is called a **byte** (also called a digital word). A byte might be four, eight, sixteen, twenty, or twenty-four bits. The larger the number of bits in a byte, the more different numbers can be recognized by the computer. This is very important in digital-audio circuits.

SAMPLING FREQUENCY AND BIT RATE

When an analog audio signal is converted to digital, the wave is **sampled** at a high rate, usually somewhere from 15kHz (15,000 times per second) up to 96kHz (96,000 times per second). Whataya mean "sampled"? Well, the computer looks at the wave at a specific point in time, tests the average level of the signal, and assigns the level a numeric value. This number is stored into memory. The signal is sampled again, and the value is again stored away. This happens at the sample rate, let's say 32,000 times per second *(see figure 12-3)*.

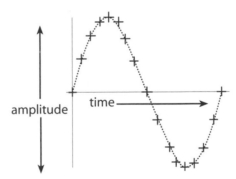

Figure 12-3: Analog audio signal with sample points marked

When the computer plays back the sound, it retrieves all of those stored numbers in the same order in which they were stored. It looks at the number, and the **digital-to-audio converter** (DAC) circuit determines what value of voltage level to output. It continues to put out that voltage until the next byte from memory tells it to change to a different value. It continues doing this at the same rate at which it was sampled, and the result is a new waveform that approximates the original wave *(see figure 12-4)* but is kind of jagged, like stair steps.

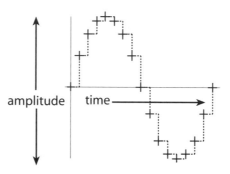

Figure 12-4: New waveform that approximates the original wave

As you can see in *figures 12-5* and *12-6,* there are two things we can do to minimize this stair-stepping problem. One is to increase the sampling frequency. The more sampling points *(figure 12-5),* the closer together the steps get. Another is to increase the number of levels we can sense and reproduce by increasing the bit rate *(Figure 12-6).*

Figure 12-5: Doubled sampling frequency

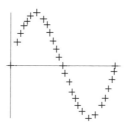

Figure 12-6: Increased sampling levels

As we just learned, the more bits there are to represent columns of numbers, the more numbers can be represented. A four-bit word can only represent sixteen different levels: 0 through 15. By increasing the bit rate to eight bits, we can have 256 different levels: 0 through 255. A higher bit-rate allows for better resolution. A higher sample rate also increases resolution. In *figure 12-7*, both the sample rate and the bit-rate have been increased. The signal looks much more like the original than does the first example in *figure 12-4*.

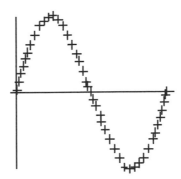

Figure 12-7: Doubled sampling rate and increased levels

Early digital sampling used low (eight-bit) bit rates and sampled at lower sample rates, so the quality was pretty poor compared to modern high-sample- and high-bit-rate units. Later units sample at 12, 16, 20, 24, or even 96 bits and have correspondingly better resolution.

The signal from the DAC still has some stair-stepping effect, especially at higher frequencies, so the signal is sent through a low-pass filter circuit, which removes the remaining vestiges of the sampling frequency and smoothes out the stair-stepping even more. By this time, the digitally repro-duced signal is pretty much indistinguishable from the original audio sig-nal. Some distortion remains at extremely high frequencies, but is unde-tectable by average human ears.

DIGITAL EFFECTS

Now that we've gotten our signal sampled and stored into memory, what happens if we change the playback sample rate? The pitch changes. What if we take the same digital information out of the memory a second time, but a little later? Digital delay! What if we reduce the level of the uppermost sampled points? Digital limiting! You can see that many effects can be easily added to a signal while it is in the digital realm.

DIGITAL CIRCUITRY

Here are a few of the electronic advantages of digital circuits. Because there are only two logic states, high and low, the components are either on or off. Most solid-state switching devices, such as transistors and diodes, use relatively small amounts of current when they are operated either full on or full off. That means lots of digital operations can be performed without generating much heat. Because the components don't generate much heat, they can be made smaller and be placed closer together, making digital units more compact. And, since they're smaller, they can be transported more easily. Now, let's have a look at base five... Just kidding.

Chapter **THIRTEEN**

How Synthesizers Work

or, wow, what a cool noise!

The evolution of synthesizers has been a long and interesting process. Most of this chapter will be a general explanation of how synths work. There isn't really any need to go into a lot of technical detail about the actual circuitry.

WHAT YOU NEED TO KNOW

There are two different types of synthesizers—monophonic and polyphonic—and it's a good idea to get familiar with their similarities and differences. That way, when it comes time to buy new gear, you'll know which type is right for your needs. You'll also want to understand about MIDI and sampling technology.

Monophonic Synths

The first music **synthesizers** were produced before the development of integrated circuits, which caused them to be large and bulky. The most famous early synth was made by Dr. Robert Moog. It was a modular design, meaning that it was produced in several sections that had to be interconnected, or **patched**, in order for sounds to be produced. Depending on how it was connected, the sound would change. These synthesizers were **monophonic**, which means they could only produce one tone at a time.

Another device that enjoyed limited popularity in the early days of synthesis was the Theremin. Invented by Professor Leon Theremin, the Theremin produced a continuous tone that could be manipulated by the proximity of the player's hands to two control antennas. The Theremin was unique in that it had no keyboard. Although, the most well-known use of this instrument took place on the song "Good Vibrations" by The Beach Boys in the mid-sixties, several pieces of classical music were also written for the Theremin, and concerts with Theremin and orchestra still occur to this day. There remains a small but fanatical group of Theremin lovers in the world.

The Moog was the first synth to be successfully mass-produced and marketed. The way it produced sound was by modifying and filtering an audio tone that was generated electronically using a **voltage-controlled oscillator** (VCO) circuit. The fundamental tone was a square wave rich in harmonic content, whose frequency could be varied depending on a control voltage. This wave would then be sent to a **voltage-controlled amplifier** (VCA) section, which enabled the operator to determine several important factors about the sound. One factor is the rise-time of the signal; in other words, the amount of time it takes to go from no output to a specified level. This is called the attack time. Another factor is the length of time it takes for the signal to get to another specified level; this is called the decay time. Other factors include the sustaining signal level, called the sustain, and finally, the release time, or the amount of time the note continues to play after the key is no longer held down, before finally going silent. The combination of these level changes over time is called the sound's envelope. This part of the synth is called the attack, decay, sustain, release, often shortened to **ADSR**. By manipulating these characteristics of the signal level, it is possible to emulate naturally occurring sounds. Current synthesizers use a similar scheme, but often there are many more points to the envelope, and the parameters of level and time can be manipulated by the user.

The signal in these original units also went to a **voltage-controlled filter** section (VCF) where the amount of harmonic content could be controlled with a multipoint ADSR design similar to the VCA's ADSR. A low-frequency wave generator could also be used to modulate the main tone. Depending on the waveform used, the signal could have vibrato or trills added to it. This was controlled by a narrow roller, called a modulation wheel, which was basically just a hand-operated potentiometer. Another similar control wheel allowed pitch changes of the fundamental signal. This control was, and still is, referred to as a pitch wheel. Instead of (or in addition to) a wheel, some synths use a lever or a touch-sensitive ribbon to control pitch bend.

The keyboard used a voltage divider resistor network to determine the voltage sent to the master **oscillator**, thus determining the pitch of the note to be played. The arrangement of the patch cables from one module to another determined the previously mentioned variables of the sound's configuration. A satisfactory arrangement of these patch cables could then be written down to be duplicated at another time and was referred to as a "patch." Because of this, the word patch is still used in modern synthesizers to describe a particular sound.

The next step in the development of the synthesizer was the use of integrated circuits that allowed them to be made smaller and more compact. This next generation of synths was self-contained, and patching was no longer done on a **patch bay** (a group of jacks allowing access to numerous points in the circuit simultaneously), but was now accomplished with banks of switches. As with most things electronic, as the size was reduced, the price also dropped, and these more portable units became more popular and numerous.

The MiniMoog produced by Dr. Moog's company is the most famous of these. They were affordable and sounded quite good, although they were difficult to keep in tune, due in part to the unstable master oscillator circuits and problems with outside radio frequency interference (RFI).

Soon after the Moog company started producing synthesizers, several Japanese companies also got into the act. UniVox (which later became Korg) and Roland Corporation both designed improved oscillators and had very respectable mono-synths of their own. Yamaha and others also began producing interesting units. This competitive marketplace sped the rate of innovations, and soon they were all making synths with very precise oscillators, some of them digital. Suddenly, there were synthesizers on the market that would play four, six, and even eight notes at a time.

Polyphonic Synths

These multichannel **polyphonic** units were popular in the late seventies and early eighties. They were much more versatile than the old mono-synths, but each "patch" still had to be set up manually. Most of the popular production synths in the eighties had digitally controlled oscillators, filters, and amps. The synth-makers found that, by adding a small, basic computer chip and some memory, they could allow the user to create and store patches digitally, to be called up immediately and at random. This enabled musicians to use the units in live performances without having to reprogram after every section of the song.

Midi

Soon, keyboardists started imagining how convenient it would be if the computer in one synth could be used to tell the computers in other synths what to do. Roland's engineers incorporated a data port on some of its models to allow the units to interface with outside equipment, such as a digital note sequencer. They called this port DCB for Digital Control Bus. It worked quite well, but it would only work with other Roland equipment. The synth manufacturers got together to discuss the feasibility of an industry-wide standard that would allow any brand or model of microprocessor-based synth to communicate with any other microprocessor-based unit, regardless of who made it. Roland had put a lot of time and money into the DCB interface, and suggested that everyone adopt it as their standard, but the other manufacturers saw too many limitations with that system. They set out to devise a communication standard that would not be likely to get outmoded soon. The result was called MIDI: Musical Instrument Digital Interface.

There are dozens of good books already in print that deal with MIDI, so I'm not going to go into much detail of how MIDI works, other than a few basics. MIDI uses a 16-channel system transferring eight-bit serial data on a single data line (as opposed to Roland's DCB, which was a parallel data system, requiring nine wires to transfer the data). MIDI can be transmitted using three lines: One for data, one for ground, and the other for power supply. A five-pin connector was chosen, both because it was a standard cable connector already in use, and because the two additional lines could be used if there were future upgrades to the MIDI standard.

More Innovations

Velocity sensitivity began to be incorporated into synth design in the late seventies. Because most synths were now using computers, it became possible for the units to be able to detect how hard, or how fast, a note was being played. This greatly increased the expressiveness of playing and the realism of the sounds. Here's how velocity-sensitive units work: The microcomputer in the unit sends digital pulses to the key switches in the keyboard. In some keyboards, the switch is a fairly standard SPDT switch. The computer would detect when the n/c switch contact opened, and measure the time before the n/o contact closed. (If you didn't understand that, go back and read Chapter 2, Components.) The faster the switch went from normally closed to normally open, the louder the synth would play. Some synths use two n/o SPST contacts, but the theory is the same. The computer measures the time between the connection of contact 1 and the connection of contact 2.

Also around this same time, Yamaha was experimenting with what they call FM synthesis. FM stands for frequency modulation. In designing multichannel synths, they found that if you used several pure tones and mixed them together, some very interesting sounds could be created. When two frequencies are mixed together, the resulting sound consists of four distinct frequencies: The original two, plus the sum of those two, and the difference between them. For example, if you add a 1,000Hz tone to a 1,500Hz tone, you get 1,000Hz, 1,500Hz, and 2,500Hz (the sum) plus 500Hz (the difference). This phenomenon is called **heterodyning** and is also used in radio transmission. The very popular Yamaha DX-7 six-operator (oscillator) synth is the most well-known example of **FM synthesis** and changed the sound of contemporary music at the time. The pure, clean, bell-like tones were totally different from anything being produced by analog or even digital synths of the same era.

The next big advance in synthesizer technology to come along was **multitimbrality**, or the ability to produce the sounds of more than one patch at a time. As manufacturers produced more units, the size and number of the components got smaller and smaller. With large-scale integration technology advancing at a fast rate, soon the contents of an eleven by fourteen-inch circuit board could be manufactured as one large-scale, integrated circuit, taking less than one square inch of space on a circuit board. The manufacturing costs went down accordingly, so it became more feasible to produce units that could play not just eight notes, but sixteen or thirty-two notes simultaneously. This gave birth to the notion that one single keyboard could be used to produce two or more sounds at the same time. For example, the keyboard could be divided so that the left hand played an upright bass sound while the right hand played a piano or string sound. With digital sequencers becoming popular, the possibilities expanded even more. A single keyboard could play the bass, drums, piano, guitar, strings, etc. The only thing really lacking at this point was the sound quality. Players longed for a synth that actually sounded like the instruments it was trying to emulate.

Sampling Synths

Enter the digital **sampler.** By this time, sampling technology was already fairly advanced. The high-end audio industry had been working with digital audio for some time, trying to decide on the "next big thing" in home stereo. The technology that eventually won out was the audio Compact Disc. (See Chapter 12, How Digital Electronics Work.) The way music is encoded for use on a CD is very similar to the way a sampling synthesizer works *(refer to figure 13-1)*. An analog musical wave has its level sampled at a high rate. In CD players, it's 44.1kHz. That's 44,100 times per second.

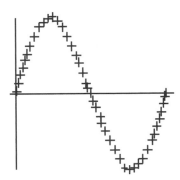

Figure 13-1: Illustration of a wave showing sample points

Early samplers used much lower sample rates: 16kHz or 32kHz were common. Generally, the higher the sample rate, the better the final sound quality would be. Each of the sampled points is assigned a digital numeric value according to its level and is then stored into a bank of memory I.C.'s. When the sound is played back, the computer pulls these digital numbers out of memory in the same order in which they were stored. The digital-to-analog converter (DAC) turns the digital numbers back into an audio signal. This signal then goes to a low-pass filter to remove the noise generated by the sample-rate frequency. The resulting wave is extremely close to the original sampled signal.

So, the technology was there, but the cost of the components, especially the memory I.C.'s and the DAC chips, was very high. This resulted in low sample rates in the early machines to reduce the memory requirements. Ensoniq produced the first affordable and widely popular samplers in the late eighties. Sampling technology has been improving ever since, and good-sounding samplers are no longer too expensive for the average keyboardist to own.

Samplers solved the dilemma of poor-quality sound, but it seems that every good solution to a problem presents a few problems of its own. The trouble at this point was that samplers were still relatively expensive, and due to the cost of memory I.C.s, they didn't have room for more than a few sounds at a time. Also, most people didn't use samplers to sample very much. Samplers came from the factory with a few good sounds, and that's what most people used—not many did much sampling on their own. This opened up a huge market for after-market samples. Joe Average didn't want to take the time to sample every instrument in a symphony orchestra, so a few small companies went out and did it for him, and sold the results for a profit. Manufacturers saw what was happening and came up with their own sample libraries, which their customers could either purchase or copy for free. This turned on lights in a few corporate brains, and they thought, "Why put in all of the expensive sampling circuitry if all the consumer really wants is to play prerecorded samples?"

It was just about then that Roland introduced its D-50 synthesizer, using LA (Linear Arithmetic) synthesis technology. The first part of the sound, the attack, was produced by playing a very short, sampled waveform of an actual instrument. The rest of the tone was produced using synthesized waveforms. The real beauty of this technique lies in the fact that there was very little digital memory required for the samples, because they were mostly less than half a second long.

Previous to this, Korg had begun to add digital reverb and delay effects to its synths. Roland borrowed this idea, and added effects and onboard tone controls to the D-50, making it one of the best-sounding synthesizers ever produced. Korg soon followed suit with a true sample player with built-in effects, the M-1. This unit played back entire samples of instruments. To extend the tones, the samples were looped, meaning that a portion of the sample, usually after any initial attack of the sound, was told to play over and over again. Getting the looped portion of the sound to be free of pops and other ugly noises isn't always easy, and seamless looping of samples is considered almost an art form in itself.

Most synth manufacturers now have very high-quality sample player synths. As of this writing, many are 64- or 128-voice and multitimbral. Many, called music workstations, have integral note-sequencers with 3½-inch floppy disc drives for storage. Even as this is written, new innovations are being taken from the drawing board and placed on the assembly lines. I can't wait to see what's next!

MAINTENANCE

The first generations of synthesizers required periodic tuning to keep them sounding right. Most modern digital keyboards are maintenance-free, but there are a few things you should keep in mind if you own one.

Retaining Memory

The user-programmable patches in most digital synths are stored in digital **random access memory** I.C.'s. Many of these RAM chips require a small voltage to be present when the power is off in order to maintain their data. This is accomplished with the use of a lithium memory back-up battery, usually 3 or 3.6 volts. The memory battery is installed at the factory and has a life expectancy of seven to ten years. In actual use, they may last as long as twenty years, but in rare cases, they have been known to fail after only a few years. If the battery fails, the patches stored in the internal memory will be lost, and are not recoverable. If you own a synthesizer that has an internal back-up battery, it should tell you this in the owner's manual. Keep track of how long you've owned the unit, and if at all possible, back up your custom patches to an external memory card or floppy disk. Any MIDI-compatible synth should allow you to perform a MIDI Data Dump to a computer equipped with a MIDI interface or to any type of MIDI sequencer. This could save you a great deal of work and/or money should the internal battery fail, or if the unit has a problem and must be manually reinitialized by a service center. Factory patches are often available either from the manufacturer or from other owners on the internet, but once your custom patches are gone, they are gone forever, and you'll have to start from scratch reprogramming your instrument if you haven't backed up your patches.

Keeping It Clean

Many common keyboard problems are dust- and dirt-related. Keeping dirt out of the keyboard will help keep it working properly. If the unit is set up in a home or studio, it is a good idea to keep it covered with a plastic or vinyl cover when it's not in use. (Avoid using cloth covers; the lint from the cloth might be worse than the dust from the room.) Dust in the key switches can cause notes to stop playing, or to play at full velocity. Some panel switches are also susceptible to dirt and dust.

If you do any glides or glissandos up and down the keyboard, do them on the white (natural) keys only. This could save you some money in broken key repairs. The keys are made of plastic, and the black (sharp) keys tend to break if they are hit from the side. The white keys seem to hold up better under this kind of use. Clean the keys and the keyboard using a nonabrasive glass cleaner and a soft cloth. Spray the cleaner onto the rag, not the keyboard, to avoid getting excess moisture inside the unit.

Transporting It Safely

Use common sense in moving and storing a keyboard. Don't move a keyboard with a bunch of cables plugged into it. That can break the contacts on the jacks that the cords are plugged into. Remove any memory cards that plug into card sockets. If a keyboard is going to be moved frequently, invest in a good-quality, hard-shell case. Don't cheap-out and buy a budget-priced "gig bag." If you're spending major money on a quality instrument, it just makes sense to protect it properly. As with any instrument, extremes of temperature and humidity should be avoided. Treat it right and most electronic equipment will last a long time with minimal problems.

Chapter FOURTEEN

HOW RECORDING GEAR WORKS
or, how'd you fit all of that music on that little bitty tape?

Audio recording has been around for a long time, ever since Thomas Edison figured out how to reproduce voice vibrations on a wax cylinder with a needle hooked onto a megaphone. The forerunner to the phonograph was crude, and poor quality, but it enabled people to do something they'd never done before: Hear themselves talk and sing. People have been fascinated by it ever since. Fortunately, the technology has improved since the early days, and the latest generation of audio recorders reproduces sounds that are almost indistinguishable from the original.

From the humble beginnings of wax cylinders, recording technology has advanced through the ages of lacquer discs, to polyvinyl chloride records, to iron-oxide coated recording tape, to compact discs, right up to today's digital audio tape, CD-Rs and hard-disk recorders. There are still some old phonograph players out there—I've still got one, along with a closet full of 12-inch LPs—and cassette tapes are far from being extinct, but digital is not only here to stay, it's become the state of the art.

ANALOG TAPE RECORDING

For the present, however, many of us are still using analog tape for at least some of our recording projects, so let's have a look at how it all works. The basic premise is that sound is converted into electronic form by a transducer of some sort, usually a microphone or the pickup on an instrument. This tiny current is processed by amplifying equipment, often in the form of a mixing console. The mixer increases the level and might add or subtract some selected frequencies, or add an effect or two—like reverb, delay or compression—to make the signal sound better, and then the signal is sent from the output of the mixer to the inputs of the recording machine.

The Recording Process

Inside the recorder, the signal is sent to a record amplifier and level control section and part of the signal is diverted to the metering section. The meters tell the recording engineer how much signal is present in the record amp. Too much signal will overdrive the electronics and saturate the tape, causing unwanted distortion. Not enough signal will result in a noisy recording. The idea is to put just as much signal on the tape as possible without distortion. The noise level on playback will be the same, regardless of how "hot" the recorded signal is, so the higher the audio signal, the less noticeable the noise. This is what the term "signal to noise ratio" means.

The recorder sends the signal out to the record heads, but first it is mixed with a high-level, high-frequency signal called a bias signal. This bias signal is usually around 75kHz to 100kHz in frequency, and somewhere around 100 volts peak-to-peak. This signal acts as a carrier for the audio signal. Without the bias, very little audio would get recorded on to the tape, and the frequency response and signal quality would be extremely poor. The level of bias is very critical. Too much bias will cause the high frequencies to not be recorded properly, and not enough bias will cause the signal to be distorted and weak.

The Tape Transport

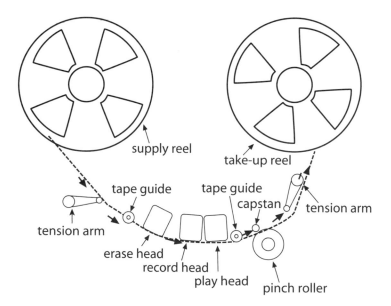

Figure 14-1: Tape path of a reel-to-reel tape deck.

On a reel-to-reel deck or a cassette recorder *(see figure 14-1),* the tape is pulled from the supply reel on the left, past the erase and record/playback heads, then to the drive mechanism and on to the take-up reel on the right (micro-cassettes record and play right to left). The tape is pulled at a constant speed by the small shiny post, called a **capstan**. A larger rubber roller, called the **pinch roller**, presses the tape against the capstan so the speed will be as consistent as possible. The cleaner these surfaces are kept, the better they work. The tape is re-spooled on the take-up side. When we start recording with a full reel of tape, there is a lot of tape on the supply spindle, and very little on the take-up spindle. The supply spindle will move very slowly compared to the take-up side. When the tape is about halfway through, they will move at about the same speed, and as the tape nears the end, the supply spindle will move much faster than the take-up spindle. The take-up side must have enough pull strength, called **torque**, to allow it to keep pulling tension on the tape at all of these speeds, yet it can't have so much torque that it pulls the tape past the capstan and pinch roller, or the speed will vary, and the tape might stretch.

Some tape decks have separate record and playback heads. These three-head decks are usually higher-priced or professional units. Lower-priced consumer decks use the same head for record and playback. The overall quality is usually better with a three-head machine. The heads are small, electromagnetic transducers *(see figure 14-2).*

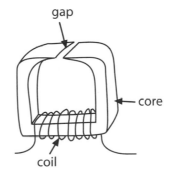

Figure 14-2: Anatomy of a tape head

Audio and bias signals are placed on a small coil of wire that is coiled around a metal core. This core is curved kind of like a small horseshoe, with the two ends almost touching. The space between these points is called the head gap. The gap in my illustration is exaggerated. The actual gap is mere microns (thousandths of a millimeter) wide and is invisible to the naked eye. The erase head and record head generate magnetic fields, and the playback head detects magnetic fields on the tape, and turns them back into electrical signals.

The Tape

The tape itself is coated with a formulation of iron oxide mixed with a binding agent. As the tape passes over the first (erase) head, a high-level bias signal causes all of the iron particles on the tape to become aligned in the same direction, which erases any information that might have been on the tape to begin with. Then the tape goes onto the record head, where the audio signal, mixed with bias signal, is placed on the tape. This rearranges the oxide into patterns of alternating magnetic polarity that exactly correspond to the frequencies of the audio signal being recorded.

When we rewind and play the tape back, these same magnetic fields run across the playback head's gap and generate tiny currents in the head's coil. This signal is then amplified, the high-frequency bias content is removed, and the signal is sent out to the monitoring system to be heard and enjoyed by all, along with a slight hissy noise.

ANALOG TAPE NOISE

This hiss is a by-product of the bias signal used during the recording process, and the high degree of amplification required by the signal. It could be removed, but the removal process would also remove some of the high-frequency content of the audio signal. Several methods have been used to try to control this problem. One thing that helps is to increase the speed of the tape across the heads. A standard cassette player runs at 1 $\frac{7}{8}$ inches per second (IPS). Many multitrack cassette units run at twice this speed, or 3 $\frac{3}{4}$ IPS. Most professional reel-to-reel machines run at 15 IPS or 30 IPS. The faster the tape speed, the less noise. Professional machines used for mastering do not use an erase head in order to reduce the noise. Brand-new or bulk-erased tape must be used on these machines.

Speed variations, called **wow** (lower frequency error) and **flutter** (higher frequency error) are also much less noticeable at higher tape speeds. Outboard noise reduction units have also been around for many years. Most of these units operate by compressing the signal before recording, and decompressing it during playback. By compressing the signal, the overall dynamic range of the signals becomes reduced; loud portions become quieter, and soft portions get louder. Because music generally has less high-frequency than low-frequency content, compressing causes the high-frequency content to have a higher amplitude before going onto the tape. Decompressing the signal during playback allows the hiss noise to be removed without having as much effect on the high frequency levels. This actually works pretty well, but some distortion is introduced in the compression/decompression process. Also, the decompress stage doesn't always remove all of the compressed effect, and some changes in frequency response can often be detected. If the encoder (compressor) section is not very well-matched to the decode (decompression) section, strange swells of volume can occur. This is called "pumping," and it can easily ruin a recording. Professional opinions vary on the best way to deal with the noise. Some engineers prefer outboard noise reduction systems, while others prefer to use high tape speed and deal with the noise through filtering.

DIGITAL RECORDING

Digital recorders go about things in a much different way. The recording process is similar to the digital audio sampling described in Chapter 12, How Digital Electronics Work, but the digital information is stored differently. The audio wave is sampled a specific number of times per second; this is the sampling rate. The sampling rate in professional machines is usually selectable. Most units will sample at 44.1kHz (the standard sampling rate for compact disc), or 48kHz (currently the accepted "pro" sampling rate). Some machines have a "long-play" mode at a lower sample rate such as 32kHz, and the newest generation of digital audio recorders at the time of this writing are sampling at even higher rates—some as high as 96kHz and 128kHz . The higher the sampling rate, the less distortion will be introduced into the signal, but the more memory is required to store the digital information.

In a sampling keyboard, the digital information is stored in Random Access Memory (RAM) I.C.'s. Digital audio recorders also use RAM, but only as a temporary buffer, or **cache,** to hold the information until it is passed along to the main storage device or devices. Because of the longer recording times and higher sampling rates involved in digital audio recording, the amount of data is more than a few, or even a whole bunch, of RAM I.C.'s can handle, so some other higher-capacity storage medium must be used to store the digital information. Most digital recorders currently use either videotape or a computer-style hard drive for data storage. Minidiscs are also getting more popular, and some machines can record directly to rewriteable CDs (CDs that can be recorded on, erased, and rerecorded) and DVD RAM (Digital Video Disc—similar to rewriteable CDs, but with more storage capacity). The technology changes daily, so I'm not going to try to guess what we'll be recording to in the future (read trade publications like *Mix* magazine to keep up with the newest trends). Digital recording isn't without its problems, however. As long as there are human beings running the equipment, there will be bad recordings made. I know. I've made plenty.

MAINTENANCE

Like any piece of machinery, you'll need to maintain your tape machine to keep it running well. The next section discusses cleaning, alignment, power conditioning, and making back-up recordings.

Cleaning

Tape recorders operate and sound better if they are clean. Reel-to-reel and cassette recorders should have the tape path cleaned and demagnetized at regular intervals. As the tape runs across the heads, the magnetic field from the recorded tape will begin to magnetize the metal parts of the tape heads and guides. This small magnetic field will eventually start to erase the tape as it passes across these parts, degrading the signal quality. The manual for the machine should outline the cleaning and maintenance advised for your particular unit, but as a rule, most tape recorders should be cleaned and demagnetized after every ten to twenty hours of use.

Alignment

Recorders are aligned at the factory for good performance with a variety of tape brands and types, but they are usually not optimized for any one in particular. If you're serious about getting the best-quality recording you can with the equipment you own, it is a good idea to have the tape machine aligned for the type of tape you plan to use. These adjustments to the levels and bias make the machine perform at its maximum quality level. Stay with this particular brand and type of tape for all of your recording. Over time, these adjustments will need to be "touched up" due to minor changes in component values. Have the machine calibrated as soon as you detect any loss of fidelity in your recordings.

Power Conditioning

Digital recorders don't normally need much in the way of maintenance, other than periodic head cleaning in the case of tape-storage units. Hard drive-based units have no maintenance requirements at all. Because they are computer-based, however, it is important that the power source is properly protected and filtered. An EMI /RF (electromagnetic interference/radio frequency) filtered power strip with surge protection is recommended. These units are available from any computer store. As with everything else in the electronics world, you usually get what you pay for, so don't buy the cheapest one you find. It might save you twenty bucks today, just to cost you several hundred next week.

The filtering section of the power conditioner removes spikes and noises that might get into the power supply of your digital equipment. These noises, if at high enough amplitude, can cause the microcomputers in your equipment to lock-up, or lose data. The surge suppressor can save your equipment if there is a high-voltage surge sent into the power line by lightning or other external source. One of the best ways to avoid problems like this is to unplug everything when it is not in use. Just shutting equipment off will not save it if you have a direct hit from lightning. (Lightning travels tens of thousands of feet through the air; the $\frac{1}{8}$-inch gap in the switch of a power strip will not slow it down a bit!) Never use the equipment during a storm.

Back-up Recordings

Tapes and equipment can fail at any time, so make back-up copies of everything. That way, if you do have problems, all of your previous work is not lost forever.

Chapter FIFTEEN

How P.A.s Work
or, what'd ya say, sonny?

I f you play music for fun at home, or if you only play for small groups of people, you may never need a sound system. However, if you play in public venues, sooner or later you'll find yourself in a situation where you need to be louder, so that more people can hear you play or sing. Sound reinforcement, or public address (P.A.) systems are the solution. Many venues have permanent sound systems installed. Some musicians contract out the sound and stage lighting, and thus never have to move, set up, or tear down a system, but even if you never have to own or operate your own system, you'll still have to use one, and the more you know about how it works, the easier it will be.

In this chapter we'll take a look at various sizes of sound systems, **feedback** problems and how to solve them, cabling, power requirements, and troubleshooting a system.

SMALL SOUND SYSTEM

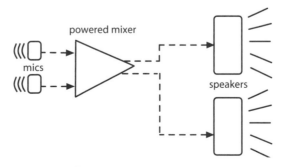

Figure 15-1: Block diagram of a small sound system

Figure 15-1 shows a block diagram of a typical small sound system. Let's say this particular sound system is for someone who plays acoustic guitar and sings in small coffee shops. The system might consist of two unidirectional microphones, a small **powered mixer**, and two full-range P.A. speakers. The dashed lines in *figure 15-1* show the signal path. The two microphones pick up the vibrations in the air from the singer's voice and the acoustic guitar. In most cases, unidirectional microphones are used for live-sound applications. Unidirectional microphones, such as **cardioid** or **hyper-cardioid,** pick up sound mainly from the front and reject sounds from the sides and the rear. This helps prevent unwanted feedback (more about feedback and polar patterns later in this chapter). The mic signals are transferred through cables to the input of a powered microphone mixer. A powered mixer has its own power amplifier built in, so there is no need for a separate amp. Each of these two mic signals goes into separate channels of the mixer section of the powered mixer, where they are amplified, and the tonal qualities can be adjusted by the tone controls in the individual channel's equalizer sections. The signals then go to the channel volume controls, called **faders,** where the levels can be set for a proper blend of the two signals. This way, the signals can be balanced so that one signal doesn't get so loud that it overpowers the other. The two signals are then mixed together and sent to the output stage of the mixer. They are amplified again, sent through a main or master-level control to adjust the overall volume, and then sent to a main tone-control section—in this case, a graphic equalizer. This allows the overall tonal quality to be adjusted. The equalized signal then goes to the main power amp, and then out to the speakers. And the crowd goes wild.

MEDIUM-SIZE SYSTEM

That system was pretty basic and simple. This next one *(figure 15-2)* is a little more complex.

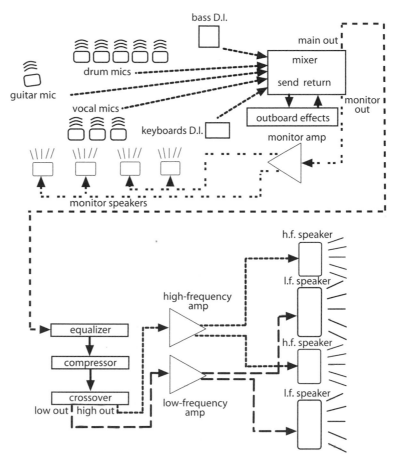

Figure 15-2: Block diagram of a more complex sound system

Here we have a sound system for a small, imaginary band consisting of an electric guitar, electric bass, a keyboard, a drum kit, and three vocal mics. This group of musicians plays small-to medium-size clubs, with audiences in the range of 100 to 200 persons. Obviously, the small powered mixer from our first example isn't going to cut it here. For one thing, we're going to need at least ten channels to get everything miked up properly, and the relatively low power of a built-in amp might not be enough to get over the audience noise. Also, some **monitors** will be needed so the singers can hear themselves. They don't really need a sound operator in this situation, so we'll assume they'll control the sound system from the stage.

The vocal microphones will plug into the mixer's mic inputs just as the one from the small system did. The guitar amp will need to have a microphone, also. The most common method of miking a guitar amp is to place the mic a few inches from the speaker, and off-center somewhat. The drums will get anywhere from a couple to several mics, depending on the size of the room. In a small room one mic on the bass (or "kick") drum, and maybe an overhead mic or two for general pickup would be adequate. In larger rooms, there might also be a a snare mic, one for each of the toms, plus a hi-hat mic, and one or more overhead mics to pick up the cymbals. Sometimes, the overhead and hi-hat mics might not be necessary, and often one mic will be used to pick up two closely spaced toms. It just depends on the situation. The room size, open channels in the mixer, and the number of microphones available all combine to determine the set up. Each of these mics will get its own channel in the mixer. If the keyboard player uses an amp onstage, the amp can be miked, but the preferred method is to use a **direct box**. The same goes for bass guitar. A direct box (also called a **splitter**, or **direct interface**), takes the high-impedance signal directly from the instrument and divides it. Part of the signal passes along unchanged to the stage amp. The other part is converted to a low-impedance, balanced signal (either passively, with a small transformer, or in the case of an active unit, electronically), and sent to the mixer. This allows the tonal quality of the instrument to be optimized for the main (front house) speakers, while at the same time permitting the musician to tailor the sound to his or her preference onstage. (One thing you'll learn early on in the sound business is, a signal that sounds good to the musicians onstage might sound really nasty out of the front house speakers.)

So now we've got all of our mics and D.I.s plugged into the mixer. As with the first system, each channel has tonal control with its EQ section, as well as a level control. We also have a couple of other controls we'll be using this time: The monitor-level control and the auxiliary level control. The monitor control sends the signal to the monitor bus inside the mixer, where all of the channels' monitor signals are combined (a bus is an electrical path that is common to several parts in the mixer; the main-, monitor-, and aux buses are where the actual mixing occurs). These signals are sent to a monitor-send master-level control, and then to an output jack which will be connected to an external amp to power the stage monitor speakers. Because each channel of the mixer has its own monitor control, we can send only those signals that are essential to the stage monitors (such as vocals), and not send signals we don't need (drums, guitar, bass).

Monitor-level controls are referred to as **pre-fader**. That means they get their signal before it is sent to the main channel level control, and consequently, they operate totally independently. The auxiliary (usually just called "aux") level control is **post-fader**. It takes its signal after the main level control. The reason for this is that aux outputs are often used to drive **effects** units, and if they were pre-fader, the effect would still be activated by the signal, even when the channel level control was turned down. With a post-fader send, the main channel level control also adjusts the aux signal output proportionally to the overall level. Then why have an aux control at all? There might be times that you want the same effect on two or more inputs, but you want more of the effect on one than the others. An example of this would be reverb on drums. The kick drum can have a little bit of reverb, the toms sound good with a little more, and the snare gets even more. Or you may want some delay on the lead vocal, but not as much, or any, on the backing vocals.

The aux level controls send their signals to the aux bus, where all of the channels' aux signals from the input channels are combined. They proceed to the aux send control, and the signal goes to a connector to be sent out to the input of one or more signal processors. Any line-level signal processing unit, such as an exciter, digital effects processor, compressor, or equalizer, may be utilized, either individually or chained together, output to input.

The output of the effects unit(s) then is connected back into the mixer at the aux return jack. The signal then goes to yet another control, the aux level, before being sent on to the master section of the mixer where it is combined with the channel signals. This may seem like an awful lot of controls, but control is good!

Sometimes, if enough channels are available, it is preferable to use an input channel as the effects return. This allows the sound operator tone adjustment over the effected signal, as well as a channel fader for better control. The only drawback to this method is, if you accidentally turn the aux level control up on your return channel, it will send the effect signal right back into the effect input, creating a feedback loop. This will show itself by squealing or howling when the channel level is increased, and can easily damage speakers and sound persons' egos!

Now we have our instruments, our vocals, and our effects all mixed together. This signal goes to the main output fader and on to the mixer's main out jack. Some mixers have an onboard graphic equalizer, but most do not, so our next connection from the mixer main out is to the input of an external graphic EQ. This allows us to fine-tune the overall tonal quality of the sound. The EQ output then connects to a compressor to control the dynamics of the sound. The compressor is optional, but highly recommended. If used properly, a compressor can help smooth the whole band's sound, as well as act as a peak signal limiter, which might save your speakers if somebody knocks over a mic stand or some disorderly yay-hoo hops onstage and yells as loud as he (or she) can into one of the mics. (In my experience, this happens much more often than a mic stand being accidentally knocked over.)

Finally, our signal can go to the amplifiers, right? Well, no. We're going to be using a multiple-amplifier system with active crossovers. The signal goes from the compressor's output to the crossover input, where the signal is frequency-divided. This particular system is a two-way configuration, which means the frequencies below a certain point are sent to one amp and speaker, and the frequencies above that point are sent to a different amp and speaker. In our little sound system, the crossover frequency is set at 120Hz. All of the sound from 120Hz down to 20Hz is sent to the subwoofer amp and then to the subwoofers. The frequencies above 120Hz are sent to our mid-high amp and out to the mid-high speakers, each of which contains an additional passive crossover. This passive crossover removes the high frequencies above about 800Hz from the signal being sent to the midrange driver, and removes the frequencies below that point from the tweeter, or horn, signal.

ARENA SYSTEMS

Larger sound systems operate in exactly the same way as the one we just got done discussing, with some notable exceptions. The main mixer will be located out in front of the main speakers. The mikes will be connected to it by a long **snake cable** (or fiber-optic multiplex cable in the case of some digital mixers), and the mixer will be operated by a sound engineer. A large-venue sound system will have a separate monitor mixer (operated by another soundtech), located just offstage with inputs for everything being used onstage, and each member of the act will have their own monitor mix. That way, the lead vocalist doesn't have to hear the backing vocals too loud, and vice versa, and the keyboard player can have lots of keyboards without too much guitar, etc. Some pro monitor boards have as many as fifty-six inputs and twelve or more output mixes. The main mixer would have a similar 40- to 56-input configuration, and the EQ section for each channel will be extensive, often with four or five frequency bands and **sweepable** (selectable) center frequencies. This type of EQ is called parametric. Pro sound mixers usually have from six to twelve aux sends for all of the effects and submixes used. Many soundtechs on tour will have three or four different digital reverbs just for vocals, and more for drums and other instruments, in addition to delays, exciters, subharmonic synthesizers, and myriad other devices. The sound system may be three-way, four-way, even five-way. Even the monitors are multi-amped, two- or three-way.

Remember way back when I told you that learning terminology was half the battle in understanding things? Well, one thing I personally find kind of humorous is the fact that, once you enter the realm of pro sound, a lot of the terms change. A mixer that costs more than a few thousand dollars is no longer referred to as a mixer; it is called a "board" or a "desk." Monitors are "wedges." Speakers ("front house boxes") aren't just hung from scaffolding, they're "flown." I think it's a status thing, the way you don't just call a Rolls Royce a "car."

TROUBLESHOOTING

It is fairly common to get a sound system set up, start to test all of the microphone lines, and find that something isn't working properly. Here's how to go about finding out what's not working and why.

From Output to Input Only

You'll notice that I always refer to connecting "from" an output and "to" an input. This helps to reinforce in our minds the path and direction of the signal. Never connect an "out" to an "out," or an "in" to an "in." Not only will it not work, but it just might damage something important. Keeping the signal's directional flow in mind helps you think logically when you are troubleshooting problems in a system.

Go With the (Signal) Flow

Always keep in mind the path of the signal flow. The signal originates at the microphone or the instrument and D.I. box, goes through the signal cable to the snake, out to the mixer, etc. If you have four mics connected, and three of them work, it doesn't make any sense to test the main equalizer. The problem must be somewhere before the signals are mixed together: Either the mic, the cord, the snake, or the mixer itself. Checking anything past the point where the mic signals are mixed is a waste of time. If you have a tri-amped system and the sub cabinets aren't working, it makes no sense to check the crossover input; obviously, there is signal present there, or the high speakers would also be dead. Thinking about the signal flow before you start to search for the problem, using logic and common sense, will keep you from wasting time and effort.

Substitution

Any time you have more than one of something, such as speakers, amps, cables, or mics, you have a means to determine if one is bad by substituting another "known-good" one. If one mic doesn't work and you have another one, try it on the "bad" mic cord. If this mic also doesn't work, the problem is obviously not the mic, and you should progress down the path to the next logical point. If your system is stereo, and one channel is working normally, you can use the working channel to solve the problem by substituting a section at a time. If, for example, the entire right side of the system is not working, you can reverse the mixer output cables—plug the left cable into the right mixer output and vice-versa. If the right side starts working and the left side is now dead, the problem is before this point in the signal path. If the problem stays in the same side, the signal is being interrupted somewhere farther down the signal path.

CABLES AND WIRES

The typical sound system has three types of cables: Low level and line level signal cables, such as instrument cords, mic cords, and patching cables; AC power cables, like extension cords and multiboxes (power strips); and speaker cords. Here are some tips about cabling.

Signal Cables

Signal cables have the potential to introduce the largest amount of unwanted noises and hums into a sound system. One thing that helps keep these noises to a minimum is to keep your cable runs as short as possible. Having a variety of cable lengths lets you choose the best cord for the job. Mic cords seem always to be too short or too long. Keep a few short (12-foot or less) mic cords for those times when a standard cord is just a few feet shy of reaching. Carry a couple of extra-long cords to reach things that are inevitably on the far side of the stage from the snake box.

Try not to run signal cables next to AC power wiring, especially wall-wart-type power adaptors. AC cables and transformers produce electromagnetic fields, which can be picked up by signal cables and amplified by the sound system. This is especially important in rack-cabinet wiring, and anywhere the signal cables are not balanced. If signal carrying cables and AC cables must cross each other, it is best if they do so at right angles to each other. Signal cables may get noisy if they are mishandled. Don't roll over cords with amps or racks. Don't pull hard on them when you're wrapping them up at the end of a gig. If they get stuck, don't yank on them; this stresses the shield and creates small breaks under the insulation. You might not be able to see them, but you might hear noise when the cord is moved, and the hum will increase due to the reduced shielding effect. Don't tie cables in knots; the sharp bends will have the same effect on the wires.

AC Cords

The same basic rules of handling apply to power cables. Any wire that is bent repeatedly in the same place will eventually break. Always unplug power cords by pulling on the plug, not the cord. Yanking them out by the cord will break the connections to the plug. If a plug sparks when you plug it in or unplug it, it needs to be repaired. If you put your own plugs on power cords, use the best ones you can afford. They will actually save you money by holding up longer. Wire them correctly: Black is "hot," white is neutral, and green is ground. The brass, gold-colored screw on the plug is hot; the steel, silver-colored screw is neutral; and the green screw is ground. If you aren't sure of the wiring, don't do it! If you're wrong, you may not find out until you fry something (or someone). Use extension cords that are large enough gauge to handle the load. Smaller-gauge cords under high loads get hot, and can melt and start fires. On high-current cables, such as those for amp racks or lighting, the shorter the cable, the better. Longer cords have higher internal resistance, which limits the current supplied to the load: Your gear.

Speaker Cords

As with power cords, speaker cables should be of a large enough gauge to provide adequate current to the speakers without losing too much power in the wires. Don't crimp, crush, bend, fold, or mutilate. The shorter, the better. Be nice to your cables, and they'll last a long time. Beat the heck out of them, and they'll get even with you at the worst possible moment!

ABOUT FEEDBACK

Feedback is a term used to describe an acoustic oscillation, or tone, that is generated by the electronic devices used to amplify the signals. The signal from the mic is amplified, sent to the speakers, and out into the surrounding air in the form of sound waves. If enough of the sound waves from the speakers re-enter the microphone, that creates a feedback loop: Out of the speaker, into the mic, through the amps, out of the speaker. The result is an audio tone that builds until it overpowers the original signal. Feedback can be at any frequency in the audio spectrum, from a low-frequency hum to a mid-frequency squeal, on up to a piercing, high-frequency screech. None of them is desirable, and all of them are annoying, and potentially damaging to your hearing and/or speakers. Feedback is best avoided by preventing the speaker's signal from getting back into the microphone. There are several ways to prevent feedback. One is to use highly directional microphones that reject signals coming from behind the mic. Another is to use very precise equalizers to reduce the frequencies that tend to feed back the most. Yet another way is to have the speakers pointed away from the microphone, and not parallel to walls. The more bouncing the sound has to do before it can enter the mic, the less the chance of feedback. Many equipment-makers are now producing feedback eliminators—devices that sense feedback, identify the frequency, and automatically reduce the level at the offending frequency. Using a combination of all of these methods allows us to have extremely high signal levels without feedback.

MICROPHONES

There are a bunch of different kinds of mics, made to serve a variety of purposes. Here are a few guidelines about which ones are used where and why. Several parameters should be considered when you are deciding which mic to use for a particular application.

Microphone Type

Most microphones used for live sound reinforcement are dynamic, condenser, or ribbon mics. The descriptions below of these types of mics are generalizations, and there will always be exceptions, but this should provide a point of reference. Ribbon-element mics are often the best-sounding and most expensive microphones, but they are fragile and can't handle much bumping or jarring, although some still find their way onto stages. Condenser mics are often used to mike acoustic instruments, such as pianos, drums, horns, and voices. They sometimes have better high-frequency response and sensitivity than many dynamic mics, and can be smaller in size than dynamic mics, and less obtrusive. They do, however, require a DC voltage (48 volts for optimal performance) to operate, either from an internal battery or an external phantom power supply. Dynamic mics used in live sound have a large diaphragm area, and work better in high-output, low-frequency applications like kick drums and guitar miking. They are often preferable for vocals, too.

Frequency Response

A mic with poor low-frequency response won't work as well on an instrument with a lot of low-frequency content, such as a bass guitar or kick drum, as one with really good low response will. Likewise, you will be better off miking an instrument with a lot of high frequencies, like violin or cymbals, with a mic that reproduces those frequencies well. Some mics have a particular midrange peak in their response curve that makes them sound better on male vocals than on female vocals *(see figure 15-3)*. Others may sound great on acoustic piano, yet sound poor on congas. A mic that sounds killer on a guitar amp may not have enough highs to sound good on a snare drum, and a great-sounding snare mic might sound thin and tinny on a floor tom.

Most directional microphones also have different frequency response characteristics, depending upon how close the diaphragm of the mic is to the sound source. Low frequencies will increase and higher frequencies decrease as the sound source gets closer to the mic. This phenomenon is called proximity effect.

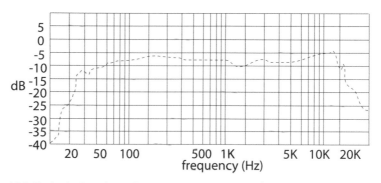

Figure 15-3: Typical microphone frequency response curve chart

Pickup Pattern

All microphones have what is called a "**polar pattern.**" The polar pattern, or pick up pattern of a mic *(see figure 15-4)* tells us from what directions sound will be best picked up (and rejected) by a given mic. An omnidirectional mic will pick up sound waves coming toward it from just about any direction. In live sound reinforcement situations, unidirectional microphones are preferred. Unidirectional mics will pick up sound coming toward the front of the diaphragm, while rejecting most of the sound coming from the rear. The polar pattern of unidirectional mics is often called cardioid, which means heart-shaped. Some, like the example in *figure 15-4*, are hypercardioid, or exaggerated heart-shaped. This directionality of the pickup pattern allows stage volume to remain relatively high without causing feedback.

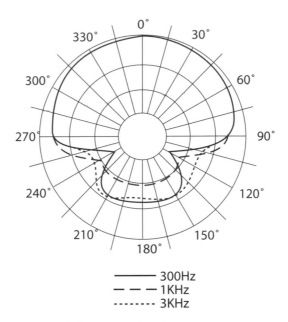

Figure 15-4: The polar pattern of a hyper-cardioid microphone

Impedance

We talked about impedance in an earlier chapter, but let's just touch on it again. High-impedance, unbalanced mics work okay, as long as the input of the mixer is also high-impedance, and the cable runs are quite short. For any mic cord runs of more than fifteen or twenty feet, low-impedance, balanced microphones are recommended. Long runs of high-Z mic cable tend to pick up noise and hum. Virtually all mics used with mid- to large-size systems will be Lo-Z, balanced.

Quality

It's hard to tell by looking at a microphone if it's a gem or junk. The only way to judge a mic's quality is to educate yourself. Read the specification sheet, look at the frequency-response curve. Shake it, listen to it, check the price. Some cheap mics sound good, but they won't hold up under the rigors of being moved repeatedly. It is usually true that you get what you pay for. It's a good bet that an expensive mic will outperform most cheaper mics. Also as usual, there are exceptions to this rule.

What Mic to Use Where?

The following recommendations are just that. Recommendations. They are just examples and are not the only way or necessarily the best way to do things. Miking techniques for live sound and studio recording differ greatly.

Drums and Percussion

Most microphone companies have a line of mics that are designed to be used for drums. These generally work very well. If these are not available to you, choose mics that can handle the high sound-pressure levels of drums, and try to match their frequency response to the drum being miked. Many vocal mics will work well on drums. Larger-diaphragm mics are preferred for kick drum and floor toms. Condenser mics work well on cymbals and hi-hat. Drum mics should be durable. Even the most accurate drummers accidentally hit one every now and then. Drum mics should be able to take a few hits.

Electric Guitars

Dynamic mics sound good on guitar amps. Again, most companies make a model or two designed for instrument miking. Most good vocal mics also work well on electric guitars.

Acoustic Guitars

Due to their flatter response curves, condenser mics help prevent feedback; plus, their high-frequency sensitivity sounds nice on acoustic guitars. If it has a good pickup built in, a D.I. box works well instead of a mic. Sometimes mixing the guitar's internal pickup with an external mic sounds good, particularly in recording situations.

Piano, Harp, Mandolin, and Banjo

Two mics on piano, one for the low end and another for the high range will usually work well. Grand pianos are generally best miked from above the strings with the lid propped open, while uprights should be miked from the rear to help prevent feedback. The brightness of condenser mics sounds good on piano and most acoustic stringed instruments.

Bass Guitar

Use a D.I. box on bass, if possible, to prevent low-frequency feedback. If miking is necessary, a good larger-diaphragm mic similar to those used for kick and floor toms will work nicely.

Brass and Woodwinds

Some microphone manufacturers make clip-on mics designed for saxophones, trombones, and trumpets. These work quite well. Most good vocal mics will also suffice, as long as they can handle the high SPLs of these instruments without distortion.

Voice

The right mic for any particular singer will depend a lot on the tonal quality of the voice. A few microphone-makers have started making mics designed just for female vocalists, due to the difference in timbre (harmonic overtone content) of female voices. Some men will sound better with this type of mic, just as some women will sound better with a traditional "male" vocal mic. Selecting the right vocal mic is mostly a matter of experimentation.

Everything Else

Select the mic that matches most closely the frequency requirement of the instrument. Keep in mind the loudness of the instrument, as well as the way the mic will be mounted. Use the best-quality microphone you can for everything you mike up. A sound system is the sum of all of its parts, and a crummy mic sounds even crummier through a great sound system!

SOUND SYSTEM HINTS AND TIPS

Carrying a few extra things with you can sometimes prevent an engagement from becoming a nightmare. Here's what every sound system toolbox shouldn't be without.

TOOLS

Standard and needle-nose pliers; large and small straight screwdrivers, especially one small enough to fit the screws in XLR sockets and banana plugs; small (#1) and large (#2) Phillips-head screwdrivers; two good hex-key sets, one SAE (American Standard), one metric; an adjustable wrench, 6- or 8-inch; wire strippers; wire cutters; 35- or 40-watt soldering iron and resin core solder; AC circuit tester; meter with voltage and **continuity** testing capabilities with test leads; electrical tape; and gaffers tape (not duct tape).

Plugs and Adaptors

At least one of each of the following: Male and female XLR type plugs, ¼-inch mono, and TRS plugs; dual banana plug; Speakon or EP speaker plug (if you have them on your speaker cables); XLR "gender changers"—two each male-to-male and female-to-female (these allow you to use a mic channel for a return line or vice versa in case of emergency); male XLR to female ¼-inch adaptor; AC ground lift (three-prong to two-prong adaptor); XLR ground lift (male-to-female XLR with no ground connection); 10dB pad (male-to-female XLR connectors that decrease the signal level by 10dB using internal resistors); ¼-inch female to two ¼-inch male "Y" cord for splitting signals; ¼-inch male to two ¼-inch female "Y" cord for combining signals; and various ¼-inch to RCA adaptors for connecting home stereo gear into the system (for when the bride's mother absolutely must play the recording of the bride's very first piano recital).

Odds and Ends

Extra mic stand; extra mic clip (stand adaptor); 13- or 18-inch gooseneck; spare microphones; a few feet each of two conductor, shielded mic cord and speaker wire for emergency rewire jobs; a few feet of stiff solid wire for hanging things and tying things up; more gaffer's tape for when the first roll gets lost or stolen; white artists' tape (also called board tape) for labeling the channels on the mixer (it has tacky glue that will not leave tape-sticky-gunk after it is removed); fine-tip laundry markers (at least two—see note on gaffer's tape above); pens (same here); and spare bulbs for board lights. Looks like you might need a pretty big toolbox, eh?

Chapter SIXTEEN

How Guitar Electronics Work
or, wires, wires, and more wires!

I always recommend that you leave repairs to the professionals if at all possible, but I realize that the combination of not having money to burn and the natural American do-it-yourself mentality will often prevail. Heck, I worked on my own guitars when I was a kid, and I didn't know a capacitor from a weasel's eyelashes. I know that there are a bunch of folks out there who, despite all of my forewarnings, are going to pop the backs off of the control compartments of their guitars and try to fix or modify them. So, I figure if you can't lick 'em, join 'em. This chapter will explain how guitars are wired and how the signal is routed, switched, and modified.

PICKUPS

There are several different types of pickups, and it's a good idea to know what they are, how they are different, and which ones work best for which applications. How the pickups in a guitar function was covered in Chapter Eight, How Speakers and Microphones Work, so we won't cover that again here. Refer back to that chapter if you need to.

Single-coil Pickups

The first guitar pickups were called bar-magnet pickups. They used a magnetized bar of steel wrapped with coils of wire to pick up the vibrations from the strings. Some bar-type pickups are still sold, and they work and sound fine. The popular "rail" and "lipstick-tube" pickups are bar-magnet pickups. Pickup makers noticed that some strings seemed to be louder than others when the player is using a bar-magnet pickup, so they designed a pickup that had individual bars, or pole pieces, for each string. This allowed the magnetic pole piece to be placed closer to the strings with the lowest output, and all of the strings then produced more equal sound. Soon, someone came up with the idea to make the pole pieces out of threaded rod, so the height of each one could be individually adjustable.

All of these types of pickups are single-coil; that is, they are wrapped with one continuous piece of wire. Single-coil pickups have a distinctive tonal quality, but they also tend to pick up hum and noise from outside of the guitar.

Double-coil Pickups

One way to combat this problem is to add a second pickup in close proximity to the first, and wind the coil in the opposite direction. This configuration, called double coil, or **"humbucking"** has the advantage of higher output and reduced noise, due to the phase-cancellation effect of the oppositely wound coils (this works in a similar manner to balanced lines on microphones). A double-coil pickup also has more low-frequency output than single-coil pickups, so they sound a little thicker and less twangy than single coils. Some people prefer the sound of single coils, and others like the fatter double-coil tones.

Variations

Until the early seventies, pickups were manufactured by the guitar companies for use on their own guitars only. That changed when a few independent pickup makers came on the scene. These companies sometimes consisted of just one guy hand-winding pickups in his basement. (Seymour! What are you doing down there? Your supper's getting cold!) These aftermarket pickups caught the attention of guitar players, because they often sounded better and had higher output than stock pickups, but still fit into the original mounting hardware.

Some even had the added feature of having tapped coils. A tapped-coil pickup has an additional wire coming from the pickup. This wire connects to the place where the two coils connect together. The tapped-coil pickups allow you to remove one coil from the circuit, and make a guitar with double-coil pickups sound like a guitar with single-coils, by simply flipping a switch. Soon, on the heels of this innovation came the independently wired double-coil pickup. A wire is connected from each end of each coil in the pickup, allowing the coils to be phase-reversed, wired in series (normal), or in parallel *(see figure 16-1)*.

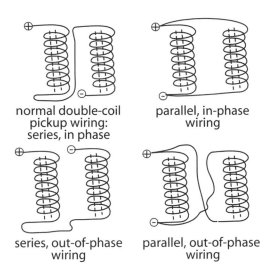

normal double-coil
pickup wiring:
series, in phase

parallel, in-phase
wiring

series, out-of-phase
wiring

parallel, out-of-phase
wiring

Figure 16-1: Double-coil pickup wiring

Guitarists have always been on the lookout for new and different sounds, and these new options were well-received. Today, many independent pickup manufacturing companies thrive.

Guitars with single-coil stock pickups sometimes had to be heavily modified to accept these tapped double-coil pickups. They often routed the body to accommodate the larger-size pickup. The independent pickup makers soon saw the need to develop a single-coil sized hum-canceling pickup. One design they came up with features two very narrow coils side by side. Another is the stacked pickup, which uses two coils on the same coil form, one above the other. These types of pickups sound more like a single-coil than a standard double-coil pickup; they reduce hum, and they feature independent wiring.

Other Pickup Types
Other types of pickups include dynamic or condenser-type microphones and piezo-electric contact-pickups. These are used mostly to amplify acoustic instruments, although there are some electric guitars that include piezo-type pickups built into the bridge to emulate the sound of an acoustic guitar. Some acoustic instruments use both a microphone and a piezo element, and allow the user to control the balance between the two.

SIMPLE GUITAR WIRING

In *figure 16-2* there is a wiring diagram for the most simple type of guitar, using just one single-coil pickup, a volume control, and an output jack. The pickup's "hot" signal wire connects to the input, or "top" of the volume pot, and the output, or "wiper" of the pot connects to the output jack's "hot" connection. The pickup's "cold" or ground wire connects to the ground, or "bottom," of the pot, and to the "cold" of the output jack. *Figure 16-3* shows the same circuit drawn as a schematic diagram.

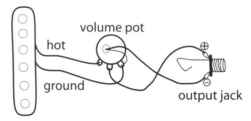

Figure 16-2: *Single pickup guitar wiring diagram*

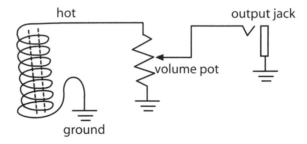

Figure 16-3: *Single pickup guitar schematic*

Here's how the signal moves through the circuit. The pickup signal goes from the pickup to the volume control. If the volume control is turned all the way down, the wiper connects directly to signal ground, so no signal goes out to the output jack. If the control is turned up, the wiper moves closer to the top of the control, and signal then is allowed to pass to the jack. (If you've already read the chapter on guitar amps, this should all sound pretty familiar.) The higher the control is turned, the more signal goes to the jack, and the less gets bypassed, or "shunted" to ground *(see figure 16-4)*.

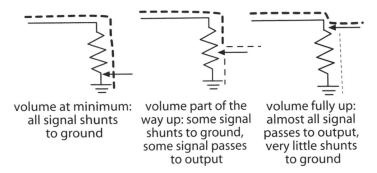

volume at minimum: all signal shunts to ground

volume part of the way up: some signal shunts to ground, some signal passes to output

volume fully up: almost all signal passes to output, very little shunts to ground

Figure 16-4

NOT-SO-SIMPLE GUITAR WIRING

Our next example *(figure 16-5)* is a typical two-pickup guitar with volume and tone controls, and a pickup-selector switch. The same circuit is shown as a schematic diagram in *figure 16-6*.

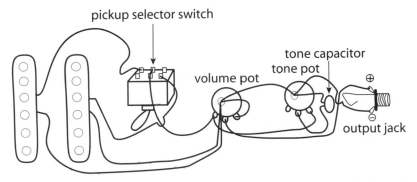

Figure 16-5: Diagram of two-pickup guitar with volume and tone controls, and pickup selector

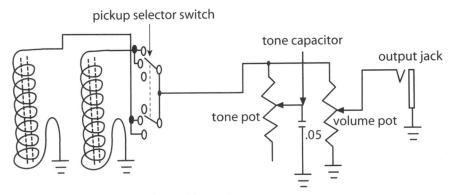

Figure 16-6: Schematic diagram of two-pickup guitar

The two-pickup hot signals connect to the pickup selector switch. This switch is a three-position "on-on-on" switch. In position one, the neck pickup only connects to the switch output, or common. In position two, both the neck and bridge pickups connect to the common, and in position three, only the bridge pickup connects to the common. The output of the switch then connects to the volume control top. This control works exactly as the one in our first example. The select switch output also connects to the bottom of the tone control. The tone control in this example is a passive **high-cut** type of control. That means it doesn't boost any frequencies; it only removes them. The capacitor connected to the wiper of the tone pot will only allow high frequencies to pass through (see Chapter Two, Components, for more information about capacitors). The other side of the capacitor is connected to ground, so the lower the control is turned, the more high frequencies will be removed from the signal and shunted to ground. (The #1 contact of the tone control doesn't connect to anything.) With the control at full up, the signal passes through to the output, almost unchanged.

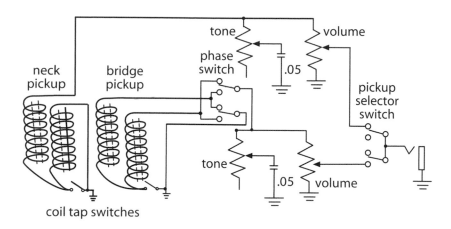

Figure 16-7: Two-pickup guitar schematic with coil taps and phase switch

COMPLICATED GUITAR WIRING

Our next example *(figure 16-7 above)* includes two tapped double-coil pickups, and a phase switch. Now things are starting to get complicated! This circuit is similar to the simple two-pickup circuit we just looked at, with the addition of separate volume and tone controls for each pickup, a coil tap switch for each pickup, and a phase-reversal switch on the bridge pickup. The volume and tone controls are identical to those in our previous example, but there are two sets, one for each pickup. In order for the pickups to have independent control, the controls must be placed before the pickup-selector switch, instead of after it.

The coil tap switches ground when the switches are engaged. In this example, the coil tap switches are push-pull switches that are part of the tone control potentiometers. When the control knob is pulled out, the coil tap is switched to ground, effectively removing one coil of the pickup from the circuit. The pickup becomes single-coil. The phase switch is a double-pole, double-throw miniature toggle switch that reverses the polarity of one pickup *(figure 16-8)*.

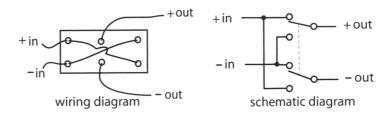

wiring diagram   schematic diagram

Figure 16-8: Phase reverse switch

In the "normal" position, the pickup's signal hot wire is connected to the positive (+) output of the switch, and the pickup's ground wire connects to the negative (-) output. When the switch is thrown to the "reverse phase" position, the positive pickup lead connects to the negative output, and the pickup ground lead now connects to the positive output.

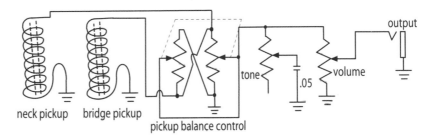

neck pickup   bridge pickup   pickup balance control

Figure 16-9: Guitar with pickup balance control

Figure 16-9 shows a guitar wired with a balance control between the pickups instead of a selector switch. This circuit is used most often in electric basses. The potentiometer used for a balance control is a dual-ganged control made especially for this purpose. This type of pot has two separate potentiometers that are both turned from the same knob. As the control turns clockwise, the first potentiometer goes from minimum-resistance, or zero ohms, and gets to maximum resistance at the halfway point of travel. As the control continues to be turned, the resistance in this pot stays at this value for the rest of the rotation. The other potentiometer acts the same way, but exactly in reverse: It is at zero ohms at full clockwise. Here's how the circuit works. Starting at full counter-clockwise, pickup 1 will be at full volume, and pickup 2 will be off. As you turn the control clockwise, pickup 1 will remain at full volume as pickup 2 starts to gain volume. At the halfway point, both pickups will be at full output. As the control continues to be turned, the volume of pickup 1 will begin to decrease, while pickup 2's level will stay at full, until finally we reach full clockwise rotation, and pickup 1 is now silent.

Musicians are known for constantly trying new things, and as you can see, when it comes to guitar wiring, dozens of variations are possible. Some sound good, and some just sound weird, but you can be sure they've all been tried at one time or another.

PART 3

EQUIPMENT FAILURES

Chapter SEVENTEEN

WHY STUFF BREAKS
or, meltdown prevention 101

There are as many reasons for things to break as there are components inside of them. There are as many reasons for equipment to fail as there are people using (and abusing) it. There isn't much we can do about random component failures, but there is a lot we can do about the using and abusing side of things.

Heat, dirt, moisture, power source, misuse, and lack of maintenance are often contributing factors to gear failure. These are all factors that can be controlled, at least somewhat, by the person operating the equipment. In this chapter, we'll explore the effect these problems have on equipment, and discuss what we can do to influence them and prevent electronic gear failures.

TEMPERATURE

Heat kills components. The output devices in amps that drive the speakers, power supply rectifiers and regulators, tubes, and many other components in the things we use to make music are heat-sensitive, some more than others. Excessive heat changes the way silicon devices pass current. Heat can also warp circuit boards and cause solder in soldered connections to become softened. Heat in the form of direct sunlight can melt plastic and warp metal. If you're performing outdoors in the summertime during the day, it may be impossible to control the temperature, but there are some things that can be done to offset its effects.

Tarps can be used to cover gear so it's not exposed to direct sun. Light colors reflect more heat, so lighter-colored tarps work best for this. Lighting stands that aren't used during daytime gigs can hold tarps up over a small stage like a roof, if there's not too much wind. This shading not only keeps equipment cooler, but prevents the warping of plastic cases on equipment. Fans are a necessity for power amps and racks of keyboard modules on hot days. In fact, even if equipment and racks have built-in fans, an additional clip-on fan or two can't hurt. The more air-flow through a rack, the better. Cooling the musicians isn't a bad idea either.

MOISTURE

Moisture is another big-time gear-destroyer. I'm not talking about 90% humidity, I'm talking about beer, soda, water, and other things that if they get into electronic equipment, cause major trouble if a liquid gets inside something electronic, it can act as a conductor and short things out. Turn off power immediately, and make sure all of the unit is thoroughly dry before turning it on again. Beer, soda pop and other drink-type liquids are also very corrosive and can eat through resistor, capacitor, and diode leads after a while. Sometimes it takes a few months, sometimes only a few days. So how do we prevent this kind of thing? This one seems obvious, but you'd be surprised by the number of units taken in for repairs because of drinking problems. Simple solution: No Drinks. No drinks on amps. No drinks on keyboards. No drinks on ledges next to amps or keyboards or mixers. No drinks anywhere near electronic gear. Murphy's law of splashing, which I just made up, states: If a drink is placed where it can be knocked, bumped, or vibrated in any way that might cause the liquid to exit the glass, it will be, and the liquid will travel three to five times farther than normal, in directions defying gravity, in order to enter electronic equipment and destroy it. Just as nature abhors a vacuum, liquids abhor music. If you don't believe me, try singing underwater.

The second rule of thumb is, if you see one rain drop, kill the power and run for cover. (Cover for the gear, not for you. You won't short out.) Water isn't as bad as beer, pop, or mixed drinks, but it'll still do plenty of damage. Even distilled water (which is not naturally conductive) will absorb dirt molecules and minerals and become conductive. If you live in an area that gets really cold in the winter, it's a good idea, if at all possible, to allow your gear to get close to room temperature before turning it on. When extremely cold equipment is brought into a warm room, condensation forms on all of the cold metal and plastic surfaces. Sometimes, enough moisture can be produced to form water drops that run into circuitry and cause problems. Usually, the condensation will evaporate without doing any damage if the equipment is allowed to warm up for a short time.

DUST AND DIRT

Dirt causes equipment to fail in a number of ways. Accumulation of dirt and dust will cause amplifier components to run hotter than normal, and heat, as we discussed previously, is a major component-killer. Dirt also has a more direct effect on gear by getting into places where it interferes mechanically with operation. Large amounts of dust, dirt, and lint have been known to cause volume controls, especially slider-type controls, to malfunction. Usually this is in the form of noise when the control is moved, but it can actually get bad enough to stop the signal entirely. Dust in keyboards may interfere with the function of the key switches. Many keyboards use conductive rubber or plastic contacts in the key switches, and it doesn't take much dust to cause them to malfunction. I once had a customer who played his electric piano all night long with a lighted cigarette hanging out of the side of his mouth, and the ashes would drop into the unit through the spaces between the keys. After the third time he paid me to replace all of the key contacts, he finally trained himself not to play and smoke at the same time. Large accumulations of dirt can cause air circulation fans to stop moving, and that causes more heat and...

VOLTAGE FLUCTUATIONS

In the summertime, when everybody has their air conditioner going full-blast, and outdoor venues become more popular, we sometimes run into low-voltage problems. It might be that you are playing a party or a fair where a generator is supplying the power, or it could just be that the power company isn't able to keep up with the demands placed on their circuits, but sometimes low voltage, or brownouts, occur. What this means to musicians using electronic equipment is possible equipment failure, again.

Let's remember back to good old Ohm's law. Voltage times current equals power. If the voltage in a circuit drops, and the power requirement stays the same, then the current must go up proportionately. Say you have an amplifier that is running along just fine at fairly high volume on a hot day. It is using close to the maximum current that it can draw before damage occurs. That's usually alright, since the amp was designed to withstand this during normal use. Suddenly, the power supply voltage drops from 117 volts AC to 90 volts AC. The amp must draw additional current to compensate for the voltage drop, and now we've jumped out of the safe operating range into the danger zone. The amp might put up with it until the voltage goes back up, or it just might short out an output transistor or two (or ten).

The power supplies in all of the other equipment will drop as well. In some pieces of gear, especially digital keyboards and signal processing equipment, the power supplies could drop low enough to cause the gear to shut down. It could be just temporary until the voltage rises again, or it could damage components in the unit. I remember playing a county fair in August once, when the temperature was around 85° in the shade (of which there was none), and every few minutes, the voltage would sag. Our keyboard player's instrument would shut off, and he'd have to manually turn it off and back on to get it to play again.

Much of the time, there isn't much you can do to prevent voltage problems, other than make sure the person who does the main AC wiring knows what he's doing, and be sure your extension cords are large-enough-gauge wire, and as short as possible. And shut off what you don't absolutely need to have on. Fans on equipment have priority; fans on musicians should be sacrificed. Drastic problems call for drastic measures.

MAINTENANCE

About maintenance and proper use of equipment: We humans are lazy by nature. We're all guilty of putting up with things because we just don't want to mess with getting them fixed. There's that power-strip-that-if-you-fold-the-cord-to-the-left-it-will-usually-work; and the extension-cord-that-sparks-when-you-plug-it-in-but-it-works-most-of-the-time; or the speaker-cord-that-failed-and-was-replaced-by-a-guitar-cord-just-to-get-through-the-gig-six-weeks-ago...you get the idea. These things may eventually cause problems. Not necessarily major ones, but it's the little aches that add up to big pains.

I recommend having equipment-maintenance days, when all of your cables get checked and cleaned, all equipment gets the dust blown out of it, and basically everything that isn't operating at 100% gets fixed. Keep a list in your gig bag or toolbox, and try to write yourself a note every time you notice something that needs repair. When a week rolls around when the stuff is idle, fix everything on the list. That way, your maintenance days aren't such major projects.

Sometimes, stuff just fails, and even the guy who fixes it can't tell you why. It just quits. Somewhere inside of something, an electron went on strike or bumped onto the wrong atom, and something somewhere fried. There is always a reason, but you don't always get to know what it is. Keeping stuff in the best possible working condition will sure make these failures happen less frequently. Now go buy a spare clip-on fan for yourself! You deserve it!

Chapter EIGHTEEN

WHY'D MY AMP BLOW UP?

or, buzz, hum, poof, hiss, pop!

A mplifiers can fail for a lot of reasons. If you haven't already done so, now would be a good time to read Chapter Eleven, How Amplifiers Work. It's much easier to understand why something doesn't work if you know how it is supposed to work. First, let's talk about solid-state (or transistor) amps.

SOLID-STATE AMPS

There are three common causes of failure in solid-state amps. The first and most likely would be thermal component failure due to excessive temperature and/or current. The second most likely cause is equipment being adversely affected by outside forces, such as heat from dust build-up or a fan not rotating; moisture getting into the amp from rain or a spilled drink; line voltage problems; or impact from someone tripping over the cables or the amp falling out of a moving vehicle. The third most common cause of gear meltdown is random component failure, meaning the part that went bad wasn't under any undue stress, it just quit, possibly because of being slightly out of factory tolerances or being infested with micro-gremlins from outer space.

Sometimes there is more than one cause, or the causes may be related. For example, if the fan in the amp (assuming it has one) fails, the components in the amp will begin to get hotter than they should, especially the ones covered with dirt (which was sucked into the amp by the fan in the first place). These components will then begin a contest to see which one will fail first. This would be a combination of external forces and thermal component failure due to excessive current.

Generally speaking, the parts of an amp that are most likely to fail are the ones that must handle relatively high amounts of current. These would be things like power transformers, power supply rectifiers, voltage regulators, and output devices. Power-supply components fail most often because of external factors, such as heat, low line voltage, or liquid spills. Also, vibration can cause the solder connections of heat sink-mounted components to crack, causing poor or broken connections. Any of these things may affect the amount of current through the power supply parts. When the current rating of a device is exceeded, it will most likely fail sooner or later.

The same is true of output devices. These are the things that actually transfer audio, in the form of AC current, out to the speakers. Output devices fail most often due to speaker line problems, such as damaged speaker cables, blown speakers, low impedance loads—too many speakers connected to one amp (see Chapter Five, Speaker Impedance), and something I call E.C.W.R.O.T.V.C. (Excessive Clockwise Rotation Of The Volume Control), also known as TLS (Too Loud Syndrome), and Deaf Musician's Disease. Just because the knobs go all the way to "ten" doesn't mean the amp will stand to be run that way for very long, anymore than your average car would run for hours at a time pegged out at 120 miles per hour.

TUBE AMPS

Tube amps are subject to the same failures, plus several others of their own. The very nature of tubes makes them prone to a whole set of quirks and foibles that don't plague solid-state amps. A tube is an evacuated envelope (meaning, almost all of the air has been sucked out of it), usually made of glass. So, it isn't too much of a stretch to say that carrying a tube amp is like toting around a box of light bulbs. Tubes are fragile and can break if the amp gets dropped or jarred. A tube amp, in addition to having a power transformer, also has an output transformer. Add this to the list of things to go bad. Tube amplifiers usually have much higher power supply voltages, which makes them more susceptible to arcing problems, since higher voltages tend to arc more easily than lower voltages. Tubes plug into sockets, so with every tube in an amp there are from four to twelve potential bad connections. Usually, these will not cause the amp to fail; they'll just make a lot of strange, unwanted noises. But bad tube socket connections can put a strain on the other components surrounding the tubes. Common tube amp failures include worn, cracked, or internally shorted tubes, bad connections, output transformer failure, and most of those already listed for solid-state amps.

FAILURE PREVENTION

Here is a list of potential problems that may cause amp failure, and some ways to help prevent them.

Heat

If possible, let a tube amp cool down to room temperature before moving it. Hot parts are more fragile than cool ones, and hot solder joints are softer than cool ones. Carry a small clip-on fan for those occasions when the temperature where you are playing gets too high: Outdoor gigs when the sun is shining, bars where the owners cheap-out on the air conditioning, house parties where there are two bodies for every square foot of floor space...

Abuse

Don't try to get the amp to do more than it was designed to do. If it's not loud enough, put a mic on it; don't crank it to infinity. If you don't know the impedance of speaker cabinets, don't hook them up to the amp. Don't try to connect multiple cabinets to an amp unless you know exactly what you're doing. Don't use a guitar amp as a bass amp, or a keyboard amp as a guitar amp, etc. It's a great way to blow speakers, and blown speakers will often destroy an otherwise perfectly functioning amp. Don't plug the whole band's guitar(s), bass(es), keyboard(s), and mic(s) into one amp and expect it to live to tell the tale. If your amp won't play loud enough, you need a bigger amp. Period. Never try do-it-yourself amp modifications unless you're doing it just for fun to an amp that you don't care much about. Non-factory mods usually do more to degrade an amp's performance than they do to enhance it.

Fuses

Carry spare fuses—the correct value! If a user-replaceable fuse blows while you're playing, there is always a chance that the reason it blew was something transitory, like a power line voltage drop or surge, and it may work again if you replace the fuse. If the fuse blows a second time, do not continue to try new fuses. The amp is already blown-up. Every time you put in another fuse, you run the risk of making the damage worse. The purpose of a fuse is to prevent the unit from catching on fire, and the rating of the fuse is important. Never use a higher-value fuse; never use foil around a fuse. Don't grab a fuse out of your car; they usually have a much higher current rating than musical-instrument equipment fuses. Most likely, it will damage an already-damaged amp more severely, plus you'll to have to drive home from the gig without dash lights or something.

Transporting Equipment

Transport your amp carefully. If you use a trailer, a little bump in the road can be a bone-jarring amp-killer. I've seen an amp (one of mine, once) where a transformer was literally ripped out of the chassis after our converted school bus hit a particularly nasty set of railroad tracks a little too fast. Put your amp in the car, truck or van. Put the drummer in the trailer; he won't mind.

Chapter **NINETEEN**

BLOWING SPEAKERS
or, how to cook a 200-watt speaker with a 100-watt amp!

Maybe it's never happened to you. Maybe it never will. Maybe it has, and you didn't know it. I'm talking about "blowing a speaker." If you are a guitarist, a bassist, or a soundtech, you have probably been around when someone discovers they (or you) have blown a speaker. It's not a pretty thing. This chapter discusses how to keep from blowing speakers, and what to do about it if you do.

ABOUT SPEAKERS

First, a few notes on speakers in general. Speakers range in size from tiny (like in a hearing aid) to really large. (Electro-Voice used to manufacture a 30-inch speaker for movie theaters.) There are several different types of speakers, but the ones we musicians are usually concerned with are called dynamic speakers. They have a magnet and a voice coil that make them work. It's this voice coil that makes the cone move, which moves air, which produces sound. (See Chapter Eight, How Speakers and Microphones Work, for more details.) Lots of variables about the voice coil determine how loud a speaker will play and at what point it will overheat the voice coil or move too far (**over-excursion**) and stop working properly.

SPEAKER FAILURES

Let's face it, at some point, your speakers are going to fail on you. Now's the time to learn what can go wrong, so you can fix it...if and when it happens. And, believe me, it *will* happen.

"Blown" Speakers

Several things happen to speakers when they are "blown." First, they make that buzzing, cruddy, distorted sound that most people associate with the term. This is the sound of a voice coil that has gotten so hot that either the voice coil form has warped, or the insulating enamel coating on the voice coil wire has melted and become liquid enough to form small bubbles, but the coil itself hasn't opened up; that is the wire hasn't burned all the way through, yet. These irregularities on the voice coil scrape against the sides of the magnet gap where the voice coil hangs out, and no longer allow the voice coil and speaker cone to move freely. This, in turn, causes the sound from the speaker to be distorted. If the speaker is played this way for a while, the wire may eventually rub completely through, and the speaker will stop playing entirely. This brings us to...

Open Voice Coil

The second most common speaker affliction is the open voice coil, or the "dead" speaker. No sound comes out. Nothing. Zip. Zilch. The cause of this phenomenon is usually just a higher degree of the over heated voice coil, as stated above, but this time, the voice coil got so hot that the wire itself melted into two pieces, causing an open circuit. This can also result from the speaker being bumped or dropped too hard. The voice coil is a continuous coil of wire, and if it breaks, it stops being continuous, so the speaker stops speaking. Sometimes if the amplifier has an output problem and it doesn't have good protection circuits, the speaker cone can actually catch on fire. This is only fun to watch if it's not happening to your speakers.

Over-Excursioning

Occurring about equally in the world of nonfunctional speakers are the over-excursioned voice coil and the shifted magnet. The voice coil in a speaker moves forward and backward. It is attached to the cone, which is attached to the speaker basket at the front and at the back of the cone. The cone is surrounded by flexible materials at points called the surround and the spider, in order to allow the cone to move forward and backward. No movement, no sound!

Occasionally, a speaker will move farther than it was designed to. The voice coil will then come completely out of the magnet gap where it has been happily residing, and things will break. Often, the cone will fold and wrinkle when this happens, and the voice coil will fail to find its way back into its cozy magnet gap, and so it stops moving at all. Again, no movement, no sound!

Sometimes humidity and old age can be a factor in this, but usually it is caused by a transient. No, not some old guy with a bottle in a brown paper bag. In tech talk, a transient is an audio signal that rises and decays very quickly. Dropping a microphone or bumping your electric bass into a cymbal stand are swell ways to generate big, ugly transient signals.

Shifted Magnet

A shifted magnet occurs when a speaker is dropped hard enough to break apart the epoxy that holds the magnet's various parts in place. Inside the magnet gap on the inside of the voice coil is a smaller magnet, called the plug, which makes up the inner wall of the gap. If it breaks loose, the magnetic attraction pulls it to the outer magnet, and this pinches the voice coil so it can't move. Once more, no movement, no sound. I don't know of any cause for this other than rough handling.

Under Powering

To keep from overheating voice coils, it is important that the speaker voice coil is not either overpowered or underpowered. Most folks understand the concept of overpowering: You turn it up too loud, and it fries! All speakers have a power rating. If you give them more than their rated power for very long, they will cook their little coils. However, few people realize it's just as bad or worse to underpower a speaker. When a power amplifier runs out of power, it is called "clipping." Most people have heard this term. It means the amp has reached the limits of its power supplies and the signal, when viewed with an oscilloscope (a piece of test equipment that allows you to see a graphic representation of an AC audio signal), looks like it has been chopped off on the top and the bottom *(see figure 19-1)*.

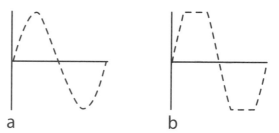

a   b

Figure 19-1: Normal signal (a), clipped signal (b)

This is a form of distortion that speakers, especially tweeters and smaller speakers, really hate. Speakers work well when the correct-frequency AC is sent to the speaker, but they don't like DC, or steady-state current. The clipped part of an audio signal is a steady-state signal, and power-supply voltage in most large amps runs from 35 to 85 volts, and sometimes even higher. This type of voltage connected directly to a speaker will overheat and destroy a voice coil in fairly short order.

SPEAKER REPAIRS

If you do happen to blow a speaker, it's not the end of the world. Most good-quality speakers can be repaired and made to be good as new. This process is called reconing. There are a few things to remember if you're having a speaker reconed. Many places that do speaker reconing use generic parts for most repairs. These parts are perfectly fine for most speakers, but if you have premium-quality, name-brand speakers, such as Electro-Voice, JBL, Altec Lansing, Cerwin Vega, or many others, you should insist on factory recone kits. Some speakers made by Peavey have replaceable baskets. They feature a bolt-on magnet, and when replacing the basket assembly, everything except for the magnet and the bolts gets replaced. You get a new basket, surrounds, cone, and voice coil, which simply bolt onto the old magnet assembly. These repairs cost about the same as reconing, but can be done by a repair shop or even by the consumer in just a few minutes. Most speakers can be repaired, but some lower-quality speakers, and most ordinary speakers under 8 inches in diameter, are cheaper to replace than to repair. A properly reconed speaker is equivalent to a brand-new speaker. Reconing a good-quality speaker typically will cost about one-third to one-half as much as purchasing a new one. Add the cost of shipping if it has to be sent away to be reconed.

If you have a blown speaker or horn driver, do not take it apart. Removing the cover and voice coil and diaphragm from a horn driver, or tearing out the cone and voice coil of a speaker, allows dust and tiny chunks of metal to get into the magnet gap. These can be difficult to remove, and will increase the time required to install the new parts, and consequently increase the cost of repair when you finally get the thing fixed.

So, that's how to blow up a 200-watt speaker with a puny little 100-watt (or smaller) amp. The keys to speaker life are: If you hear any distortion, turn the amp down. If you are playing in a larger room (or outdoors), be extra attentive and careful. That's where people often try to get more out of their speakers than they were designed to give. Try not to store speakers where it is damp or humid. Eat your vegetables. Look both ways before crossing the street... Yikes! I'm starting to sound like my mom!

PART 4

SERVICING

Chapter **TWENTY**

MAKING A REPAIR
or, so you think you wanna try this yourself...

Sometimes things break and it seems like you should be able to fix the stuff yourself and save the time, effort, and money of hauling it down to the local repair guy. There are things that go wrong that you can fix yourself, and there are others you should leave to the professionals. The following pages will offer some guidelines, so you'll know when to do which. I'll also try to impart some information that will help you deal with your repair person if you do have to take in the broken piece.

Here is a list of malfunctions you may be able to repair yourself: Broken wires in cables; burned-out light bulbs; intermittent connections, especially on signal jacks and power sockets; bad tubes in tube equipment; dirty (oxidized) connections and controls. Things you don't want to mess with include: Everything else, especially if smoke came out of the unit, the unit gets too hot to touch, or if finding where the problem might require major disassembly. More do-it-yourself repairs are botched by incorrect reassembly than by anything else I can think of.

GIVING A REPAIR A GO

To illustrate the principles I'm trying to convey about equipment repair, let's say we're going to fix something: You've got a guitar amp that sometimes just stops playing, for no apparent reason. You don't have much money, so you're going to try to fix it yourself. What do you need? A screwdriver to start with... Aah, that was tasty! Maybe you should have another one, this time with less orange juice and more... Wait! We better backtrack and lay down some ground rules!

Rule #1

Don't ever try to work on anything that plugs into the wall if you've done anything to impair yourself physically or mentally. That means no beer, wine, liquor (including screwdrivers), or controlled substances of any kind. This is for the protection of the equipment as well as to keep you from killing yourself. (Many electronic units, especially tube equipment, have large-value capacitors that can hold a charge for quite a while after being turned off and unplugged. Just because it's unplugged doesn't mean it can't zap you!)

Rule #2

Use the right (good-quality) tool for the job. A #1 Phillips screwdriver will fit into a #2 Phillips screw, but it will strip the head out if much pressure is applied. Once you strip out the head of a screw, you're out of luck. A soldering iron that is not hot enough might melt solder, but it will not make a good solder connection. Conversely, a soldering iron that is too hot can damage switches, jacks, and circuit boards. A 25-watt iron is usually about right for doing small wiring jobs and circuit board work, but you'll need a hotter iron, 30 watts or more, if you're going to be connecting heavy-gauge ground wires on the backs of volume controls, or wiring large speaker wire to connectors. An ohm meter can be used to make sure point A is connected to point B like it's supposed to be, and is a handy addition to your toolbox if you know how to use it.

Rule #3

Use the right screw for the right screw hole. To someone who has never taken apart an amp, the screws that hold it together might all look about the same, but they often are not. There are several styles of screws, and they are not interchangeable. All of them will either strip-out the screw or the screw hole if you try to put them in the wrong spot. Machine screws won't fit in tapping screw holes, but tapping screws (they tap their own threads, hence the name) will go into machine screw holes...and ruin them forever. There are fine-thread tapping screws for metal and coarse-thread tapping screws for plastic that look very much alike, but if you get them mixed up, your gear will no longer fit together properly.

Rule #4

Don't spend too much time looking for bad components. More than 90% of the units I work on have what I call mechanical problems. By that, I mean something has physically broken or come loose. Often, there are no burned electronic parts.

REPAIRING THE VIRTUAL AMPLIFIER

So, back to our project! We're going to fix the virtual amplifier that stops playing seemingly at random. By following these steps and thinking logically, there is no reason that we can't find the source of our problem, and make this amp as good as new. If we know how something is supposed to work, and can get replacement parts if we need them, there is nothing that we cannot repair.

Step One: The Visual Inspection

Okay, so you've got a well-stocked toolbox, you've got a good-quality soldering iron, and you're ready to go. The first thing you're going to do is look at it. That's right, don't plug it in, don't turn it on, just get it in a place where the lighting is good, and visually inspect it. It frequently happens that a piece comes in for repair and I can see what is wrong with it before I ever get around to turning it on or taking it apart. Look for anything that seems out of place. On an amp, are all of the knobs sticking out the same amount from the front of the faceplate? Are any of them dented, tilted, or bent? These things might indicate a broken control. Inspect all of the input and output jacks and sockets. Are any of the control nuts loose or missing? Are there broken-off plugs stuck inside of them? Many jacks contain switch contacts that perform various functions in the unit, and broken off plugs or foreign objects stuck inside of them can make the amp malfunction. Check the power cord, and, if the plug on a cord has been replaced, check the new one to make sure it was properly wired; it is surprising how many are not.

Examine any user-accessible fuses to see if they are blown, and make sure they are the right type and value. Try to notice if any screws are loose or missing. Look at the wires that run to the speakers, if it has them. Are they wired correctly and tightly? Are there any connectors that should have something plugged into them that are empty? Is the outside of the cabinet damp or sticky, or does it look like the unit may have gotten wet? Look it over carefully.

Step Two: The Sound Check

Let's assume the unit passes the look-see test. Now what? Now, turn it on, after first making sure the volume controls aren't cranked to arena levels. Plug in a signal source (guitar, bass, keyboard), preferably the same one you were using when you noticed the problem. Check to see if it is still malfunctioning. If it is, that's half the battle. If it's not, the fun is just beginning.

If the amp is malfunctioning, most people's first response is to try to make it work. Resist this urge! Once it starts to function normally, there is nothing you can do to figure out what the problem was until it malfunctions again, and getting it to mess up might be nearly impossible. Listen carefully to the amp. Is it totally silent, or is there normal amp idling hiss and/or hum? Is there some signal present? Is it distorted? These indicators will help to pinpoint the likely cause(s) of the problem. A totally dead output means that either the output section of the amp isn't functioning, or the speaker isn't working. Some signal means that at least part of the amp works. If the signal sounds distorted, it could be a bad component just about anywhere in the circuit, or it might be a broken connection somewhere.

Note that at this point, we haven't touched an ohm meter or a screwdriver. Folks who grab a driver and immediately start to take something apart often cause themselves lots of extra work.

Step Three: Substitution

Now it's a good idea to try a different signal source, even if you're positive your guitar or bass or whatever is fine. Never take anyone else's word that something has been tested! Test it yourself. This is the voice of experience speaking. Try another cable, too. It just takes a few seconds, and it might save you from feeling like a total fool three hours later when you're putting the screws back into a perfectly good amp.

Step Four: The Vibration Test

This phase of the inspection process is extremely useful for intermittent problems, but it also can be helpful on nonintermittent ones as well. Tap lightly (don't pound) on the unit with your fingertips, while listening to the amp. Listen for any change in the signal: Increased or decreased volume, decreased or increased distortion, hum or buzz. Tap on the top, the sides, the front, the back. Tap close to the input jacks, the output jacks, any send/return, preamp in/out or effects loop jacks. Tap lightly with a fingernail on the tubes if it is a tube amp, but be careful because they can get really hot. If there is no change, tap in all of the same places again, harder (except for the tubes, which can break). If this causes any change in the symptom, you've narrowed it down to a mechanical problem, which is good, because they're the easiest to track down and repair. If there still is no change in the symptom, well, it's on to...

Step Five: Divide and Conquer

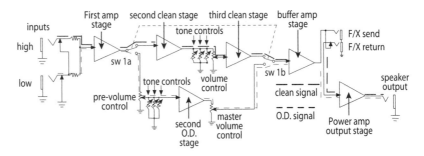

Figure 20-1: A block diagram or flow chart of a two-channel guitar amp

At this point, it helps to know the signal flow of the amp. The diagram in *figure 20-1* is called a block diagram or flow chart. It might look familiar to you, because it's the same one I used in Chapter Eleven, How Amps Work. If we think of the amplifier in sections—the input, the first preamp stage, the tone controls, etc.—and keep in mind the direction of the signal flow, then we can divide it into halves. It's much easier to troubleshoot half of an amp than it is to do the whole thing at once. Beginners often signal-trace a broken amp from the input jack, stage by stage, to the speaker. This works great if the problem is close to the input end of things, but it wastes a ton of time if the problem is close to the output. We can see in the block diagram that the effects loop is about halfway between the input jacks and the speaker. That means if our missing signal is present at this point, the front half of the amp is okay! We can test this by running a cable out of the effects send (output) jack into another amp that we know works. If there is no signal present, we then know the problem is before this point, and we can assume the output half is okay. Just like that, we've eliminated half of the components and connections in the amp from the list of possible problems. Applying this principle whenever possible enables us to narrow down the problem to smaller and smaller sections of the amp. If there was no signal at the effects send, we can move back to the next halfway point, the volume and tone controls. If you vary these controls, does the sound of the amp change at all? If we were to turn the treble and volume controls all the way up, would the hiss of the amplifier change level or tonal quality? If it does, that tells us the preamp section is working from that point on out to the speaker. If not, then that section is before the point where the problem is occurring. Now we've narrowed down the "bad" section to one-fourth of the amp. By repeating this division process, we'll eventually narrow the possible defective parts down to: The One With The Problem.

Step Six: Logical Thinking

Let's assume the volume and tone controls were working, which means the problem must be between the input jacks and the tone/volume section. At this point, without a device for looking at signals in the circuit, such as an oscilloscope, there really isn't another good place to divide this section of the amp, so we have to start thinking. Since (A) the problem is intermittent, and (B) we know that intermittent problems are most likely to be connection-related, which things between the input jack and the volume and tone section are most likely to cause an intermittent connection? Intermittents occur most often when something gets moved a lot. They also tend to occur at connection points where the components are larger and/or heavier, which causes them to move more during normal vibration. The first possibility that comes to mind is the input jack, followed by the controls themselves. Jacks and potentiometers are heavy compared to most components, and are under stress from being attached to the front panel and being switched on and off or plugged in and out of frequently. Most of the mass-produced amps made in the past several years use jacks that solder directly into the circuit board, and they are notorious for breaking those solder joints. Chances are, in this imaginary case, if we check the connections on the input jack, we'll find at least one of them broken.

Step Seven: Disassembling the Unit

So, what do you suppose we do now? Make sure it's unplugged, grab a screwdriver, and start taking it apart, right? Well, no. Actually, it's time to look at it again. Last time, we looked closely at the amp to see if anything looked funny or out of place. This time, we're looking at it to see if we can tell how it was put together. If we just start removing screws, there's no telling what parts might be removed that don't need to be removed, or worse, shouldn't come off. So, we look it over. Try to imagine the metal chassis sliding out of the case. Looks like it's either got to go forward or backward, because the top, bottom, and sides are blocking those paths, and there aren't any screws to take the cabinet apart. It won't go forward; the opening in the cabinet is too narrow. It can't go backward for the same reason. Wait! there's a panel on the back with screws in it. It looks like if it comes off, the chassis might just fit out of the cabinet that way. You get the idea. Look before you unscrew. If you can't tell what a screw is for—holding on a panel or something—don't unscrew it! Very often, there are screw heads showing that hold things like the power transformer in place, or connect a ground wire to the chassis. If we unscrew these before the chassis is out of the cabinet, we might just loosen something that can't be tightened from the outside, or something heavy (like a transformer) might fall off inside and break components on the circuit board. Once again, this is the voice of experience speaking. If you can't figure out how to get it apart, stop right there and save yourself and the local repair guy a lot of trouble.

If you're mechanically inclined and see what needs to come off to get it apart, then it's time to start drawing. Draw a picture of the amp, showing the location of every screw you remove, and if any of them are different sizes or types, write yourself a note telling which screw went in which hole. You can't make too many notes or draw too detailed a diagram. This important step of the disassembly can save you incredible headaches when it's time to put the thing back together.

Step Eight: The Fix

Assuming we've gotten as far as taking the chassis out of the amp, we should now be able to take a good, close look at the solder connections on the input jack. You may have to loosen or even remove the circuit board to do this. Follow the same guidelines as before to continue the disassembly process. If you get to the point where you're not sure what to do next, stop. Look at it. Think about it. Visualize it. There's no shame in knowing enough to stop before you mess something up. If it looks like you have to disconnect or unsolder a lot of wires to get where you need to go, you might want to hold off and let a pro take care of it. If you're continuing on, resume your note taking. Draw a picture of the circuit board showing where all of the wires and connectors go. Label the colors of the wires. Take a fine-tip marker and mark any connectors you pull loose. If there are a lot of them, number them and mark them so you know which way they were facing. Some connectors will go on in both directions, but one direction is correct and the other one is *ka-blooie!*

Okay. Let's assume you've gotten the circuit board out, and you are looking at it. A lot of bad solder connections don't look bad at first glance. On the actual circuit board are holes that the leads of the components go through. On the other side of the circuit board are metal (usually copper) traces that go from one lead-hole to the next. These are the interconnections between the components. A good connection has the component lead (wire) coming through just a little bit above the surface of the circuit board, and this lead is then surrounded by solder. The copper around the hole is called a solder pad. The solder should completely cover the solder pad. The surface of the solder should be smooth and satin-finished. If the surface of the solder doesn't cover the entire solder pad, or if the solder surface is dull or lumpy, or if it seems to have a "halo" around the lead, it might be bad. If it looks even marginally bad, fire up the old soldering iron, grab the 60/40 solder, and... You do have a soldering iron, right? Of course you do! You wouldn't ignore Rule #2, would you?

Some people don't realize there are also several different types of solder. Don't run downstairs in the dark, dirty tool room and grab a roll of solder, unless you know what it's made of. Most solder for electronics use is made of lead and tin in a mixture of 60% tin to 40% lead. Some solder contains a small amount of silver to improve the flow and appearance of the solder joints. Most solder is hollow with an anti-oxidation agent, either rosin (pronounced ROZZ-un) or acid, added in this hollow core. Rosin-core solder is used for electronics. Acid-core is used in plumbing. Both the rosin and acid perform the same function of removing the oxidation from the metals to be joined, but rosin core is a much mellower agent, and only does its cleaning while it is hot. Acid core solder will seem to work to solder electronic stuff, but the acid continues its corroding action even after it cools, and a couple of months down the road, it may eat right through the component leads that you soldered. Rosin core *good.* Acid core *bad.*

Soldering

I guess now would be a good time for your basic soldering tutorial. Soldering is quite simple and complex at the same time. On the one hand, you're connecting two pieces of metal together by melting soft metal around them; that's pretty simple. On the other hand, properly soldered connections form an actual molecular bond of the two metals being soldered. Pretty complex! Also, note that some circuit boards have printed foils on both sides. Do not attempt to de-solder anything from this type of circuit board. These require either special de-soldering equipment or extraordinary skill.

But let's say we're soldering a resistor lead into a printed circuit board. The two pieces of metal should be touching each other, like the wire and solder pad in *figure 20-2,* below.

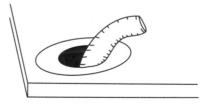

Figure 20-2: A good connection

The ones shown in *figure 20-3* are not touching, and will not make a good connection if soldered that way.

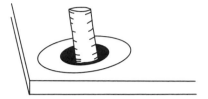

Figure 20-3: Not a good connection

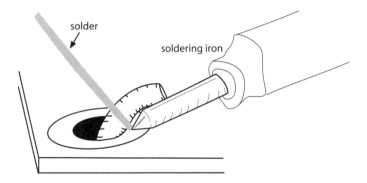

Figure 20-4: Soldering iron touching both the solder pad and the lead

When soldering, the soldering iron (like the one in *figure 20-4*) should be touching both pieces of metal, the solder pad and the wire lead, so that both are about the same temperature. By the way, solder melts at around 450° Fahrenheit; most soldering irons will heat up to between 600° and 800°. If the connection is made when only one piece of metal is hot enough, the solder will not bond and adhere properly to the cooler piece. This is what is known as a **"cold" solder joint**. The solder is touched to the pieces being soldered until it begins to melt. Don't leave the iron there any longer than you have to in order to get a good joint, as excessive heat can damage things close to where you're soldering. Add just enough solder to form a slightly concave joint. Too much solder may blob over to adjacent solder pads or traces, and too little solder might break with normal vibration.

Figure 20-5 shows examples of good and bad solder joints.

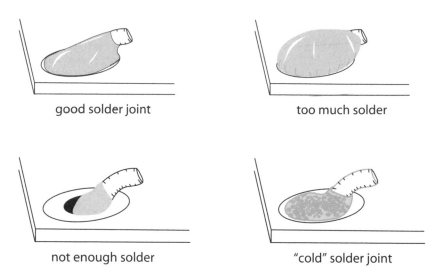

good solder joint   too much solder

not enough solder   "cold" solder joint

Figure 20-5: Solder joints

The most common problem I run into with people doing poor soldering is that they do not have a hot enough iron. The iron must be able to get hot enough to heat both pieces of metal to the right temperature, quickly. A 25-watt iron is fine for circuit board work, but musicians normally don't solder much on circuit boards. We solder connectors and potentiometers and other larger chunks of metal. A 30- to 35-watt iron works better for this kind of soldering. Good soldering is easy, with some practice.

I suggest you practice soldering some scraps of wire, before trying it on something important. Always use wire-strippers to strip the insulation from the wire, not a pocket knife (bad), or the heat from the iron (worse), or your teeth (yikes). Any time you are going to solder a wire to something, it is a good idea to tin the wire. This means that the part of the wire from which you have stripped the insulation is heated with the iron and enough solder is melted onto the wire to just cover it. This will make the actual soldering process much faster, because the iron doesn't have to heat both surfaces as much. Also, if you tin them, the solder's rosin core will remove most of the oxidation from the wires. Tinning the terminal or solder pad you're soldering to is also a good idea. This might seem like an unnecessary extra step, but it will prevent a lot of bad solder connections and melted parts if you get into the habit of doing it.

Back to our virtual amp. Now we've found the bad connection through the use of logical troubleshooting, we've taken the thing apart, and we've resoldered the bad connection. We're getting close! Before you put the chassis into the cabinet, you should take this opportunity to ask yourself if there were any other little problems that you'd been ignoring that you should take care of now, like noisy controls. If so, there isn't a better time to get the thing in perfect working order.

Cleaning Controls

Now might be a good time to learn the right way to clean controls and switches. The noise generated by a "dirty" control is the result of poor contact between the wiper and the element. This is usually caused by oxidation of the carbon-resistive element and the metal contact point of the wiper. First, we'll need a good-quality control cleaner. What we're looking for is a deoxidizing spray. The ideal cleaner is one that will deoxidize the contacts without adding any lubricants. Tuner cleaner available from your local electronics parts store has oily grease in it, which is alright for old-fashioned television tuners, but is not good for controls. The grease will attract dirt and hold it, so the control will very likely get dirtier than it was before, in a very short time. There are several good contact cleaners available, including De-Ox-It made by Caig, and De-Ox-Id, made by GC Electronics. Some of these cleaners are not available to the general public, but your local chain electronics part store should have something that will work. Read the ingredients and do not take the recommendation of a store clerk until you verify that there is no lubricating agent such as silicon, oil, or grease in it.

Controls, or potentiometers, come in a wide variety of shapes, sizes, and styles. Most of the ones used in electronic musical equipment look like the one in *figure 20-6*.

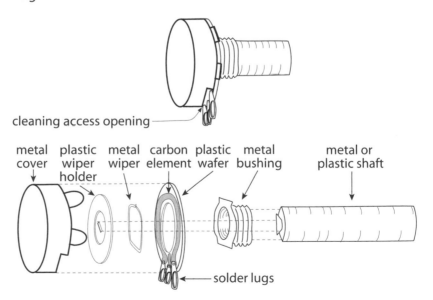

Figure 20-6: Standard potentiometer

The access opening is where the cleaning agent will be applied. If the control doesn't have an access hole, it is a sealed control, and cannot be cleaned by ordinary means. The element and wiper contact are the surfaces we are trying to deoxidize. Some controls are now made using conductive plastic. Many spray cleaners will destroy plastic, even if the cleaner manufacturer claims the product is safe on plastic. So, if you're not sure the cleaner is safe for your particular control, don't use it. Controls often are mounted in such a way that getting to the access opening is difficult. This is why spray contact cleaners come with an extension tube. You might even have to place the chassis upside-down and use gravity to help get the cleaner where it needs to go.

Our goal when cleaning controls is to use the least amount of cleaner that will do the job. A drop or two is all it takes to clean most controls. Saturating the control with cleaner will also get the job done, but the cleaning agent will destroy any damping grease in the control, making it feel stiff when it is turned. Plus, the cleaner will go all over the place inside the amp. Before spraying the control, spray a little bit into a rag or paper towel to see how fast it comes out of the tube. Once you have a feel for how to get just a little cleaner out of the can, you can put a couple of drops into the access opening of the noisy control, then turn the control through its full range of motion a few times. Eight to ten turns back and forth should do it.

Slider-style potentiometers also get dirty, but using spray cleaners on these is not a good idea. Sliders rely on their damping grease to move smoothly, and any cleaner strong enough to clean them will also destroy this grease, leaving them stiff and jerky, and sometimes they will not move at all. The best thing for noisy sliders is to either replace them or clean them manually by removing them from the circuit board and taking them apart. Leave this to a pro. In some cases, if you are extremely careful, you can use a single drop of cleaner applied through the opening in the top of the slider to clean the contacts, but it's not recommended. Most good-quality sliders have plastic shields that are designed to keep dust and dirt from getting inside, and these shields will prevent spray cleaners from getting where they need to go. Lots of sliders also use conductive plastic elements, and they can be easily destroyed by cleaners. Then, instead of a control that works but is noisy, you will have a totally nonfunctional slider.

Cleaning switches is not as tricky, although if they have plastic parts, they might be damaged by the spray. Again, if in doubt, don't do it. When cleaning switches, the idea is to get the actual contacts damp with cleaner, and then move the switch through all of its positions several times. As with potentiometers, the less contact cleaner you use, the better.

The amp is finally ready to be put back together. Reassembling an amp is pretty much like taking it apart in reverse order, but there are a couple of things you need to do to make sure the amp still works when it's all back together. Make sure, before you put the amp chassis back into the cabinet, that you have reconnected every wire and connector you had previously taken loose. Go slowly, take your time. Refer back to the pictures you drew as you took it apart. Here are a few helpful tips:

Never tighten any screw on an assembly until you have all of them started. If you had to remove five screws to get the circuit board out, get all five started, then tighten them down. Otherwise, you'll probably find that four of them go in, but the last one won't start, and you'll have to loosen all of them up again.

Never force a screw into place. If it doesn't seem like it belongs where you're putting it, it probably doesn't. Recheck your notes. I once worked with a guy who screwed in a plastic-thread screw that was "a little stiff," only to find it poking half an inch out of the front of the plastic case of the boom box he had just finished "repairing." He had to buy the customer a new plastic cabinet.

When starting a screw, turn it counter-clockwise first. When you do this, you will be able to feel a little click as the thread of the screw finds the thread of the hole. Then, you'll be able to screw it in knowing you're in the right place, and not just making new threads (and in the process stripping out the old ones). Note that sometimes you'll feel two clicks as you turn the screw in reverse. Usually, it's the first click that is the correct spot, even though the second click might feel more "solid." Go slowly, try them both. You'll be able to tell the right one: The screw will go in with the least resistance. Once you've gotten the chassis in place, but before you put in the case screws, you should test the amp to see if it's fixed. If you completely reassemble it and find it still isn't repaired, you'll have to take all of those screws out again. Okay, let's say it's all better. Now you can put in the case screws and you're done. Whew! We got our broken virtual amp virtually repaired. Shut it off, unplug it, grab your screwdriver, and celebrate! Ah, that's tasty... Bartender, we'll have another round over here!

ADDITIONAL INFORMATION

This last servicing section will give some basic tips on how to use meters and other pieces of **test equipment** if you happen to have access to them, as well as give a few hints about troubleshooting. I'll also give you some insight so that, if you do have to take something in to your local Mr. or Ms. Fixit, you can avoid a lot of time-wasting trouble and misunderstandings.

Test Equipment

As mentioned in a previous chapter, ohm meters are handy test aids if you know how to use one. I'm going to tell you how to use one, but first I'm going to explain what meters are and what they do. The ohm meter is actually just one part of a device called a Volt-Ohm-Milliammeter, or VOM. A VOM is a self-contained unit whose main feature is a large analog, or needle-type, meter. An example of a typical VOM is shown in *figure 20-7*.

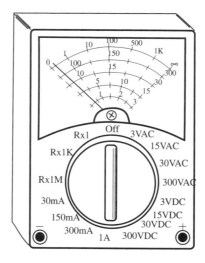

Figure 20-7: Typical VOM

These units are designed to measure AC and DC voltage, current, and DC resistance in electronic circuits. They are also called multimeters. Most come equipped with a pair of wires, called test leads. One wire is usually black for negative, and the positive one is usually red. Polarity is important when measuring DC voltage or current. AC measurements are not polarity-sensitive. That is, it doesn't matter which lead goes where. There is a rotary switch on the front panel, which is used to select the function (what it is you'd like to measure) and range (approximately how much you will be measuring).

There are also a couple of other types of meters. One, the Vacuum Tube Volt Meter, or VTVM, isn't seen much anymore, as they are less portable than other types of meters. VTVM's were extremely popular during the fifties, sixties, and seventies, because they were highly accurate and very precise, and had a high input impedance. (A high input impedance prevents the meter from loading the circuit, which would result in an incorrect reading.) The VTVM was all but replaced in the eighties by the Digital Voltmeter, or DVM.

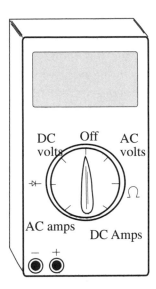

Figure 20-8: Typical DVM

These digital meters have a numeric display instead of an analog meter movement *(see figure 20-8)*. They are more accurate than VTVMs, and some have even higher input impedances. DVM's are useful when measuring small voltages, currents, and resistances, because they are so much more accurate in these lower ranges. All of the previously mentioned meters are called multimeters, because they measure several different things. Basic analog VOM-type multimeters can be quite inexpensive. A functional (but inaccurate) meter, can be had for a very small amount of money, but for a bit more, you'll get one you can trust. Digital multimeters range greatly in price, depending on the features offered; some may include capacitor checkers or frequency counters, which you may or may not use.

The voltage-measurement function is useful if you need to know if the correct voltage is present at any particular spot, be it in a circuit or at an AC outlet. Sometimes, checking AC voltage before you plug into an outlet can save major equipment problems, especially if your power is coming from a generator or an unknown source, such as a power distro box wired by person or persons unknown.

Multimeters are also capable of measuring current. This function is helpful in determining if a circuit is consuming more current than normal, and it is useful in setting the bias level in amplifiers, but the average musician will probably never need to do any current measurements.

The resistance, or "ohms," function can be helpful in finding broken wires, testing cables, and checking for broken circuit board foil traces. Also called a continuity tester, the ohm meter contains a voltage source, usually in the form of a single AA cell. The cell places +1.5 volts DC on one of the test leads. The other lead is at ground, or zero volts. If you touch the two test leads together, the needle of the meter will swing all the way to one side of the meter scale, reading zero ohms. This indicates a closed circuit, or continuity between the positive lead and the negative lead, with no measurable resistance between them. Most analog meters have an adjustment so you can set the needle exactly on zero when the leads are touching. Many meters have several ohms scales where the number one on the meter scale may correspond to 1 ohm (Rx1), or 10 ohms (Rx10), or 1,000 ohms (Rx1k), etc. When using the meter to test for continuity, use the lowest scale available. If you are testing components like resistors or diodes on a circuit board, you should be aware that the meter will measure the value of not only the component, but also anything parallel to it in the rest of the circuit. This can cause erroneous measurements, so to be sure, lift one end of the component being tested to isolate it from the rest of the circuit components. Capacitors are not effectively tested by an ohm meter, as they do not pass DC voltage.

It seems like cords and cables are always going bad. There's a reason for this. They get moved a lot, and just like any other piece of wire, if they are bent enough times in the same place, they will break. To test a guitar cable for open wires, place the red meter lead on the "tip" connection of one end of the cable, and the black lead on the "tip" connection of the other end. If the cord is good, there should be almost full-scale deflection of the needle, much like when the leads were connected directly together. The meter might register a small amount of resistance due to the resistance of the wire, but unless the cord is extremely long, it should be less than 1 ohm, if you're using the Rx1 scale. This tests only the inside, or center conductor of the cable. To test the outer conductor, or shield, move the test leads to the "sleeve" part of the two plugs. Moving the cable while testing it can sometimes reveal intermittent connections. One drawback to this method of testing cables is that audio signals, which are normally carried by the cable, are very low voltage AC—usually in the 50mV to 100mV range, compared to the 1.5 volts DC being sent through the wire by the VOM. Some tiny breaks will not be detected by this method of testing, because the higher voltage of the meter is enough to bridge across the break. The best way to check a cable for possible intermittent problems is to run a low-level audio signal through it, using an audio tone generator (see below), or music from a radio, tape, or CD player, and wiggle the cable around while listening for signal dropout.

A couple of things to remember when using an ohm meter: Never try to measure the resistance of anything that is turned on. Any voltage present in the wires other than the battery voltage from the meter itself can damage the meter's electronics. Also, an ohm meter measures only DC resistance, not AC impedance. You can tell if the voice coil of a speaker has continuity, but you can't tell the exact AC impedance of the coil with an ohm meter. There are impedance meters available, but they are fairly expensive, so unless you need to test impedance often, they're probably not something you need to own.

Another helpful piece of test equipment is the audio **tone generator**. Also called a **function generator**, this piece of equipment produces audio frequency waves, which can be used as steady, unvarying signal sources for testing equipment. Some tone generators only put out one frequency; others may give you a choice of several, or dozens, and yet others are sweepable. That is, they can generate any frequency from 20Hz to hundreds of kHz, and you can dial in the frequency you want with a knob. Some generate only square waves; some will give you the choice of sine, square, or even triangle-waves. Signal generators are useful when you need a signal that doesn't vary in pitch or level in order to track down an intermittent, like the cutting-out signal in our virtual broken amplifier from the previous chapters. Sometimes a blown speaker will distort badly, but only at a particular frequency. A sweepable signal generator can help determine whether the speaker is indeed bad, or the amp, cables, or instrument might instead be the cause.

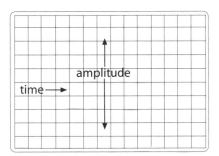

Figure 20-9: Oscilloscope display

Oscilloscopes are used to "look" into circuits and "see" what the signals are doing in there. Waves, as you remember from earlier chapters, emanate in all directions—360° in three dimensions—from their point of origin. In order to understand how they work, however, we graph them in only two dimensions: time and amplitude, as seen in *figure 20-9*. An oscilloscope is similar to a little television, and has a pinpoint of light, called a **trace**, that crosses the center of the screen horizontally from left to right. The trace also moves vertically from top to bottom if an AC signal is connected at the scope's input. Most audio signals occur too quickly to be detected by the human eye, moving positive, then negative, then positive again hundreds or thousands of times each second. The oscilloscope gets around this by slowing the horizontal trace movement down, enabling us to see a graphic representation of a wave, in real time. This graphic representation is called a waveform. A sine wave's waveform is shown in *figure 20-10*.

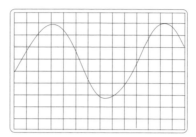

Figure 20-10: Oscilloscope display with sine wave

If we place a sine-wave signal from our signal generator on the input of an amplifier, we can then connect the test lead of an oscilloscope, called a **probe**, to various places in the circuitry to see what the signal looks like after being amplified. This is useful for finding out where the signal is present and where the signal is missing if an amp has no output, or finding out where in the circuit distortion is being introduced if a piece of gear has too much distortion. Again, unless you have excess money or are serious about learning the repair business, oscilloscopes are much too costly. Locating the cause of a nonfunctional channel can be perplexing, but there are some tricks you can use to make it easier to find the source of the problem.

Troubleshooting Hints

One of the best methods for troubleshooting a missing signal, ranking right up there with "divide and conquer" is called, "compare with channel X." Many times, you'll find that only one channel of a stereo amp or a multi-channel mixer is nonfunctional. That's great news, because that means you have at least one more channel that is working perfectly. Say you have a stereo amp that has no signal from one speaker. You can compare the bad channel with the good channel to pinpoint the cause of the problem. By switching signal sources—plugging the good signal into the nonfunctional channel, while simultaneously plugging the questionable signal from the bad channel into the good channel—you can determine whether the problem is before the amp's input or further along the signal path. If you switched the signal input lines as outlined above and the same channel as before is still not working, you know the problem isn't the source signal, because you just plugged a known good signal into the channel that is still nonfunctional. Conversely, if the problem switches channels, the problem is located somewhere further up the signal path. You repeat this simple procedure until you've isolated the piece or section that has the problem. This seems simple enough, but it is easy to get confused, especially in a live gig situation when you're under pressure and racing the clock. The best advice I can give you is to remain calm, block out the background noise, ignore everybody's "helpful advice," and think it through. Only switch one pair of inputs at a time. As soon as you make your determination, switch them back. Don't switch outputs. (The theory is the same, but the logic is reversed, which will just add confusion.) Go on down the signal path to the next set of inputs.

Dealing With a Service Center

There will probably come a time when you have to take your broken whatchamacallit to someone like me to have it fixed. Here are some ways you can make the experience more pleasant.

What's Wrong?

Know how to describe the problem. Don't just drop off a piece for repair and say, "It's broken." That's fairly obvious; no one brings a perfectly functional piece of gear to the repair shop. Here are some common descriptions of complaints, and what they mean. "Dead" means no lights, no sound, no functions of any kind. "No sound" means at least some of the indicators or display functions work, but the unit doesn't produce any audible output. "Cuts out" indicates intermittent signal output. It helps if you can detect any pattern to this behavior, such as "…after 30 minutes," "…only when it's hot," or "…only when my wireless is on," etc. "Noisy" means the unit produces a hiss or static noise, even when the instrument is not being played. "Hum" indicates a low-frequency, constant humming tone is present, not to be confused with a "buzz," which is a constant, raspy, mid-frequency noise. "Distortion" is an ugly sound you hear only when the signal is present; not a constant noise, but a degradation of the signal. "Blows fuses" would indicate that the main, user-accessible fuse has blown and been replaced and blown again. (Don't keep replacing fuses. If a second fuse blows, the unit has a definite problem and no number of new fuses will make it better. Continuing to burn out fuses until every component in the unit is toast will just cost you more money to get it fixed.) "Smokes" means just what it says: smoke has come out of the unit. There are many other potential scenarios, of course, but those are the basics.

Bring Everything

Bring in everything associated with the problem. You wouldn't take the steering wheel off of your car and take it to the garage to fix a high-speed vibration problem, so don't bring in just the transmitter part of your wireless system. Do not assume the repair shop has every frequency of wireless receiver in the known universe. If the unit uses an outboard power supply or AC adaptor, bring it in with the unit. Not only might the repair shop not have the right one for the gear you bring in, but the problem may well be caused by the power adaptor. If you haven't eliminated other accessories, including your instrument, stomp boxes, cables, etc. as being possible causes of the problem, bring them in, too. A repairman would much rather have stuff he doesn't need to troubleshoot your unit than need stuff he doesn't have.

Don't Take it Apart

Bring the unit in completely assembled. Rarely do repair people welcome a box of parts that the customer has disassembled. Often, there will be parts missing, screws stripped-out, wires broken, and the like. And it's hard enough to put things back together if you're the one who took them apart, but if you've never seen the unit fully assembled, it can be darned tricky. Customers sometimes think they'll save the tech time, and consequently save themselves money, but this is not the case. Some shops add an unstated "basket-case fee" or " idiot charge" of anywhere from 5% to 25% in these cases.

Paperwork

If the unit is covered by a warranty, have the necessary paperwork with you when you bring the unit to the shop. Whenever you buy a piece of musical gear, keep the receipt somewhere that you'll be able to find it (inside an envelope in the back of your amp, for example). Send in the warranty return card; with some manufacturers, the warranty will only be activated if you've returned the warranty reply card and registered the purchase with the factory. The factory warranty is an agreement between you, the consumer, and the manufacturer of the piece of equipment. The repair technician is just a go-between, authorized by the manufacturer to do the work. When you take a broken item in for repair under warranty, the tech is actually working for the manufacturer, not the customer, since that's who is paying for the fix. The manufacturer pays the technician (usually a lot less than he normally charges), and they will only pay him if he meets all of their criteria, one of which is POP, or proof of purchase. Supplying this to the repair station is the customer's responsibility. It doesn't matter if the owner of the store himself sold you the item in question or if the repair tech personally delivered it; the manufacturer won't pay him unless you provide paperwork to prove it is still within the factory warranty period.

Some retailers have an in-store limited warranty on used gear purchased from them. You need the bill of sale for these, too. Don't expect the repair department to know when you bought something; have the paperwork with you. Warranties most often only cover "defects in materials or workmanship." That is, if the factory screwed up the unit when it was being built. Don't try to get a repair station to fix something under warranty if you broke it. You wouldn't expect to buy a car, smash it into a tree, and have the dealer cheerfully repair it at no charge.

Estimates

Let the repair department know how much money you're willing to spend on repairs before you leave the unit. As the old saying goes, "Time is money." This is especially true in the repair shop. Most shops charge an hourly "bench rate." The more time a technician spends repairing your equipment, the more the total repair bill will be. The less time the tech spends talking to you about the repair, the more of this time is actually spent finding and repairing the problem. Decide what it is worth to you to have the piece fixed before you take it to the repair tech. Tell him to call you if repairs look like they might exceed that amount. You're well within your rights to request an estimate, but an estimate will usually increase the cost of the repair.

Here's why: Technicians charge for the time spent troubleshooting, disassembling, repairing, and reassembling the unit. They also charge for the time it takes to write the estimate, put the unit back together so it can rest on the shelf until the estimate is approved or declined, call your answering machine, talk to you when you call back, and take the unit back apart to finally fix it. Some tech's charge a flat estimate fee to cover this "non-productive" time, while others just add it to the total, but it is charged one way or the other. So, if you slmply say they should go ahead and fix it if it's less than "X" dollars, you'll save yourself from being charged extra for an estimate. In the same vein, repeated calls to the shop to check on progress will also cost you more. I charge just as much to talk on the phone as I do to troubleshoot a broken piece of gear. I've never had a part that I ordered arrive any sooner because the customer called ten times, but I have charged for the extra time spent on the phone explaining this.

Honesty

Do some research before you leave a prized possession with any repair tech. Some customers are afraid that if they set a dollar limit on a repair, the tech will automatically charge that amount, even if it could have been repaired for less. Most repair techs are honest. Dishonest repair people don't stay in business very long, because their reputations soon catch up with them. The best way to avoid unscrupulous service people is to ask other musicians for their opinions and experiences related to the technician you're considering. Ask the tech for some references. If he's honest and knowledgeable, he'll gladly give you the names of some satisfied customers. If he won't, then go elsewhere.

Contact Information

Give the repair tech accurate personal information, including your real name. Nicknames and stage names make it too difficult to track you down if one means of communication fails. Leave a telephone number where you can be reached during business hours. If you aren't near a phone during the day, leave a number where the repair shop can leave a message that you will be sure to get. Give an address, so if your telephone or answering machine doesn't work, the tech can drop you a postcard. It's amazing how often people give out their own phone numbers incorrectly.

Factory Returns

Occasionally, an item will have to be returned to a factory service center to be repaired. Some manufacturers will consider a product warrantee voided if the product is serviced or repaired by non-factory technicians. Others might simply recommend that certain models be returned for service and updating. Factory service centers generally do very good work, but they also tend to be expensive, and sometimes take a long time to repair and return a piece of gear to the dealer who sent it. The dealer, in this case, is merely the agent that sent the unit in, and he has no control over how long it takes or what it costs.

Pick Up Your Repair

If you want to stay on your repairman's good side, pick up your repaired unit promptly. If I had a nickel for every time someone told me they needed rush service and then left the repaired gadget sitting in my shop for months, well... I'd have some nickels, by golly!

PART 5

ADDITIONAL BITS AND PIECES

Chapter TWENTY-ONE

BITS AND PIECES WORTH NOTING
or, why can't I use a guitar cord for a speaker cable?

When I was first beginning to play music and operate sound and lighting systems, I often wished that there were some reference book available that would save me the trouble of learning everything the hard way. This chapter includes a bunch of general knowledge, bits and pieces of information about cable gauges and types, power wiring, speaker crossover points, grounding, and other things that would normally take years of experience to learn. You're welcome.

WIRE AND CABLE GUIDE

Guitar cables *(see figure 21-1)* are shielded, which means that there is a thin, stranded (several tiny wires all wrapped together) center conductor surrounded by a coating of insulation. This insulated wire is surrounded by another stranded conductor, called a shield, which is either braided or spiral-wrapped around the inside wire's insulation.

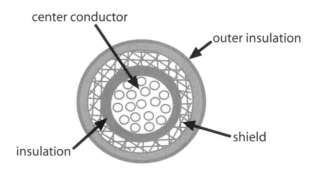

Figure 21-1: Single conductor shielded cable cross section

Then, the whole thing gets another flexible, insulating covering. The shield is connected to the amplifier's ground. This is to prevent the wires from picking up stray noises, such as electromagnetic fields (EMF) and radio frequencies (RF). Most instrument, microphone, and line-level signal cables use shielded wire in order to reject unwanted noises.

Okay, so why can't I use a guitar cord for a speaker wire? Well, the reason it's not a good idea is because of the gauge, or thickness, of the wire. As you learned earlier in this book, wires have some resistance, and it's known that thicker, heavier-gauge wire has less resistance than thinner, lighter-gauge wire of the same length. Because a shielded cable is constructed the way it is, and the current through this type of cable is usually minuscule, cable manufacturers use very small wires in order to keep the cable flexible and the outside diameter small. Sometimes the center wire is so small, if you tried to run much current through it, such as the current required to drive a speaker, the center wire could become hot enough to melt the insulation and short to the outer shield wires. As pointed out in Chapter Eighteen, Why'd My Amp Blow Up?, this is not a good thing.

Speaker cables, on the other hand, normally are not shielded, which is why speaker wires shouldn't be used as instrument cables. (There are some exceptions to this; notably, commercial speaker wiring and some used in recording and broadcast studios.) They are handling a much higher current signal than instrument or line cables. Also, as there are usually no additional stages of amplification past this point, any noises the wires pick up will be so small in comparison to the signal level that they will be undetectable. Speaker wiring is also stranded wire. In fact, almost any cable for nonpermanent installation of audio or AC power wiring will use stranded wire. The main reason for this is flexibility. Multiple small wires bend more easily than thick single conductor wires, and can be moved repeatedly without breaking. As I've repeatedly mentioned in this book, any wire will break if you bend it at one spot too many times, but having multiple, highly flexible wires takes the stress off of individual conductors and makes breakage less likely.

There is another reason stranded wire is preferred for power and speaker wiring. Electron flow through a length of wire tends to be higher toward the outside "skin" of the wire than in the center core. This phenomenon is called **skin effect**. The darker-colored atoms shown in *figure 21-2* will carry more current than the medium-colored atoms, which will carry more than the light-colored ones. Multiple-strand wire has more "skin" area than similarly sized solid wire, so stranded wire can handle more current without getting as hot.

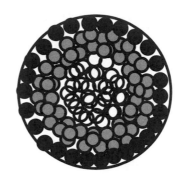

Figure 21- 2: Skin effect in a piece of wire

I mentioned wire gauges earlier without being very specific. Wire gauges used for musical electronics run from very tiny (46-gauge wire or smaller used for guitar pickup coils), to very large (4-gauge or larger cable used for high-power AC wiring). As you can see, the smaller the number, the larger the wire. The center conductors of a typical microphone or guitar cord will usually be from 20- to 26-gauge. The speaker wire used on a medium powered bass rig might be 18-, 16-, or even 14-gauge. The gauge of the wire used in speaker cables and power wiring is determined by the amount of current it will need to handle, along with how long the cable runs will be. The more current and the longer the cable, the thicker the gauge (the smaller the number).

POWER WIRING

Not to scare you or anything, but 110- and 220-volt electricity can kill you. Dead. Forever. No do-overs. Don't mess with AC power unless you know a lot more about it than you'll learn from this book. The information here is for general knowledge only. The heaviest gauge wire you're likely to see will be power wiring. Most of the smaller venues folks play have a few standard AC outlets on or near the stage area, but when we get into bigger venues where large lighting systems are used, standard 110-volt outlets with a maximum rating of 20 amps just can't provide the current needed for the power required. That's when 220-volt (or higher) power sources and distribution networks are necessary.

Lighting systems require a lot of current. Professional lighting fixtures use from 250-watt up to 1,000-watt light bulbs, called lamps. Since power divided by voltage equals current, you can see where a bunch of 500-watt lamps, drawing over 4.5 amps each, can add up to a lot of current in a hurry (16 of them would draw over 72 amps). In order to get around having to use outlets from all over the building, most professionals have a portable power distribution system, or **distro** that they use to power their gear.

The power distro gets its power from a standard 220-volt outlet, or else connects directly to the 220-volt lines inside a breaker box. The 220 volts is then divided into two **legs** and sent via circuit breakers to several 110-volt outlets. Here's how they work: The standard 110-volt AC outlet has three connections, **hot** (black wire), **neutral** (white wire), and ground (green wire). The AC voltage between the hot connection and the neutral is about 110 volts. The voltage between the neutral and ground is zero. The ground connection is at the same electrical potential as the neutral, but they are not the same. More on this later.

The 220 volts AC coming into a standard circuit breaker box also has three wires, hot 1 (+ phase, black wire), neutral (white wire), and hot 2 (- phase, red wire). Hot wire 1 and hot wire 2 are 180° out of phase. The AC voltage between the + phase hot 1 and the - phase hot 2 is about 220 volts. Current is carried by the hot wires. If a circuit is balanced properly—that is, if both hots have the same amount of load—then there will be little or no current through the neutral wire. Audible hum in sound systems is often caused by the hot legs of a circuit having uneven loads, which places unwanted current on the neutral wiring. The AC voltage between either hot wire and neutral is about 110 volts *(see figure 21-3)*.

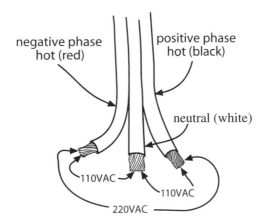

Figure 21-3: 220v AC wiring

Again, the voltage between the neutral connection and ground is zero. The + phase hot and neutral make up one 110-volt leg of the circuit. The - phase hot and neutral make up the other leg. Both 110-volt legs share the same neutral. The neutral wire is connected to ground inside the breaker box. Each leg will then run to a set of circuit breakers, and each breaker will go to one or more standard outlets *(see figure 21-4)*. This is the way most modern houses in the United States are wired.

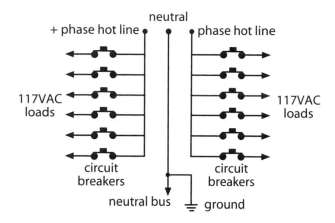

Figure 21-4: Wiring diagram of a standard distro breaker box

THREE-PHASE POWER

Three-phase power is common in places where large amounts of power are used, such as factories, schools, and hotels. Large high-torque motors for things like elevators often use three-phase power. Three phase works much like standard 220, except that three-phase uses three hot wires, each of which is 120° out of phase with the other two. A fourth wire, the neutral, is also present. There is 110 volts AC between any hot wire and neutral, and 208 volts AC between any two hot wires. Connecting a power distro to three-phase is exactly like connecting to standard 220, except one of the hot wires is not used. The resulting voltage, 110v AC at the distro's receptacles is slightly lower than when connecting to normal 220 volts (117v AC), but it is not low enough to cause equipment problems. You've probably noticed that the numbers mentioned previously don't seem to add up exactly. The fact is, the voltage from a standard outlet can be anywhere from 110 VAC to 120 VAC, and even slightly higher or lower. This can vary from section to section of town, and can even vary a little bit depending on the time of year or time of day. The "220" coming into your house is normally closer to 240 VAC than it is to 220 VAC. The terms "220" and "110" have become rather generic. The term "110" is generally accepted to mean standard wall voltage, and "220" is the name for standard two-phase power, regardless of their actual voltage levels.

ABOUT GROUNDING AND GROUND LOOPS

Ever wonder why they call it "ground"? Well, the planet we live on is conductive. In Europe, they call the ground connection of a circuit "earth." Individual rocks and dirt clods aren't very good conductors, but the metallic minerals, vegetable matter, and decomposing animal substances (yuck!) throughout the earth's crust conduct electricity pretty well. Because the earth is so huge, and it is basically all at the same electrical potential (zero volts), it makes a handy reference point for everything else. Every home, business, factory—in fact, every place that electrical current is used, should have at least one grounding point. Usually, this is a long copper rod, driven straight into the ground eighteen to twenty feet. This grounding point should be as close to the breaker box as possible.

As I stated above, the ground is a reference that never changes. This is true as far as good old planet earth is concerned, but ground levels in power circuits may vary a little due to the resistance of the wires being used. One of the most common problems in live sound systems is hum due to ground differentials, commonly called a "ground loop." The cause of a grounding hum, or ground loop, is simple: The ground level of one part of the sound system is slightly different from the ground level of another part. The solution isn't always simple. A stage power distro might be hundreds of feet from the sound board, and even though they share the same ground, the resistance of all of that wiring might be enough to cause some hum. If any "house" outlets are used—that is, outlets that are part of the building as opposed to outlets in a portable distro—they might not be connected to the same ground. In fact, they might not be wired correctly at all, especially if the wiring was done by a do-it-yourselfer, like a bar owner on a budget. The problem with finding ground loops is that the ground differential might be in any piece of gear that is connected to the system. Signal cables running too close to transformers, especially outboard wall transformers, commonly referred to as wall warts, can inductively pick up hum from the magnetic field they generate. This can sound like a ground loop, but it isn't. The best way to track these unwanted noises down is to eliminate the possible sources one by one by unplugging any connections to the system.

DIRECT BOXES

One place ground loops seem to breed is in direct boxes. Direct boxes, also called direct interfaces (DI's), are a way to take an unbalanced signal, such as that of a bass, guitar, or keyboard, and convert it to a low-impedance balanced signal so that it can be transferred through a snake cable to the mixing console many feet away. There are two basic kinds of DI's, active and passive. The passive type uses a small transformer to take the signal from Hi-Z unbalanced to Lo-Z balanced. An active DI uses small signal amplifiers to do the same thing. Active DI's require a power source such as a battery, while passive DI's do not require power to operate. Some have a switch that allows you to disconnect the ground connection from the Lo-Z side, called a ground lift switch. If there is a ground loop present at the DI, this will usually eliminate the grounding hum. Many direct boxes also allow you to switch between an instrument-level signal and a high-level source, such as the speaker output of an amplifier.

CROSSOVER NETWORKS

As we learned in Chapter Eight, How Speakers and Microphones Work, some speakers are better suited to reproduce certain frequencies than others. Small speakers reproduce high frequencies better than large speakers do, and in fact, low frequencies can damage small speakers if too much power is sent to them. High frequencies will not hurt large speakers, but since the large speaker can't reproduce these frequencies very well, sending high frequencies to large speakers is a waste of power. So, how do we keep the lows out of the small speakers and keep the highs out of the large ones? The answer is called a crossover network, or simply a crossover.

The function of a crossover is to divide the audio signal into distinct bands of frequencies so the speakers can deal with the signal more efficiently. Adjusting an audio signal by reducing or increasing certain frequencies is called filtering. This can be done actively, using transistor or I.C. filtering circuits before the signal is sent to the input of an amplifier, or passively (using large, high-power capacitors and coils), after the amplifier's output. There are advantages and disadvantages to both methods. Passive crossovers are handy in that they can be installed directly inside of a speaker cabinet. All of the interconnections are permanently wired in the speaker cabinet which saves cabling and time setting up a system. There are no adjustments to be made, and they cannot be set for the wrong frequency. On the other hand, the components required to handle high power levels are expensive and tend to add weight to the speaker. Also, passive crossover systems are inefficient. Some of the current of the audio signal is sent to ground (via the filters) and is wasted.

A passive crossover consists of one or more capacitors and/or coils. Capacitors, by their nature tend to block low frequencies and pass high frequencies. An inductor (coil) tends to pass low frequencies and block high frequencies. By placing a coil in series with the positive speaker terminal *(see figure 21-5),* fewer high frequencies will get to the speaker.

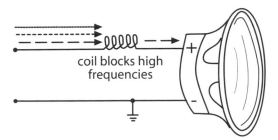

Figure 21-5: Coil in series with positive speaker terminal

A single inductor in this configuration will reduce the high frequencies by a factor of six decibels per octave, starting at a particular frequency, called the **center frequency.** What frequency this is depends upon the value of the coil, and the impedance of the speaker. A typical two-way crossover network does two things: It removes the low frequencies from the high-frequency driver(s), and it removes the high frequencies from the low-frequency driver(s). There are two factors involved when this takes place. The first is the crossover point, or center frequency. The center frequency is determined by the size and efficient operating range of the speakers being used. The second is the degree of filtering, called the "Q" (which stands for quality). No electronic filter circuit works perfectly, so some frequencies above or below the center frequency will be allowed to pass through the filter. The "Q" determines at what rate they drop off.

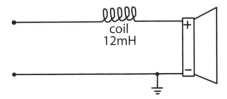

Figure 21-6: Coil in series with positive speaker terminal

In the 100Hz low-pass crossover filter circuit in *figure 21-6,* the center frequency is 100Hz. Frequencies below 100Hz are unaffected, but frequencies above 100Hz are decreased or rolled-off. The faster the high frequencies roll-off, the higher the Q. In the single-element, 6dB-per-octave crossover, the next octave above 100Hz to 200Hz will be 6dB lower than a

100Hz signal. The next octave is 400Hz, and it will be 6dB less than 200Hz, and so on. By adding a capacitor *(figure 21-7)* from the output of the coil to ground, the capacitor's tendency to pass high frequencies will remove even more high-frequency content from the signal before it gets to the speaker.

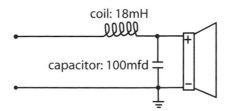

Figure 21-7: 100Hz low-pass crossover filter circuit, 12 dB/octave

If the values of the coil and capacitor are calculated properly, this configuration will increase the Q of the circuit to 12dB per octave. Adding a second coil after the first one will increase the Q to 18dB per octave. *Figure 21-8* shows a typical 12dB/octave two-way crossover. Some formulas for finding the correct component values for crossovers are given in Appendix D, Formulas and Miscellaneous Information. The power a passive crossover can handle is determined by the maximum voltage rating of the capacitors and the wire gauge of the inductors.

Active crossovers generally do a better job of filtering than passive crossovers, and since they use amplifier circuits to filter, they have no signal loss. In fact, they can add signal gain. Active crossovers are used in the low-level stage before the power amplifiers, instead of after the amp like a passive crossover. This eliminates the problem of power wasted by the passive crossover, but it also means you must have separate amplifiers for each frequency range you wish to reproduce.

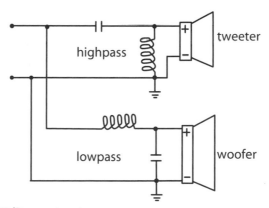

Figure 21- 8: Typical 12dB-per-octave two-way crossover

The best crossover method depends upon individual needs. Many lower-power speakers remove the lows from the tweeters to prevent them from being damaged, but run the woofers full range. It isn't as effective, but there are fewer parts required, so it's less expensive.

CONNECTORS AND HOW THEY ARE WIRED

Here's some more handy information about some commonly used audio connectors, their uses, and correct wiring:

The standard microphone connector is commonly called an **XLR** or **Cannon connector.** Designed for use with balanced lines, these normally have three wires and come in a male or female type. Also available in four- and five-pin configurations, these are used frequently with push-to-talk-type microphones. We're only going to concern ourselves with the three-pin type used in pro audio.

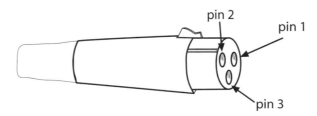

Figure 21-9: Female XLR connector

As you can see in *figure 21-9,* the pins are numbered one, two, and three. Pin one is always the ground, or shield, connection. Pins two and three are signal positive phase and negative phase. Many pro audio applications use pin three as positive phase, but not all companies do, so you need to know the preference of the particular equipment manufacturer. This information is usually given somewhere in the owner's manual of the equipment in question. When wiring mic cords or snake cables, it is important to make both ends the same. If you use a red wire for pin two on one end, use the same red wire for pin two on the other end, also. A simple trick when wiring cables is to use the alphabet position of the first letter of the wire color as a guide. If the two wires in your cable are black and red for example, B (for black) comes before R (for red) in the alphabet, so black should connect to pin two and red to pin three.

There are many different manufacturers of XLR-style connectors. Most of them are pretty good quality, and each different kind of plug comes apart and goes together a little differently. Most are fairly easy to figure out, but some Switchcraft XLR connectors (and some copies of them), have a set screw that is left-hand threaded. That means to loosen this set screw you must turn it clockwise. This can be maddening the first time you run into one unless you know about it beforehand.

Soldering to XLR connectors is pretty straightforward. Don't get them too hot, or the plastic that holds the pins might melt. Remember to tin your wires and the pin terminals, and don't forget to put the parts of the connector that need to be on the wire side of the connector on the cable before you solder the terminals, or you'll have to unsolder your beautiful solder joints after you're done and start over.

Quarter-inch plugs are called phone plugs, because they were invented for use by the telephone industry. They are the plugs on the ends of guitar cords. They are also found on a whole bunch of other audio cables, including patch cords on rack cabinets, speaker wiring, high-impedance microphone cables, and many others. Stereo versions (like the ones found on professional-grade headphones) are called tip/ring/sleeve or TRS connectors. Most good quality ¼-inch plugs have some type of strain relief to take the stress off of the soldered connections. Some cheap plugs use little screws to connect the wires. These have no strain relief. Don't use them; they will not hold up, and they tend to have problems with the wires fraying and shorting. The barrel (outer cover) part is made of either plastic or metal. Use the metal ones if possible. They act as an extension of the shield to reduce hum and noise. The plastic ones do not, plus they break easily.

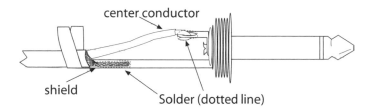

Figure 21-10: How to solder a cable to a mono ¼" phone plug

Figure 21-10 shows the correct way to solder to a mono phone plug. Strip only enough insulation—about ¼-inch—from the cable in order to leave insulation where the cable strain relief clamps will be crimped. Again, tin the terminals and the wires, and put the barrel on the cable before you solder on the connector. The procedure for a TRS plug is similar; it just has one more wire. Large-gauge speaker wires sometimes use oversize ¼-inch plugs. The barrel is larger to accommodate the large wire, and the connections are larger, but the actual connections are the same as a standard ¼-inch plug.

Speakon plugs, made by Neutrik, are designed for use with higher-powered multispeaker systems. They come in two-, four- and eight-pin types. Speakon connectors are twist-lock-type connectors and are solderless. That is, they use small copper sleeves and tiny set screws to hold the wire in the terminal. This method works quite well, but it is still a good idea to tin the wires to keep them from fraying. They can be soldered, but a fairly hot iron is required. The terminals on a Speakon connector are labeled in pairs: 1+, 1-, 2+, 2-, etc.

EP connectors are similar to XLR connectors, but are larger. Like Speakon connectors, EP connectors are designed to be used with higher-power multiple speaker systems. They also come in four- and eight-conductor styles. Connections are soldered much like a standard XLR connector, but a higher-powered soldering iron is a major plus, due to the larger wire gauges that are often used in these types of applications.

The banana plug is another "solderless" connector. They are available as single plugs, but most often are of the dual-banana type shown in *figure 21-11*. The wire is stripped and pushed through the connector where a small set screw tightens it and holds it in place. As with Speakon connectors, it is a good idea to tin the wires to keep them from fraying.

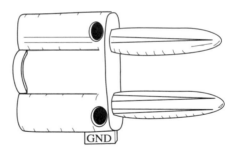

Figure 21-11: Dual banana plug

Phono plugs (also called RCA plugs), not to be confused with the previously described phone plugs, are the connectors used on most home stereo equipment for line-level signal ins and outs. I personally wish they would be declared illegal because they fail very frequently.

Well, I'm sure I missed a bunch of stuff, but it's a good start.

Chapter TWENTY-TWO

PRODUCT SPECIFICATIONS
or, eat your alphabet soup.

When you look in the owner's manual for a piece of electronic music equipment, often you will find a page with a list of specifications on it. Specification information can be both useful and confusing. To help you comprehend the information commonly included in product specs, here is an imaginary spec sheet for an imaginary unit: Model 700 Super Duper Audio Thingamajig Specifications.

INPUT SENSITIVITY: 75MV

This figure will be a voltage. Depending on what the unit does, it will vary from very small (5mV), as in a microphone input, to fairly large (1.4 to 2.5v), as for an audio power amplifier. Things like synth modules that have no inputs will not have this spec listed. Other things with many inputs, such as mixers, may have several different specs for the different types of inputs.

INPUT IMPEDANCE: 7.5K OHMS

This specification basically tells if a unit has low or high impedance inputs. Low Z is usually around 150 to 600 ohms. High Z is typically 5 to 50k ohms, although some gear may have extremely high input impedances up to several Megohms. Knowing the input impedance helps us connect things correctly. High Z outputs should not be connected to Low Z inputs. It probably won't hurt anything, but the sound quality can be degraded if they don't match up correctly.

OUTPUT IMPEDANCE: 300 OHMS

This spec tells us to what kind of load impedance the output(s) of our imaginary thingy would prefer to be connected to. *See* Input Impedance, above.

FREQUENCY RESPONSE: 24HZ TO 19.6kHZ

This spec tells us what kind of performance to expect from a piece of gear. This is useful in determining the crossover frequencies of speakers, for example. If a speaker has a frequency response of 38Hz to 1kHz, it would be best not to use it as a tweeter. If you want to be sure of audiophile-quality sound when recording your newest demo CD, don't use a signal processor that rolls off the high frequencies at 10kHz. You get the idea.

SAMPLING RATE: 44.1kHZ

Digital signal processors and recorders use various sampling rates. The sampling rate is instrumental in determining the way the computer inside the gear handles the data. The current school of thought is the higher the sampling rate, the better the sound quality. (Of course, some folks do not agree. You'll have to decide for yourself.) Sometimes, a piece that uses one sampling rate cannot be used with another piece with a different sampling rate. It's nice to know this before you buy two expensive units and find they are incompatible.

DAMPING FACTOR: >450

This specification is found in power amplifiers. Damping factor is a measure of how well an amplifier deals with the **back-EMF** produced by a speaker. As we learned in Chapter Eight, How Speakers and Microphones Work, the current from the amplifier causes a speaker's voice coil to move inside the gap of the speaker's magnet. That is how the cone moves air, producing sound. The movement of the coil inside the speaker magnet's magnetic field is simultaneously inducing currents into the voice coil. These small currents, called back-EMF, or back currents, cause the speaker cone to continue to move slightly after the signal from the amplifier has stopped. The amplifier is designed to eliminate most of this back-EMF. How well the amplifier accomplishes this is called the damping factor. The higher the number, the better the damping factor. An amp with a low damping factor will have mushy, poor-definition sound on low frequencies. (Note: An amplifier with an extremely high damping factor might sound too stiff and brittle, so an extremely high damping factor may be no more desirable than a low one.)

SLEW RATE: 90NS/VOLT

This spec is another one usually found in power amps. The slew rate is a measurement of the time delay between a sudden change in the input signal of an amplifier until the output changes correspondingly. Basically, this is the transfer-time of the unit. The higher the slew rate, the faster the amp will respond to quick, transient signals. Again, a high (fast) slew rate amplifier might sound harsher and more brittle than one with a lower (slower) slew rate.

NOISE (SIGNAL-TO-NOISE RATIO): -106dB (A-WEIGHTED)

The technically correct name for this specification is signal-plus-noise-to-noise ratio, because the noise is always there and adds to the signal measurement. All electronic components generate some noise. This specification tells us how much is generated by the unit at idle with no signal being produced or amplified. This measurement is usually shown as a relationship between the standard or maximum output signal level and the noise level with no signal present. "A-weighted" means the measurement was taken in a specific way that has been standardized so that the specification for one unit will relate directly to another. There are several standards: A, B-, and C- weighting are all used, and unweighted measurements can also be found. The main thing to remember is the higher the number in decibels, the less noise at rated or full output. Some manufacturers list the noise spec as a measurement of voltage; in that case, the lower number is the better one.

POWER SUPPLY: 117v / 60HZ

This tells us what the unit requires to function properly. It might be an AC voltage with the line frequency as listed above, or it might be a DC voltage with maximum current requirement (12v DC / 500mA), such as would be supplied by an outboard AC adaptor or batteries. If the unit will operate with batteries, the specs will list what type and how many are required.

POWER CONSUMPTION: 28 WATTS

This specification can be confusing, especially when it is listed on the rear panel of an audio power amplifier or a guitar amp. This has nothing to do with the output power provided to speakers. In fact, the power consumption specification of an amplifier will always be greater than output power produced. Power consumption is the amount of power the unit uses from the power source—either batteries or the AC receptacle on the wall.

It is good to know how much power a piece of gear uses, so you don't over-load the power source. If you have several high power-consuming pieces connected to one circuit, you might be blowing breakers all night long. Knowing the power consumption of the units helps us determine how much we can expect to draw from a power circuit. It's also good for figuring how long batteries will last. The consumption figure is usually in watts. AC circuit breakers are rated in amps. You can use the formula, "power divided by voltage equals current in amps" to determine the current consumption of your gear. A very rough rule of thumb is: 100 watts of power is about 1 amp of current. It's not really accurate, but for ballpark estimates in your head, it works.

OUTPUT POWER: 250W RMS

This is a measurement in watts. Output power measurements can be confusing, and some are often downright misleading. Audio amplifiers all produce power. The maximum power they can put out is an indication of how loud they will play. Some amp manufacturers seem to count on the general public not knowing the difference between the several various rating systems. Amplifiers can be rated in "continuous" or RMS power, peak power, peak-to-peak power, and (the very misleading) "peak music power." The number is always referred to as "watts," but there is a big difference between the different ratings. Take a look at the following graph *(figure 22-1).*

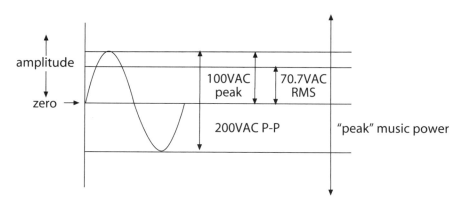

Figure 22-1: Sine wave and the relationship between RMS, peak, peak-to-peak, and music power ratings

The sine wave represents the amp's signal at full power output. The different methods of measuring this wave are shown on the chart with their associated values. The "peak" reading measures the signal from the zero reference to the top of the positive peak. Peak power is shown as 100 watts. The "peak to peak" measurement is from the negative peak to the positive peak, and thus reads twice as high as the peak reading, or 200 watts. The "peak music power" level shows another peak reading much higher than the signal level. The peak music power is an indication of the highest peak, which can be achieved by sending the amp a very short burst of signal. The amp can output this level, but only for an instant. It is arbitrary, unrealistic, and very misleading. My advice is to ignore "music power" specs.

As you can see, the smallest number is the RMS or "continuous" rating. RMS stands for Root-Mean-Square, which is shorthand for the formula used to determine this level. The RMS level of an AC signal is the "relative DC level." This means if all of the factors of the circuit remain the same, and a DC current was substituted for the AC current, the DC level would be this number. Using RMS levels for AC current allows us to use standard formulas (RMS = .707 x peak) to determine electronic values, rather than have an entirely different set of formulas for use with AC current. RMS ratings are the most consistent, and have been used as industry standards for many years. The RMS rating of our example amp is 70.7 watts. This doesn't seem as powerful as the 100-watt peak-rated amp or the 200-watt peak-to-peak-rated amp, but as the graph shows, they all equal the same thing. RMS is more useful when comparing output power ratings of different amps. A 70-watt (RMS) amp like this one might have a "peak music power" rating of 400 or 500 watts! Note: speaker power ratings can be just as dubious as amplifier ratings, so be careful!

DISTORTION: .02% THD@ 1W RMS / 1kHZ

Distortion measurements usually are included only on higher-fidelity equipment. They show the percentage of Total Harmonic Distortion (THD) at a given level and frequency. Sometimes, the specs will show several measurements made at many frequencies and output levels, or even a frequency sweep from low to high. Most of the time, anything made in the past twenty years will have distortion so low as to be undetectable by normal hearing. In the sixties and seventies, power amp and hi-fi companies competed to have the lowest distortion specs, and extremely low specifications like .002% were common. Blindfolded listening tests since then have shown that .01 or below is quite acceptable to all but the most discerning ears. Lower is better, but don't spend more for an amp based on a hundredth of a percentage point of THD. Many folks now agree that some distortion in a signal actually makes it sound better. Guitar players have known this for years.

DYNAMIC RANGE: 105dB

This is the measurement of the difference between the highest level the unit will produce and the level with no signal. The dynamic range of a piece of equipment can be important, depending on where in the signal path it is placed. You wouldn't want to painstakingly produce a digital audio recording that has a wide range of signal levels (my personal favorite: "Hummingbirds in a Thunderstorm") just to run it through a piece of processing gear that only has a 60dB Dynamic range specification.

GAIN: 3dB

This is a measurement of the difference between a standard input signal and the maximum output from a piece of equipment. Many signal processors that have line-level inputs and outputs will have very little or no gain at all. A mixer that has microphone inputs and line outputs will have much a higher gain rating.

WEIGHT: 15.5kG

This is how much the piece weighs. This is important if you're going to have to ship the equipment somewhere or move it around frequently. Sometimes this specification doesn't include things like cabinets, cases, or external power supplies, so check it out carefully.

DIMENSIONS: 19.0" (48.3CM) WIDE, 3.5" (8.9CM) TALL, 13.2" (33.5CM) DEEP

This tells us how big it is. Same warning as above. This particular set of dimensions happens to be those of a standard 19-inch rack-mountable piece that is two rack spaces tall (2U). Each rack space equals 1.75 inches.

ACCESSORIES

Power cord, ugly stickers, owner's manual, box and packing, stands, cables, toothbrush case, etc. This is the additional stuff that comes along with the unit. Sometimes this list includes things like sustain pedals, volume pedals, extra power supplies, etc., that do not come with the unit but can be purchased separately for use with the equipment.

There are other specifications you may run into, but these are most of the more common ones. Now, on with the show.

Chapter TWENTY-THREE

ODDS AND ENDS
or, now's my chance to rant and rave a little!

This chapter is sort of a "catch-all" of miscellaneous information: Thoughts, ideas, and opinions about things that didn't really fit into any of the other chapters.

ABOUT MODIFICATIONS

First, an opinion. I personally do not believe in non-factory modifications. It has been my experience that, if you have a piece of equipment that doesn't do exactly what you want it to do, there is almost always something on the market that does. Rather than try to turn the proverbial sow's ear into a silk purse, it's better to save up some dough and buy the one that was designed to perform the way you want. The reasoning behind this is, the person who designed the modification is usually somebody like me: A service tech, not a design engineer. I have built hundreds of gadgets, from switching units to pedal-boards to stereo tube power amps. Some of these have worked really well, some have been merely marginal, and others have been dismal failures. (I once tried to make a stage intercom system out of surplus telephone handsets. I spent a lot of time and effort on this little project. It didn't work).

When the guys at XYZ amps build something, they try to make it the best they can. Let's say you buy one of their amps, and decide it's just perfect, except it would be really cool if it had a variable level effects loop. So you bring it in to the local fix-it shop and ask the guy to put one in, or you see an article in a guitar magazine on how to do it yourself, so you decide to give it a try. Now, we don't know if the guys at XYZ just didn't think to put one in, or if they knew that an effects loop was not a good idea. We won't know the answer to this question until someone has built the circuit, installed it, and drilled a few holes in the amp chassis. By then, it's too late. Holes are forever. Sometimes an older Fender or Marshall amplifier will come in for repair that is in otherwise perfect condition, except that it has one or two holes drilled in the chassis for some "modification" that has long since been removed. It's sad to see a potentially "mint" collectors item reduced to "pretty good" condition, its value dropping accordingly.

It is also rare that a modification will do exactly what you want it to do sound-wise. Adding a master volume control to an older series Marshall amp will not make it sound like a JCM 800 or 900 series amp. Adding a tube gain stage will increase the distortion available, but will also add noise. I've also found that many customers want modifications done to try to over-come shortcomings in their playing. No amount of cool amp mods will make you a better player.

I once had a customer ask me to install a variac in his Marshall 100-watt head. I explained to him that a variac capable of handling the current used by his amp would be almost as big as the entire amp head and would not fit inside. When I asked him what he was trying to accomplish, he said he wanted his amp to "sound just like Eddie Van Halen's," and he had heard that Eddie used a variac on his 100-watt tube head. I tried to explain that Eddie's sound was a combination of many factors, including his guitar, its pickups, the amp's settings, and mostly just the way he plays. My customer wouldn't accept this explanation, so I told him how to make his amp sound just like Eddie's: Turn everything all the way up.

"But, won't that fry the tubes or something?" he asked me. I told him of course it would, but that's how Eddie gets his sound. He has a guy that tours with him whose job it is to retube the amp every time it needs it, and Eddie doesn't care if he has to retube the amp every night, because he's got lots of money! There is no modification in the world that will make a musician better. The real reason Eddie sounds the way he does is his hands. Most really good players have a distinct sound that has nothing to do with gui-tars or amps or pedals. I've seen Johnny Winter play quite a few times. Once he was playing a Gibson Flying V through an acoustic solid-state amp; once he was playing a Steinberger headless guitar through a Marshall stack. I saw him play a Gibson 335 through a Fender Twin reverb. His sound was the same every time. He sounded just like Johnny Winter. It's in his hands. This is true of Johnny Winter, Jeff Beck, Jimi Hendrix, Stevie Ray Vaughn, Eric Johnson, and countless others, including Eddie Van Halen.

AC/DC POWER ADAPTORS

We're talking wall warts here. They seem so innocuous, yet they are so varied and unforgiving. They come in hundreds of sizes and shapes. Some plug directly into the wall, some have a power cord that connects to a box with another cord that goes to the piece of equipment it is designed to operate...and yet, they all look much the same.

Because AC adaptors look so much alike, people tend to think they are interchangeable. They aren't. There are two basic types of AC power supplies: AC to DC and AC to AC. The voltage output from an AC/AC type is alternating current. These adaptors are used to power units that have the rectifiers, filters, and regulators built into the main unit, not the adaptor. AC/DC adaptors have the rectifiers and filtering, and occasionally some regulating devices built into the adaptor. These two types of adaptors are not interchangeable, even if the voltage rating is the same. Another variable we encounter is the voltage output. Adaptors range from 1.5 volts to 40 volts or higher. Most AC/DC adaptors have outputs in the 6- to 12-volt range.

Adaptors are also rated by how much current they can safely provide. A device operating from an adaptor will use only as much current as it needs. If the adaptor can provide this much current, or more, and the voltage and polarity are correct, then all is well. If the power adaptor is rated lower than the unit's current requirement, the adaptor will try to provide the additional current, overheat, and eventually fail.

Power adaptors come with a wide variety of connectors. Some look almost exactly the same, yet they are different. Barrel-pin-type connectors come in many sizes; they can vary by as little as half a millimeter, so they can be extremely difficult to tell apart. The polarity of the output plug can be positive or negative. Connecting a positive-polarity adaptor to a unit requiring a negative one could destroy either the adaptor, the unit, or both, unless they are protected against reverse polarity. The bottom line is, if a unit is powered by an outboard adaptor, use only the adaptor that came with the unit. If you must use a generic replacement adaptor, be sure the connector, voltage, current, and polarity are all correct before trying to use it, or you are likely to experience problems. Also, do not wrap the power adaptor's cable around the adaptor; it bends the cable at a sharp angle and will eventually cause the wires in the cable to break (this rule applies to amplifier footswitches, too).

OVERDRIVING

Many guitar amplifiers have overdrive built into them to generate pleasing distortion effects. That is not what I'm talking about here. The overdrive I'm referring to is an unpleasant, gritty distortion caused by trying to shove too much signal into an input. Many signal processors have the ability to amplify signals. That means you can get more signal level out than you put in. If we chain effects together and each one increases the signal level a little bit (or a lot), eventually we will get to a point where the level is higher than the input of the next device can handle. This overdrives the input stage of the effect, or mixer, or whatever, producing that ugly, gritty distortion. The obvious solution is to try to keep the input and output levels equal. Input overload can happen quickly in multi-effects processors, where the output of one stage feeds directly into the input of the next stage. The best way to tell if a processing stage is increasing the signal level is to compare the effected signal with the dry (no effect) instrument signal. Most of the time, these effects can be bypassed individually. If the effected sound seems louder than the dry signal, adjust the output level of the effects stage down until they match. This is called unity gain: "X" in equals "X" out. Running line-level effects into instrument-level inputs can also cause overdrive distortion. See Appendix B for more information about signal levels.

OPEN-BACKED GUITAR AMPS

If you own a combo-type guitar amplifier, one that has the amp and speaker(s) all in one cabinet, it is common practice to use the back of the amp to store things like pedals, extra strings, picks, slide bars, chewing gum wrappers, etc. One word of advice: Don't! It's a guitar amp, not a suitcase. Go to the local thrift store and buy a small suitcase if you need somewhere to keep things. Anything in the back of an amp other than the power cord is a potential problem. If it is a tube amp, cables and switches can loosen or break tubes. Anything metal stands the chance of getting into the amp or a speaker and shorting wiring or components. Small things like picks, matchbooks, business cards, etc. can get into the speaker basket and cause unwanted noises. Many older Fender amp head units also have an open back, and most owners of these amps store the power cord in the back. This is not a good idea, as the frequent stuffing and unstuffing of the cord loosens the tube sockets and can even break the tubes. Wrap the cord up and lay it on top of the unit, or stick it under the handle, instead. It could save lots of money in repairs. If you don't want to go to all of that trouble, you don't have to. I can always use the business.

BUYING GEAR FROM CATALOGS OR ON LINE

There are a lot of places to buy top-quality electronic music gear at reduced prices. Often these are mail-order outlets, and with the growth of the computer industry, Internet retailers have become major players. I'd like to share a few thoughts with you about buying electronic gear by mail or on line. As with everything, there are advantages and disadvantages to buying in person and sight-unseen. If you do not have a good music store near where you live, mail-order discounters are the way to go. You can save money buying from a large chain, and sometimes they carry a wider variety of gear than a small shop.

If, however, you do have a music store in or close to your town, I recommend you give them your business, even if it costs a little more. If you develop a solid relationship with your local store, it can come in real handy sometimes. They will go out of their way to stock your favorite picks and strings, for example, and money spent at a locally owned store stays in your town. If the local store goes out of business because of outside competition, you'll have to mail order everything, and you'll never be able to try stuff out before you buy it.

DUCT TAPE

Duct tape is for taping sheet metal ductwork together. Duct tape on anything else is a sticky mess! Use gaffer's tape, if tape must be used at all. The glue on gaffer's tape doesn't leave as much residue. Board tape or artists' tape is useful for marking things like the inputs on a mixer. It is designed to come off without leaving sticky gunk behind. Art supply stores and good full-service music stores carry this kind of tape. Use zip ties or Velcro strips to wrap cables, not duct tape.

MEMORY BACK-UP BATTERIES

Many digital electronic signal-processing units and synthesizers have a battery inside. The purpose of this battery is to maintain a voltage on the dynamic RAM (random access memory) I.C.s so they will not lose their memories when the power is off. The current required to do this is minimal, so most units use a small lithium battery. Lithium batteries supply low currents for amazingly long times: Seven to ten years! Equally amazing is how fast seven to ten years goes by. Some units use a ni-cad rechargeable battery that is recharged each time the unit is turned on. The drawback to this is, if the unit is not turned on frequently, the battery can go dead. If the battery in one of these units fails, the memory presets will be lost. The back-up battery prevents this from happening, and that is the only thing the battery does. The result of a dead back-up battery is a jumbled display—strange characters that make no sense, and strange sounds or no sounds at all. These are the only symptoms a dead battery will cause. Missing notes, cutting out signals, poor MIDI transmission, and hot power supplies are not caused by a dead battery. The only way to prevent battery failure is to have the battery replaced every five to seven years, and always back up your patches. Usually, this can be done via MIDI to a sequencer, or some older units had a tape interface built into them for this purpose. Many synths allow you to back-up patches to memory cards, but they are expensive (and some memory cards have back-up batteries, too).

BUYING VERSUS RENTING GEAR

There is a rule of thumb I use when it comes to deciding if I really need to own something: If I'm going to use it every day, once a week, or several times a month, it pays to buy it. If I only need it once a month or less, I rent it. If you have a sound system that works fine for 90% of the dates you play, but you do a few street dances during the summer where you need more gear, it is much more cost-effective to rent the extra stuff on those few occasions than to own it (and store it) the rest of the time.

SUMMING UP

Well, that about does it. I hope you found this book to be interesting and informative. Thank you for reading it. As far as I know, all of the electronic theory I've described here is correct, and I have gone to great pains to see to it that there is no misinformation being spewed forth. There are plenty of folks doing that daily on the Internet. I've done my best to be certain that the contents of this book are accurate, but some of the opinions expressed might not agree with popular thought. That's okay. I've never worried too much about my personal opinions being popular. They are based on personal experience, and everyone's personal experiences are different. I haven't told you everything there is to know, but hopefully there's enough useful information here to help you understand how your electronic music gear functions, and to help prevent it from messing up. As far as electronic theory goes, we've just scratched the surface. If you find that you'd like to get deeper into the nuts and bolts of how electronic circuits works, there are good books on every aspect of electronic theory and application that you can check out at your local library, as well as a lot of good websites you can access on the Internet. Some of these are listed in Appendix C, Suggested Reading. Now, go out there and do what's really important: Make your music!

FREQUENCY CHARTS

Sound waves and radio waves are measured in Hertz, or cycles per second. The total spectrum of frequency includes all frequencies from 1Hz to infinity. Zero Hertz is the lack of any frequency. The following charts illustrate just where things lie in the frequency spectrum.

Standard concert pitch in the U.S. is A440, which means middle A is 440Hz. This varies from country to country and even orchestra to orchestra. The standard in much of Europe is 441Hz.

The frequencies of bass and guitar open strings are:

6-string guitar:
Low E: 83Hz; A: 110Hz; D: 147Hz; G: 196Hz; B: 247Hz; high E: 330Hz
(Low B on a 7-string guitar is 62Hz.)

4-string bass guitar:
E: 41.5Hz; A: 55Hz; D: 74Hz; G: 98Hz
(Low B on a 5-string bass is 31Hz.)

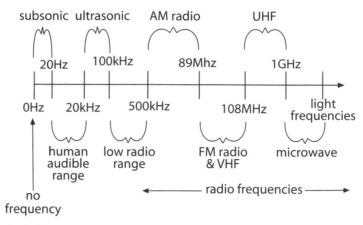

Figure A-1: The full frequency spectrum

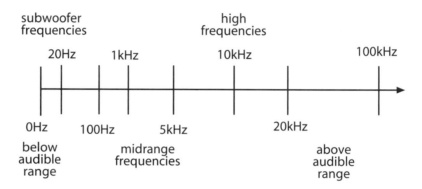

Figure A-2: Audio frequencies

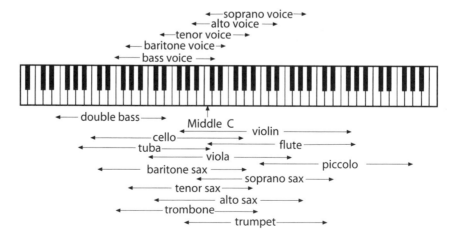

Figure A-3: The ranges of various musical instruments

Appendix **B**

AUDIO SIGNAL LEVELS

Audio signal levels vary greatly. Most of the time, they are expressed as a voltage. These voltages vary from zero (no signal) up to 70.7 volts RMS (constant voltage speaker-distribution systems) and higher in high-power sound systems. Because the voltage of an audio signal varies with volume level, these voltages are constantly changing, but certain standard level ranges have been established as a reference. The following chart shows standard audio reference levels, arranged from low to high. (These levels are average voltage levels, and the audio signals in actual use might be higher or lower than the numbers listed below.)

*Phono:
(moving coil cartridge) 5mV
(moving magnet cartridge) 20mV
(ceramic cartridge) 500mV

Microphone: 20mV to 50mV

Instrument: 50mV to 100mV

Line levels: 0dBu: .775V RMS
**-10dBV (consumer standard): .316V RMS
**+4dBu (professional standard): 1.23V RMS
0dBm (power reference): 1mW

* phono levels may soon be a thing of the past. Digital technology is quickly making the phonograph a rarity. I've included these reference levels just because I happen to remember them after all of these years.

215

** Mixer levels are sometimes referred to as -10 or +4. These numbers represent the 0dB reference operating level of the device. Plus four is usually considered "pro" level, and -10 is used mostly in consumer-level gear.

SUGGESTED READING

H ere are some good books and interesting websites, in no particular order. There's no guarantee that all of these books are still in print, but they should be available at any good library; that's where I found them. The websites and pages were all functional and current as of this writing.

BOOKS

Lee, Dr. William F. *The Music Theory Dictionary: The Language of the Mechanics of Music*. New York: Hansen Educational Music and Books, 1966.

Horn, Delton T. *Basic Electronics Theory With Projects and Experiments*. New York: McGraw-Hill/TAB Electronics, 1993.

Bell, David A. *Fundamentals of Electronic Devices*. Reston, VA: Reston Pub., 1975.

Horowitz, Mannie. *Elementary Electricity and Electronics: Component by Component*. New York: McGraw-Hill/TAB Electronics, 1986.

Seippel, Robert G. *Fundamentals of Electricity: Basics of Electricity, Electronics, Controls and Computers*. Chicago: American Technical Society Publishing, 1974.

Graf, Rudolf, F. *The Modern Dictionary of Electronics*. Burlington, MA: Newnes, 1999.

WEBSITES AND PAGES

Audio Glossary
www.audioc.com/information/audio_glossary/glossary.html

Rane Pro Audio Reference
www.rane.com/digi-dic.html

Rane Reference Books Page
www.rane.com/par-book.html

Tomi Engdahl's Electronics Page
www.hut.fi/Misc/Electronics/index.html

Rane's Audio Links
www.rane.com/hotlinks.html

Other Electronics Webpages
www.radiosky.com/learn.html
science-ebooks.com/electronics/basic_electronics.htm
www.maxmon.com/glossary.htm
www.iserv.net/~alexx/glossary.htm
www.uswi.com/glosmain.htm
home.teleport.com/~bdnewman/Sound.html
www.hmusic.com/newsletter/sound_related.htm
www.whirlwindusa.com/tech04.html

Note: Things change fast on the Internet, so some of these addresses may no longer be there by the time you read this. Any good search engine will provide you with zillions of electronics websites. However, keep in mind that just because it's out there where you can read it doesn't mean it's accurate.

FORMULAS AND MISCELLANEOUS INFORMATION

RESISTOR COLOR CODE

Resistors are often marked with colored stripes to designate their value. Each color corresponds to a number value:

black = 0
brown = 1
red = 2
orange = 3
yellow = 4
green = 5
blue = 6
violet = 7
gray = 8
white = 9

There are usually four or five of these stripes. The first stripe indicates the value of the tens column of a decimal number. The second indicates the value of the ones column. These first two stripes will each be one of the colors listed above. The third stripe is called the multiplier. This represents a number that is the power of ten that the previous numbers will be multiplied by. It sounds a lot more complicated than it really is. Take a look at *figure D-1*.

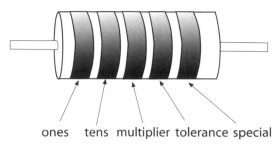

ones   tens multiplier tolerance special

Figure D-1: Typical resistor color code

Let's say the first stripe is brown, and the second stripe is black. That corresponds to a 1 in the tens column and a 0 in the ones column, or the number 10. Now let's say that the multiplier band is orange. Ten to the third power is 1,000, so we multiply 10 times 1,000 and we get 10,000. That is the value of the resistor: 10,000 ohms. Now, notice that orange equals 3 in our color code, and when we multiplied our numbers, we effectively tacked three zeros onto our first two-digit number. The multiplier is the number of zeros that get added to the original number. This works on all resistor values of more than 1 ohm. Now that we're armed with that little bit of information, let's do another one. This time, all three of the first three stripes are red. Red is equal to two, so there's a 2 in the tens column, a 2 in the ones column, and on our multipliers band two 0's. That makes it 2,200 ohms.

In the case of resistor values of less than one ohm, there are two more colors that are used in the multiplier band.

Gold = -1

Silver = -10

Ten to the -1 power is .1; if we multiply the 22 (from our example above) by .1, the resulting number will be 2.2, or 2.2 ohms. Ten to the -10 power is .01, so if we multiply the 22 by .01, the resulting number will be 0.22, or 0.22 ohms. The fourth band on the resistor is the tolerance rating. This stripe will be either silver, gold, red, or black. Silver indicates a 10% tolerance, meaning the resistor will be within plus or minus 10% of the color-coded value. A 100-ohm resistor will have to fall within 90 and 110 ohms to have a 10% tolerance rating. A gold stripe indicates a 5% tolerance (95 to 105 ohms); a red stripe is 2%, and a black stripe is 1%. Some older resistors don't have any tolerance stripe. These are assumed to have a 20% tolerance and are seldom seen anymore.

The fifth stripe on some resistors is a temperature rating. Sometimes it indicates the resistive material used in the device. Some manufacturers recommend replacing specific resistors with the exact same type, due to the way they open when they fail. Power supply resistors are often flame-proof, meaning that they will not produce actual flames when they fail. These special requirements will normally be indicated on the schematic of the unit. If in doubt, use flameproof resistors.

OHM'S LAW

E (voltage) divided by I (current in amps) equals R (resistance in ohms). Notice that the values used in this formula, as with all other electronic formulas, are expressed in whole units: Amps, not milliamps; ohms not Kilohms. Any deviation from this rule will get you a (very) wrong answer.

$$E=volts, I=amps, R=Ohms, P=watts$$

$$E \div R = I \quad E \div I = R \quad R \times I = E \quad I \times R = E$$

Figure D-2: Ohm's Laws

$$P \div I = E \quad P \div E = I \quad I \times E = P \quad E \times I = P$$
$$I \times R = P \quad E \div R = P$$

Figure D-3: Power formulas

To find the frequency (f) of a tuned LC circuit: where L = Inductance in Henries and C = capacitance in Farads:

$$f = \frac{1}{2\pi \sqrt{LC}} \quad or \quad f = \frac{159.2}{\sqrt{LC}}$$

To find the capacitance of a tuned LC circuit when frequency and inductance are known:

$$C = \frac{1}{4\pi^2 f^2 L} \quad or \quad C = \frac{25,330}{f^2 L}$$

To find the inductance of a tuned LC circuit when frequency and capacitance are known:

$$L = \frac{1}{4\pi^2 f^2 C} \quad or \quad L = \frac{25,330}{f^2 C}$$

Figure D-4: Resonant frequency formulas

CROSSOVER NETWORK CONFIGURATIONS

Figure D-5a

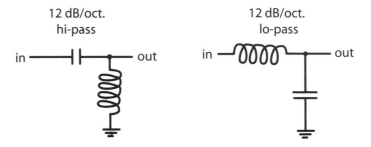

Figure D-5b

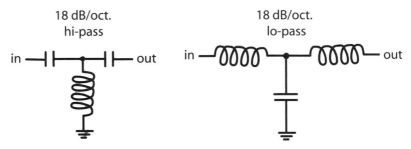

Figure D-5c

RESISTANCE FORMULAS

$$\text{Resistors in series: } R_{total} = R_1 + R_2 + R_3 + \ldots$$

$$\text{Resistors in parallel: } R_{total} = \frac{1}{\dfrac{1}{R_1} + \dfrac{1}{R_2} + \dfrac{1}{R_3} + \ldots}$$

Figure D-6: Resistance formulas

Here is a speaker fuse formula to effectively protect a speaker or horn from being overpowered. Find out the power rating of the driver or drivers you wish to protect. Take the power rating of the speaker times .8 to get 80%. Using your calculator, find the square root of this number, then divide it by the speaker's impedance. The result is the current at that power rating. The fuse should be a fast-blow type, as close to this number as you can find, without going over it.

Wavelength (represented by the Greek letter lambda: Λ) is the distance a wave travels in the time it takes for one complete cycle of its frequency to occur. Antennas for transmitting or receiving radio frequency signals work best if they are the same length as the wave. Sometimes it is not practical to make the antenna a full wavelength long. Half-wave or quarter-wave antennas are often used. Radio waves travel at the speed of light: 300,000,000 meters per second. Wavelength measurements are also used in recording studios to adjust microphone placement, and by acousticians in the design of listening rooms and recording studios.

The formula for finding wavelength is V (velocity in meters per second) ÷ f (frequency).

GLOSSARY

W ords included in this glossary are followed by a definition and a sentence using the word, as an example of usage. Many of these words have several meanings. I've only concerned myself with the ones pertaining to the text of this book. If I've missed any terms, or you didn't understand my definition, you might want to check out the other glossaries and dictionaries I have listed in Appendix C, Suggested Reading.

active: adj. having the ability to add gain to a circuit
> The bass player was able to increase the high frequencies in his signal, because his bass had active electronics.

adaptor: n. any device that allows one type of connector to be used with another type
> Using an XLR to ¼-inch adaptor, he was able to plug the balanced output of the mixer into the unbalanced input of the amp.

ADSR: n. the section of a synthesizer that controls the dynamics of a sound over time, also called the envelope.
> By adjusting the ADSR, she was able to make her keyboard sound just like a dying pigeon.

algebra: n. the name of a certain branch of mathematics
> In high school, I disliked algebra, but it sure comes in handy in electronics.

alternating current: n. a changing voltage that varies from positive to negative with respect to a reference point
> The electrical outlets in most houses provide alternating current to operate electrical devices.

AM: *see* amplitude modulation

ampere: n. the unit of measurement of current

One volt through a one-ohm resistor equals one ampere of current.

amplification: v. to increase, as in level

Some of the transistors in my stereo system provide amplification to the audio signals.

amplitude: n. the level of an alternating current signal or wave

By increasing the gain of the circuit, the signal's amplitude was made higher.

amplitude modulation: n. a method of adding two signals together, resulting in a variation of the original signal's amplitude, or signal level

The AM radio station adds audio to a carrier frequency by using amplitude modulation.

analog: adj. describes an electronic circuit where the signal levels are continuously variable, as opposed to digital circuits where there are only two states: On and off

Some effects units use analog circuitry instead of digital.

anode: n. either terminal of a battery or cell, also the positive terminal of a diode

She connected the negative anode of the battery to the anode of the diode.

antenna: n. a device used to transmit radio waves into, or pick up radio waves from, the atmosphere

The wireless receiver didn't work very well after she broke off the antenna.

atom: n. the basic building block of matter

The chair you're sitting on is made up of atoms, as are the molecules in the air you're breathing.

attenuator: n. a part of a circuit used to decrease the signal level

The speakers in the small room of the church were too loud before they installed an attenuator on the speaker line.

back-EMF: n. the current induced into a speaker line by the speaker's voice coil and magnet

It's a good thing they put filtering into the amp to negate the effects of the back-EMF.

balanced: adj. a circuit where the signal is symmetrical with respect to ground

A balanced system reduces the noise picked up by long signal lines.

bandwidth: n. the range of frequencies that can be produced or used by a device

My ancient television won't pick up some stations because of its limited bandwidth.

base two: *see* binary

basket: n. part of a speaker; the frame supporting the cone or diaphragm
The speaker was dropped so hard that the magnet came off of the basket.

battery: n. a source of direct current consisting of two or more cells
John had to use a cord last night, because he only had one battery for his wireless, and it was dead.

bias: n. 1) the voltage used in an amplifier circuit to keep a device, either tube or solid-state, operating at the proper idling level while no signal is present
Her amp was running too hot until she had the bias adjusted.
2) the high-voltage, high-frequency signal used to assist the audio signal in getting imprinted on tape
Recorded signals can be noisy and distorted if the record bias isn't correctly adjusted on a tape deck.

binary: n. a numbering system using a base number, or radix, of two
The base ten number 5 is 101 in base two, or binary.

bipolar transistor: n. an electrical device made of silicon or germanium, using both negative and positive charge-carriers in its construction
My amp uses bipolar transistors, but my friend prefers to use an amp with FETs.

bit: n. one single part of the data in a digital system; bits are grouped together in sets to make bytes
The microcomputer in her CD player froze up because of a single incorrect bit of data.

block diagram: n. a chart showing the various stages and signal flow in an electronic device
He could see that the tone-control circuit was before the main fader by examining the block diagram.

blow: v. to damage from over current; also to cause a circuit to open
Too much current in the circuit will cause the fuse to blow.

bobbin: *see* coil form

buffer: n. 1) a section of an electrical circuit whose function is to keep one stage from interacting with the next stage
If you place a buffer between the volume control and the tone controls, they do not interfere with each other's functions.
n. 2) a section of memory in a digital circuit that holds data temporarily until it can be transferred by the microcomputer to its permanent memory location
Even though the power went off, the information wasn't lost, because it had been stored in the temporary memory buffer.

bypass: v. to go around (and thus eliminate) part of a circuit
He wired the pickup in his guitar directly to the output jack, bypassing the controls.
byte: n. a group of data bits that form a digital word
In older computers, it only took four bits of data to make a byte.

cache: n. a high-speed buffer in a computer between the processor and the data memory; also the data stored in this temporary buffer memory
The computer seemed slow due to the small size of its cache.
Cannon connector: *see* XLR
capacitor: n. an electronic component that blocks DC voltage and passes AC current; capacitors tend to pass high-frequency AC better than low-frequency AC, making them particularly well-suited for use in filtering and tone controlling circuits
The high frequencies of the audio signal were reduced by sending them through a capacitor to ground.
capstan: n. a round spindle used by a tape deck to pull the tape at a constant rate from the supply spindle to the take-up spindle
The sound from the tape deck was fluttering due to the dirt encrusted on the capstan.
cardioid: adj. shaped like a heart
The cardioid polar pattern of the microphone helped to reject off-axis signals, thereby preventing unwanted feedback.
carrier: n. a constant radio frequency wave signal
His uncle's favorite radio station is called X107 because the station's carrier frequency is 107.5MHz.
case: n. the outer covering of a device
Transistors come in a variety of case styles.
cast frame: n. a type of speaker basket that is cast or molded rather than stamped from sheet metal
Generally speaking, she prefers the sound of cast-frame speakers.
cathode: n. the negative terminal of a diode or a tube
The tube's cathode was connected to ground through a 250-ohm resistor.
cell: n. one section of a battery that produces DC voltage
A typical 6-volt lantern battery contains four cells, each producing 1.5 volts DC.
center frequency: n. the primary frequency of an audio filtering circuit
The tone-control circuit was set up to cut and boost around a center frequency of 800Hz.
centi-: prefix used in the metric system designating one one-hundredth
One one-hundredth of a meter is one centimeter.

choke: *see* inductor

circuit: n. an electronic path from ground to a positive voltage source

By connecting the lamp to the battery terminals, he completed the circuit.

circuit breaker: n. a resettable circuit-interrupting device that opens a circuit if a certain level of current is exceeded

He got careless, plugged in too many things at once, and blew a circuit breaker.

class A: adj. a type of amplifier configuration where the entire signal is amplified by all of the output devices

His amp seemed to run hotter than most because it was operating class A.

class AB: adj. a type of amplifier configuration where the positive part of the signal is amplified by only the positive devices, and the negative signal is amplified by only the negative devices

The amp was more efficient, because it was using a class AB output section.

class G: adj. an amplifier configuration where the power-supply voltages are switched to a higher level during high power transient signals

Her amp put out higher power than other amps of the same weight because it had a class G switching power supply.

class H: *see* class G

clean: adj. undistorted

Most modern guitar amps have an overdrive channel as well as a clean channel.

clipping: v. the process of an amplifier's signal level exceeding the power supply voltage, resulting in a distorted signal

The sound quality suffered when the DJ ran his amps into clipping.

coherent: adj. descriptive term used to express when two or more signals are in the same phase.

By reversing the phase to one channel, the signals became coherent, and thus sounded much better.

coil: *see* inductor

coil form: n. the center of an inductor, which has the wire wrapped around it

High-frequency inductors often use plastic coil forms.

cold solder joint: n. a solder connection made where the two pieces of metal being joined were not close enough to the same temperature

A cold solder joint on the circuit board degraded the signal.

common: n. the terminal of a switch that is used in all positions of the switch; also another word for a voltage reference point in a circuit

The common connection of the switch was connected to common ground.

component: n. a part of something, specifically the individual devices that make up an electronic circuit

The resistors, capacitors, transistors, diodes, and other components were mounted on the main circuit board.

compress: v. to decrease the dynamic range of a signal

The band sounded "flat" because the signal was too compressed.

condenser: *see:* capacitor

conductor: n. any material that readily passes electrical current

A piece of copper speaker wire is a good electrical conductor.

cone: n. the diaphragm of a speaker

He had to have his speaker reconed after his brother poked holes in the cone with a pencil.

connection: n. the point in a circuit where two or more components are tied together

The signal cut in and out because of a poor connection at the power amp input jack.

contact: n. a moving part of an electrical device that touches another part to provide a path for current

The contacts of the switch were connected, causing current to flow through the circuit.

continuity: n. unbroken, as in a circuit

The guitar cord didn't pass signal due to a lack of continuity of the hot wire.

continuous: adj. uninterrupted

There was an annoying continuous noise in the speakers all night. Unfortunately, it was the band!

control: n. a device used to vary or adjust part of a circuit, such as a potentiometer; v. the act of varying or adjusting a parameter of a circuit

He controlled the frequency response of his amp with the tone controls.

control grid: n. one of the elements of a vacuum tube

By varying the signal on the control grid, the output of the tube changed.

crossover network: n. an electronic circuit whose components divide a signal into specific frequency bands

The speaker's passive crossover network kept the low frequencies from damaging the tweeter.

current: n. the volume of electrons flowing through a circuit

Fuses won't blow from too much voltage; they are current-sensitive devices.

current gain: n. an increase in current due to amplification

The output stage provides a lot of current gain, and almost no voltage gain.

cycle: n. one complete wave of a repeating function
Three-hundred-sixty degrees make up one cycle of an audio frequency, measured in cycles per second, or Hertz.

D.I.: *see* direct interface

DAC: *see* digital to audio converter

data: n. information, specifically that used by a digital computing device
The computer couldn't process the request due to a lack of data.

data bit: *see* bit

Deca: prefix used in the metric system indicating ten to the power of one
Ten meters is one Decameter.

deci: prefix used in the metric system indicating ten to the power of -1
One tenth of a gram is one decigram.

decibel: n. a unit of measure used to indicate degree of change
The signal increased ten decibels when he turned up the level control.

device: n. any man-made thing, any electronic component
The amp's main fuse opened, due to one shorted output device.

diaphragm: n. a membrane which when moved by an electronic driver produces sound, such as in a speaker; conversely, a membrane used to detect changes in air pressure, such as in a microphone element
Many dynamic horn drivers use aluminum or titanium diaphragms.

digital: adj. describing an electronic device using circuitry that recognizes only two states: on and off
Her synthesizer was able to reproduce sounds realistically, because it was digital.

digital-to-analog converter: n. a device, usually an integrated circuit, that changes digital signals to analog signals
The recording turned out great due to the high quality of the digital-to-analogt converters used.

diode: n. a two-terminal device, either solid-state or vacuum tube, that passes current in only one direction
A diode placed across an AC voltage rectified it to half-wave pulsating DC.

direct box: *see* direct interface

direct current: n. a current source that remains at a constant voltage level with respect to ground; zero Hertz
A battery provides direct current to the electrical system in your car.

direct interface: n. a device that allows an instrument to be connected directly to a mixing console

The bass player's signal was sent to the mic snake using a direct interface.

directional: adj. the property of being able to locate a sound's source

He could hear that the tweeters were high above the arena, because they were very directional.

display: n. the part of a piece of equipment that provides information to the user

The synthesizer was easy to use because of the large display.

distortion: n. any change in a signal from the original introduced by the circuitry of a device

The signal processor induced a lot of distortion into the signal, causing the sound quality to be degraded.

distro: *see* power distribution system

Doppler effect: n. the compression of waves in front of, and the expansion of waves behind, a moving source

The pitch of the siren seemed to drop as the police car went speeding past, due to the Doppler effect.

driver: n. a device in a speaker system that produces sound

The sound system sounded better than usual due to the new higher-quality drivers in the speaker cabinets.

dry cell: n. a voltage-producing cell using a dry paste as an electrolyte (rather than a wet acid as found in a "wet" cell), see also: cell

Her flashlight used a pair of dry cells to power the lamp.

dynamic: adj. refers to electromagnetic function in transducers

Several of the tweeters in the system were piezo-electric, but most of them were dynamic.

dynamics: n. the difference between signal or volume levels

He had to turn down his stereo because of the music's wide range of dynamics.

effects: n. a generic term meaning any signal processing, such as reverb, echo, compression, etc.

The band sounded like they were playing in the men's room of the bus station, due to the soundman's overuse of effects.

effects loop: n. a part of a circuit were the signal can be routed out to one or more external effects, and then returned to the signal path of the circuit

There was a multi-effector connected to his amp's effects loop.

efficiency: *see* efficient

efficient: adj. the relationship of work produced to power consumed

His amp was not very efficient because it used 400 watts from the AC wall socket, but only put out 25 watts to the speakers.

electromotive force: *see* voltage

electron: n. the particles that spin around the nucleus of an atom
The electrons transferring from atom to atom make electric circuits possible.

element: n. a part of an entire entity
The tube was made up of several elements: The plate, cathode, grid, and filament.

EMF *see* voltage

emission: v. the process of emitting, or outputting something, such as electrons or waves
There was good electron emission in the tubes, so the transmitter emitted a good, strong signal.

energized: adj. the state of having current flowing through a circuit or device
The solenoid pulled in when the coil was energized.

envelope: n. a sealed membrane surrounding something, such as the elements of a tube;
the level and/or timbre characteristics of a sound over time. (*see* ADSR)
The 12AX7a tube has a glass envelope, but some tubes use metal ones.

equalizer: n. a tone-controlling audio circuit
We were able to compensate for the poor low end of the speakers by boosting 35Hz with an equalizer.

even-order harmonics: *see* harmonics

farad: n. the basic unit of capacitance
The power supply filter capacitor value was 4,700 microfarads.

fader: n. a sliding type of variable resistor
The faders on a mixing console control each channel's output level.

feedback: n. an oscillation frequency generated by a signal being reamplified due to mechanical, acoustic or electronic coupling back to a previous section of the circuitry; also any signal purposely coupled into a previous section of a circuit
A loud feedback squeal resulted from the mic being too close to the speakers, and the soundman got immediate feedback from the audience.

field-effect transistor: n. a type of transistor using only one PN (positive-to-negative) junction as opposed to a bipolar transistor which uses two
Many amplifiers use FET's in their output sections.

filament: n. the part of an electron tube that heats the cathode, also the part of a light bulb that glows and produces light
You can see the glow of the filament in some tubes, and in others, you can't.

filter: n. any circuit that is designed to remove certain frequencies from the signal; v. the act of removing certain frequencies from an electronic signal

Most crossover networks include at least one low-pass filter, to filter out the highs.

flow chart: *see* block diagram

FM: *see* frequency modulation

FM synthesis: n. a method of producing sounds by combining four, six, or eight steady-state tones, utilizing the overtones and subtones produced (*see* heterodyne)

A lot of synthesizers from the eighties used FM synthesis.

frame: n. another name for a speaker basket

He knew he shouldn't sit on the speaker, because it might bend the frame.

frequency: n. the number of times per second an audio or radio wave cycles

He couldn't hear the dog whistle, because the frequency was much too high.

frequency generator: *see* tone generator

frequency modulation: n. a method of adding audio to a radio frequency carrier signal that varies the phase of the carrier (rather than producing a change of level as in amplitude modulation)

frequency response: n. a measure of what frequencies are produced, amplified, processed, or detected by an electronic device

The frequency response of most audio power amps is at least 20Hz to 20kHz.

function generator: *see* tone generator

fuse: n. a device designed to disconnect (open) when a predetermined current level passes through it for a specific amount of time

The excessive current through the circuit caused the fuse to open.

gain: n. a measure of the increase (or lack thereof) of a signal through a circuit

The signal got much louder due to the high gain of the amplifier.

gap: n. the space between the magnet and pole piece of a speaker, where the voice coil is situated

After dropping the speaker one too many times, the magnet shifted and the voice coil would no longer move in the gap.

germanium: n. a material used to make solid-state components

The diodes in some old fuzz boxes are made of germanium.

Giga: prefix used in the metric system to designate ten to the ninth power

Two million Hertz equals two gigahertz.

graphic equalizer: n. a type of tone-shaping device usually using slider-type potentiometers where each slider is assigned a center frequency
There seemed to be some phase distortion introduced by the graphic equalizers he was using.

grid: n. one of the elements of a vacuum tube
By placing a bias voltage on the grid of a tube, the flow of electrons through the tube can be regulated.

ground: n. a constant source of zero volts
He made sure his distro had a good connection to ground to prevent hum problems.

harmonics: n. overtones of waves; frequencies that are multiples of the fundamental frequency
Two thousand Hz is a harmonic of 500Hz.

heat sink: n. a device, usually metal, attached to any component that tends to get hot in order to help dissipate the heat
The power supply regulators were mounted on a heat sink.

heater: *see* filament

Henry: n. the basic unit of inductance
The wah wah pedal used a 33-milliHenry inductor.

heptode: n. a multi-element tube
Heptodes are not used much in audio circuits.

Hertz: n. the unit of frequency
One thousand Hertz equals one thousand cycles per second.

heterodyne: v. The act of adding one frequency to another, resulting in additional frequencies
Heterodyning two frequencies together results in four frequencies being produced: The original two frequencies, the sum of the original frequencies, and the difference between the original frequencies.

high shelving: adj. a description of a type of filter circuit that cuts frequencies below a certain point but doesn't change frequencies above that point
Most guitar amps have high-shelving treble controls.

high-cut: adj. a type of filter circuit that decreases the frequencies above a certain point but doesn't effect frequencies below that point
A high-shelving filter is different from a high-cut filter.

high-fidelity: adj. a term used to describe audio components that attempt to introduce as little tonal change and coloration as possible
Music sounds better through high-fidelity equipment.

hot: adj. having a high temperature;
n. the positive-phase signal carrying wires in an audio cable

The amp got quite hot when we accidentally connected the speaker's hot wire to ground.

humbucking (pickup): adj. description of a guitar pickup utilizing two coils wound in opposite directions to reduce hum

Many guitars have humbucking pickups installed at the factory.

hyper-cardioid: adj. shaped like an exaggerated heart (*see* cardioid)

The hyper-cardioid polar pattern of the microphone did a great job of rejecting off-axis signals.

I.C. *see* integrated circuit

impedance: n. the resistance of AC circuits (*see* resistance)

The amplifier shut down due to the extremely low impedance of the speaker line.

in phase: *see* coherent

inductor: n. an electronic component made of coiled wire, used in AC circuits, useful in filter circuits

The low frequencies in the speaker crossover pass through an inductor.

infrared: n. a type of light that is higher-frequency than humans can see, but is detectable electronically

The remote-control unit on most VCRs emit infrared pulses that are detected by the VCR.

integrated circuit: n. a device that contains all of the components of a circuit, encapsulated as a single unit

Instead of three transistors, ten resistors, and various other parts, they used an integrated circuit.

inverse: adj. the opposite of

In addition to the regular signal, there was an inverse signal, and the two signals canceled out.

junction: n. a place in a diode or transistor where the positive doped (P) and negative doped (N) silicon materials come together

A bipolar transistor has two junctions.

Kilo: prefix used in metric measurements to designate ten to the third power

One thousand watts equals one kilowatt.

lamp: n. a light bulb

He replaced the burned out lamp in his guitar amp so he could tell when it was turned on.

large-scale integrated circuit (LSI): *see* integrated circuit

laser: n. an acronym for Light Amplification by Stimulated Emission of Radiation, a device for transforming incoherent light rays into a very narrow, focused, coherent light beam
Laser diodes generate low-power laser beams, which are used to read the information from CDs.

leg: n. a portion of a circuit that branches off and eventually returns to ground
Each leg of the circuit had the same voltage present.

light emitting diode (LED): n. a diode whose junction emits visible light rays
The power indicators on a lot of electronic equipment are LEDs.

line level: n. a standard voltage level where 0dBu equals .707 volts RMS
Most signal-processing equipment has line-level inputs and outputs.

load: n. the resistance or impedance of a circuit or part of a circuit
As long as the total load stays constant, the current through the circuit won't change.

logarithm: n. a trigonomic mathematic function
Logarithms are used to simplify large exponential numbers to make them easier to deal with in electronic formulas, especially formulas dealing with decibels.

logarithmic: adj. *see* logarithm
Logarithmic taper variable resistors change value at a non-linear rate as they are turned because our ears don't detect changes in volume or loudness linearly.

low shelving: adj. a type of filter circuit that reduces all of the frequencies below a certain frequency without effecting the frequencies above it
Many guitar amps use a low-shelving filter on their bass control.

lumen: n. a measurement of light intensity
Many light bulbs have their light output in lumens listed on the package.

magnet: n. a piece of metal that has the property of attracting ferrous metal
The heavy part of a dynamic speaker is a permanent magnet.

magnetic field: n. the area around a magnet or current-carrying wire that exhibits the properties of magnetism
If you place a wire inside an expanding or contracting magnetic field, a current will be induced into the wire.

maintenance: v. the act of adjusting, repairing or cleaning equipment in order to prolong its useful life
Every third month we take everything out of the truck and perform routine maintenance on it.

Mega, or Meg: prefix used in metric measurements to indicate ten to the sixth power

One million ohms is one Megohm.

metric system: n. the system of measurements preferred by the scientific community, where all units are divisable by ten

Measurements made using the metric system are compatible with any other metric measurements.

meter: n. an indicating device, also a piece of test equipment designed to make and display measurements

He used a volt meter to test the power onstage before connecting it to his equipment.

micro: prefix used in the metric system to indicate 10 to the negative sixth power, or one-millionth

One-millionth of a joule equals one microjoule.

microphone: n. a device that senses changes in air pressure and converts them to an electrical current

Please speak directly into the microphone.

microphonic: adj. having the (usually unwanted) characteristics of a microphone

Those tubes seem to be microphonic, and should be replaced.

MIDI: acronym for Musical Instrument Digital Interface; a standardized serial communication method for electronic musical instruments

He played huge-sounding chords on his keyboard by linking several sound modules together using MIDI.

milli: prefix used in the metric system to indicate 10 to the power of -3

One one-thousandth of an amp is one milliamp.

modulate: v. to mix one AC signal with another AC signal, causing a variation

FM radio transmitters modulate the phase of a carrier frequency.

monitor: n. a speaker or video display placed in such a way as to allow the user to hear/see a signal that is being reproduced elsewhere; v. to listen to/see the above-mentioned signal

I'll monitor the action in studio nine on my video monitor.

monophonic: adj. having only one output

The synthesizer could only play one note at a time because it was monophonic.

multitimbral: adj. being capable of reproducing more than one sound at a time

The multitimbral synth was producing the piano, drum, bass, and organ sounds simultaneously.

nano: prefix used in the metric system indicating 10 to the negative ninth power

One-billionth of one Weber is one nanoWeber.

neutral: adj. neither positive nor negative; n. the conductor in an AC power circuit that has the same potential and phase relationship to the other (hot) lines in the circuit

With the ground and neutral lines properly connected in a circuit, there should be no shock hazard.

nickel-cadmium: n. common construction materials for rechargeable batteries

They saved a lot of money at the church by using nickel-cadmium batteries in their wireless transmitter.

noise: n. the (hopefully) low-level static sound generated by electronic equipment

With the volume all the way down, there was still a small amount of noise coming from the speakers.

nominal: adj. the average value of a property in a component or circuit, somewhere between the minimum and maximum levels

The nominal impedance of a speaker might not be its actual impedance at one particular frequency.

normal: adj. the position a switch's contacts are in before the switch is thrown

The keyboard's sustain pedal was a normally closed (N/C) style switch.

new old stock (NOS): adj. any component, especially a tube, that was made sometime in the past but has not been used yet

She felt lucky to have found some NOS tubes for her favorite antique guitar amp.

nucleus: n. the center of an atom

Electrons orbit around the nucleus of an atom.

odd-order harmonics: *see* harmonics

ohm: n. the basic unit of measurement of resistance or impedance

The resistor's value was ten ohms.

Ohm's law: n. the mathematical relationship between power, current, resistance and voltage

He found the correct value of the fuse for the circuit by using Ohm's law.

open: n. a missing or broken connection in a circuit

The speaker wouldn't produce sound due to an open voice coil.

open-load: adj. without being connected to a load device

The tube amp got hot and blew a fuse because it had been run open-load.

opto-coupler: n. a device that houses a light source and a light-sensing device in the same package

The channel switching in some amplifiers is accomplished by the use of opto-couplers.

oscillation: *see* feedback

oscillator: n. a circuit or device that produces a wave signal

Early synths used voltage-controlled analog oscillators to generate the tones.

out of phase: adj. more than one signal being in a state of incoherence, usually by 180°

The two signal lines of a balanced mic cable are 180° out of phase.

over-excursion: v. to move beyond the recommended point of travel, as in a speaker voice coil

If the speaker cone should over-excursion, it may be the last time it makes a sound.

overdrive: v. to drive an input beyond the limits of its ability to reproduce an undistorted signal

By cranking the preamp volume to maximum, he was able to overdrive the output driver stage of his amp.

oxidation: n. the thin film formed when some metals are exposed to oxygen in the air (commonly known as rust on ferric metals and tarnish on copper or brass)

The volume control of his bass sounded noisy when it was turned due to the oxidation on the wiper contact.

P.A.: *see* public address system

parallel: adj. connected to a common pair of terminals

The lights were wired in parallel, so if one was to burn out, the other would remain functional.

parametric equalizer: n. a type of tone filter circuit where the center frequency and the boost/cut are variable

Some mixing consoles use parametric equalizer circuits in their tone control sections.

passive: adj. lacking the capability of adding gain to a signal

The passive tone controls in most guitars cannot boost frequencies.

patch: n. a set of parameters that produce a specific tone in a synthesizer

Many newer synths have extensive patch memories.

patch bay: n. an arrangement of connectors configured to make it easy to connect various components together

He connected another digital reverb unit to the board using the external patch bay.

peak: n. the highest amplitude portion of an AC signal

Clipping occurs when the peak of a signal exceeds the power-supply voltage.

peak music power: n. a false power measurement used to confuse an ignorant buying public

This amp puts out 10 watts RMS, but over 1,000 watts of peak music power! Yeah, right.

peak-to-peak: n. the measurement from the highest positive peak to the lowest negative peak of an AC signal

Ten volts peak is twenty volts peak-to-peak, AC.

pentode: n. a multi-element tube

The amp's output tubes were a pentode configuration.

phantom power: adj. a type of power supply remote from the device being powered, often used with condenser microphones

The microphone got its operating voltage from the phantom-power supply built into the mixer.

phase: n. a state of an AC signal in relation to a reference or another AC signal

By reversing the phase of one microphone signal, the soundman made the snare drum sound more crisp.

phase-coherent: *see* coherent

photo resistor: n. a device whose resistance varies with exposure to light

A photo resistor senses when the sun comes up, and the porch light shuts off.

photo transistor: n. a transistor that is light-sensitive; *see* photo resistor

The auto exposure control in the camera used a photo transistor to sense the amount of light present.

pickup coil: n. a coil of wire wrapped around a magnetic pole piece used to sense vibration of metal strings on musical instruments

The guitar had a dynamic pickup coil under the strings.

pico: prefix used in the metric system indicating ten to the negative twelfth power

One trillionth of one Farad is one picoFarad.

pinch roller: n. the rubber roller that presses the tape against the capstan in a tape transport mechanism

The tape speed was inconsistent due to the dirty pinch roller.

plate: n. one of the elements of a vacuum tube; slang term for reverb (early reverb units utilized a large metal plate to produce the effect)

Due to a lack of bias, the tube's plate was glowing red-hot.

polar pattern: n. the diagram showing the directions from which sound can be picked up by a microphone

He could tell by the polar pattern of his new mic that it was omni-directional.

polarity: adj. the condition of being positive or negative in a circuit
   He forgot to check the polarity of the capacitor, and when he powered up the circuit, it exploded.
pole: n. a terminal of an electronic device
   The lamp was connected to the positive pole of the battery.
pole piece: n. the magnetic metal parts of a pickup coil
   Some pickups have two pole pieces for each string.
polyphonic: adj. the capability of producing more than one note at one time
   Early synthesizers were not polyphonic; they only played one note at a time.
post-fader: adj. occurring (in the signal flow) after the main channel volume of a mixer channel
   The auxiliary send is post-fader on most mixers.
potential: n. the difference in electrical charges between two points, like the poles of a battery
   The battery terminal had a 9-volt potential with respect to ground.
potentiometer: n. a variable resistor
   He increased the volume of his amp by turning the level control potentiometer.
power: n. the term for energy used in an electronic circuit, measured in watts
   The power rating of the guitar amp is 100 watts into a 4-ohm load.
power-distribution system: n. a device that divides 220-volt two- or three-phase AC down to 117-volt AC
   He built an 8-channel 100-amp power-distribution system for use with his lighting equipment.
powered mixer: n. a mic mixer that includes one or more onboard power amplifiers
   Although they had a large sound system, they used a small powered mixer for practicing.
pre-fader: adj. occurring (in the signal flow) before the main channel volume of a mixer channel
   Many mixers have a pre-fader monitor bus.
primary: n. the input side of a transformer
   Although there was 100 volts on the primary, the output of the transformer was only 10 volts.
probe: n. the metal end of a test lead used with a meter or other piece of test equipment
   The black probe of a meter is usually connected to negative or ground.

public address system: n. a sound-enhancement system used to enable announcements, musical performances, etc., to be heard by large groups of people

He ran his tape of dogs barking Christmas carols through a public address system, so his neighbors could enjoy it, too.

pulsating DC: n. half-wave rectified, unfiltered AC current

By connecting a diode to the AC voltage, it was rectified to half-wave pulsating DC.

pulse power supply: n. a type of power supply that uses a high-frequency oscillator instead of a standard 60Hz AC source

Some power amps have pulse power supplies to reduce their size and weight.

quality, or "Q": n. the degree of filtering in a filter circuit

Some tone controls work better than others because they have a higher "Q."

rack cabinet: n. a box for housing standard 19-inch rack-mountable equipment

All of his front of house processing fits in a 16-space rack cabinet.

radiate: v. to emit, as in heat or RF energy

The massive heat sinks on the amplifier allow the transistors to radiate their heat without being damaged.

radio frequency (RF): n. any frequency signal above about 100kHz, but below light frequencies

The speed of radio frequency signals through a vacuum is 300,000,000 meters per second.

radio waves *see* radio frequency

random access memory (RAM): n. the part of a computer's memory where data can be stored or retrieved, also called read/write memory

The user-programmable patch information in a synthesizer is stored in RAM.

receiver: n. the part of a radio system that picks up the signal from the atmosphere and converts it back to audio

Don't take only the transmitter from your wireless to the repairman, because he can't test it without the receiver.

rectifier: n. a diode or several diodes used to change AC to DC

The shorted power rectifier blew the fuse in the amp.

relay: n. an electronically activated switch

Power was directed to the circuit through a relay contact.

resistance: n. a measure of the ability of a device or devices to impede the progression of electrons in a circuit

The light glowed dimly due to the high resistance of the wiring.

resistor: n. a device that reduces electrical current flow in a circuit by converting some or all of the current into power

The current from the power supply was dropped to 12 volts by a series pass resistor.

return: n. an input signal path, usually part of a loop in an amp or mixer

The effects were routed back into the mixer through the return jack.

rheostat: n. a type of variable resistor; *see* potentiometer

A rheostat controlled the brightness of the lights on the large microphone mixer.

RMS *see* root-mean-square

rolled-off: v. having been reduced

The high frequencies were rolled-off by the filters in the EQ.

Root-Mean-Square (RMS): n. the square root of the average of several measurements taken over a specific period of time

The voltage was 100 volts peak, or 70.7 volts RMS.

sample: v. to digitize and store an analog signal; n. the name of the stored digitized signal

He digitally sampled the sound of a frog, and then played back the sample in his sister's bathroom as she took a bath.

sampler: n. a device used to digitize and store analog signals for later playback

He sampled the frog's sounds using a digital sampler.

schematic: n. a diagram showing the interconnections of an electronic circuit

She was able to pinpoint the problem in her guitar by tracing the signal path on the schematic.

screen grid: n. an element of a vacuum tube

The pentode didn't amplify because the screen grid voltage was missing.

secondary: n. the output side of a transformer

Although there were 100 volts on the primary, there were only 10 volts present on the secondary of the transformer.

send: n. the output of an effects or other loop in audio equipment

He had connected the input of his effects processor to the effects send of his mixer.

series: adj. a circuit configuration where the components are connected end to end, causing the same current to pass through all of the components

His speaker cabinet was wired in series, so when one speaker failed, they all stopped working.

seventy-volt line: n. a high-voltage speaker-distribution system that allows many speakers to be connected to one amplifier through impedance transformers

They wired the grocery store's fifty-seven speakers using a seventy-volt line.

shelving *see* high- or low- shelving

short: n. a connection from one part of a circuit to another, which bypasses part or all of a circuit

The screwdriver fell into the amp, shorting the positive power supply to ground and blowing the fuse.

shunt: v. to pass current to ground or around part of a circuit

A passive crossover works by shunting unwanted frequencies to ground.

silicon: n. a material used to make solid-state devices

Integrated circuits are often made from a single wafer of silicon.

skin effect: n. the phenomenon of electron flow tending to occur toward the outer "skin" of large-diameter wire

The use of multi-stranded wire reduces the skin effect.

snake cable: n. a multiconductor cable used to direct the signal of multiple devices simultaneously

All thirty-four microphone signals were routed to the front house mixer through the snake cable.

solenoid: n. an electromagnetic device utilizing a coil of wire and a metal plunger; the plunger is drawn into the center of the coil when current is applied to the coil

The current through the relay's solenoid pulled the contacts together.

solid-state: adj. the condition of an electronic component having no moving parts or open spaces

Two pieces of oppositely doped silicon, bonded together, form a solid-state diode.

sound: n. audible vibrations in the atmosphere

In outer space, no one can hear you scream, since there must be air to transmit sound.

sound pressure level (SPL): n. the degree to which a sound changes the air pressure, directly corresponding to the loudness of the sound

She put her hands over her ears to reduce the sound pressure level of the jet engine.

sound reinforcement: v. increasing the loudness of sounds by use of amplification devices and speakers

He made sure the band was loud enough by running all of their instruments through a sound reinforcement system.

spectrum: n. a range of frequencies

Very few people can actually hear the entire audio frequency spectrum of 20Hz to 20kHz.

speed of light: n. the speed at which light travels through a vacuum: 300,000,000 meters (186,000 miles) per second

Radio waves in a vacuum travel at the speed of light.

SPL: *see* sound pressure level

splitter: n. a device used to divide a signal so it can be sent to two different destinations

The keyboard signal was divided using a splitter, so it could be sent to the main mixer, as well as the monitor amp.

spool: v. the act of wrapping recording tape around a reel

He watched with satisfaction as the tape spooled neatly on the take up reel.

stable: adj. a state of being unchanged

The circuit became much less stable as the unit got hot.

stamped frame: *see* cast frame

standby: v. a mode of operation of some tube amps where the filaments are energized and heating the tubes' cathodes, but plate voltage to one or more stages has not yet been applied

He switched his amp to standby when the band went on break.

steady-state: adj. constant, unchanging, as a sine wave signal that doesn't vary in level or frequency

The soundman stopped using a steady-state tone to test the system's levels after the bar's customers threatened to end his life.

step-down: adj. a type of transformer where the primary voltage is higher than the secondary voltage

The AC from the power pole is reduced to 220 volts by a step-down transformer before it enters your house.

step-up: adj. a type of transformer where the primary voltage is lower than the secondary voltage

The voltage is increased at the power station by use of step-up transformers.

subwoofer: n. a speaker cabinet designed to reproduce very low frequencies, usually below 250Hz

The music sounded full and rich due to the addition of subwoofers to the system.

suppressor grid: n. an element of an electron tube

By adding a suppressor grid to a tube, the tube can direct more electrons to the plate, thereby increasing efficiency.

sweepable: adj. having a continuously variable center frequency, as in a parametric EQ

The new board had standard high-shelving controls, plus sweepable mids and lows.

switch: n. A device that opens (disconnects) or closes (connects) a circuit, or circuits

The amp came on when he turned on the power switch.

switching: adj. a type of power supply circuit; *see* pulse power supply

Some amps use a switching power supply to reduce weight.

synthesizer: n. a musical instrument that electronically emulates existing sounds, or allows the user to invent new sounds

He managed to make his synthesizer sound very much like a pair of tennis shoes in a dryer.

taper: n. the variation and degree of gradation of a potentiometer's resistive element

The new volume control seemed to jump suddenly from no volume to full volume, because it was not the correct taper.

test equipment: n. any of a variety of electronic devices used to analyze, troubleshoot, or measure the functions of other electronic equipment

An oscilloscope, VOM, tone generator, and logic probe are good pieces of test equipment for a full-service repair shop to have on hand.

tetrode: n. a type of electronic vacuum tube

Tubes with four elements are called tetrodes, and are not used much in audio gear.

thermal: adj. an intermittent problem having to do with the temperature of the equipment

The amp had a thermal problem and shut itself off when it got too hot.

thermo-coupler: n. a temperature-dependent circuit breaker

The heat sink got hotter than 160°, so the thermo-coupler opened, shutting off the amp.

throw: v. the act of engaging a switch

You'll have to throw the switch if you want the light to come on.

time-aligned: adj. description of a multiple speaker system where the drivers are placed in such a way that the different frequencies arrive at the listening position in phase with each other

The tweeters were placed back from the woofers a bit in order to time-align the system.

tin: n. a type of metal used (with lead) to make solder; v. the act of putting some solder on a contact or wire before soldering the connection

It is a good idea to tin contacts with solder made of a mixture of tin and lead.

tolerance: n. the percentage of error allowed in the manufacture of electronic components

No two production amps will ever sound exactly alike, due to tolerances in the components used to manufacture them.

tone: n. the timbre of a signal, also a steady-state signal

His guitar's tone was very similar to that of a chainsaw.

tone generator: n. a signal-producing piece of test equipment

He found that the power amp section of his amp was functional by injecting a tone generator signal into the effects return jack.

tone shaping: *see* filtering

torque: n. a measurable amount of rotational pressure

The cassette deck was chewing up her tapes because it didn't have enough take-up torque.

trace: n. a copper circuit path on a circuit board; v. to follow a signal path to discover where a signal is missing

He placed the probe of the oscilloscope on the trace of the circuit board to try to find his missing signal.

transducer: n. any device used to change energy from one form to another

A speaker is a dynamic transducer, which changes electrical energy (current) to mechanical energy (sound).

transformer: n. an electrical device consisting of two coils of wire wrapped around a common core; the electromagnetic field generated by the current through one coil transfers into the other coil, generating a proportional current

The AC voltage from the wall socket was reduced for use in the calculator by using a transformer.

transient: n. a short attack, short decay signal

There was a loud transient generated when the tipsy woman tripped and knocked over the microphone stand.

transistor: n. a solid-state device, usually made of silicon or germanium, used to control the flow of current in a circuit

The power-supply voltage was stabilized by using regulator transistors.

transmitter: n. the part of a wireless system that generates radio frequency waves

The wireless mic stopped functioning because the transmitter had been dropped too many times.

transmission: n. a signal or current sent from an originating point to a different destination

The metal building was blocking the antenna from receiving the wireless transmission.

trimmer: *see* potentiometer

triode: n. a type of electronic vacuum tube

Many of the preamp tubes used in tube guitar amps are dual triodes.

troubleshooting: v. the act of finding out what the problem is in a piece of equipment

She found the intermittent problem in her P.A. system by using the logical troubleshooting techniques learned in this book.

tube: n. an electronic device that transfers electrons from one element to another, through an evacuated space

Many amplifiers use vacuum tubes instead of transistors.

tune: v. the act of adjusting a component to work with a specific frequency or band of frequencies

The operation of your wireless receiver is best if it was properly tuned at the factory.

Ultra High Frequency (UHF): n. a specific frequency band as specified by the FCC

Many FM wireless units operate in the UHF range.

vacuum: n. any space having very few or no atoms present

Radio waves move at the speed of light through a vacuum.

valve: *see* tube

variable resistor: *see* potentiometer

variac: n. a variable autotransformer, useful as a level-adjusting device for AC signals

He simulated low-voltage conditions on the test bench by using a variac.

Very Large Scale Integrated circuit (VLSI): *see* integrated circuit

Very High Frequency (VHF): n. a set frequency range established by the FCC

Some television signals are transmitted in the VHF range.

voice coil: n. the current-carrying part of a speaker, situated in the gap of the permanent magnet

Too much current can damage a speaker's voice coil.

voltage: n. the measurement of the potential between two electrical points

As the battery slowly went dead, the voltage dropped to zero.

voltage-controlled amplifier (VCA): n. a circuit used in the ADSR section of a synthesizer, or in the gain circuit of some audio mixers, which uses a voltage to control the gain of an amplifier, and hence the level of an audio signal

He was able to adjust the level characteristics of each tone in his synth with the voltage-controlled amplifier.

voltage-controlled filter (VCF): n. a circuit used in the ADSR section of a synthesizer that controls the tonal quality of a signal
He was able to adjust the tonal characteristics of his synth with the voltage-controlled filter.

voltage-controlled oscillator (VCO): n. a circuit used in the ADSR section of a synthesizer that controls the frequency of a signal
She was able to adjust the pitch of her synth with the voltage-controlled oscillator.

voltage gain: n. a measurement of the increase of the voltage of a signal through a circuit, or circuits—usually measured in decibels
His preamp produced a voltage gain in the neighborhood of 55dB.

wall-wart: n. a slang term for a power supply or adaptor that plugs into an AC outlet
When he set up his equipment he was careful to use the correct wall-wart adaptor for each of the pieces of equipment in his rack.

watt: n. the unit of measurement of power
The light bulb produced 60 watts of power.

wave: n. one cycle of any repeating frequency
One wave of an audio frequency is made up of 360°.

wavelength: n. the distance a wave will travel in the time it takes to complete one cycle of its frequency
The higher the frequency of a wave, the shorter its wavelength.

wiper: n. the movable part of a variable resistor that contacts the resistive element
The output of the guitar decreased as he moved the volume control's wiper closer to ground.

wireless: n. synonym for radio transmission/reception
A common table radio is a wireless receiver.

word: n. a collection of bits of data, usually in groups of eight, also called a byte
MIDI transmits at least three digital words with every key played.

XLR connector: n. a locking, multi-pin audio signal connector
XLR plugs and sockets are often used to connect microphone and line-level audio signals in sound systems and recording studios.

zener: n. short for zener diode, a device that passes current only above a specific voltage level
The voltage in the power supply was stable, thanks to the zener diode regulator.

INDEX

Total Harmonic Distortion (THD), 205
trace, 181
transducers, 117, 119
  dynamic, 67–71
  piezo-electric, 71–72
transformers, 38–39
  direct boxes and, 195
  in power supplies, 101
  for seventy-volt line systems, 52
  tube amps and, 98, 156
transients, 161
transistors, 19, 23–24
  case styles, 24
  photo, 29
  preamps and, 90
  in solid-state amplifiers, 99–100
transmitters, wireless, 75–78
triacs, 29
triodes, 79–80, 82–83
troubleshooting
  hints on, 182–83
  signal flow and, 131–32, 169–70, 183
  substitution and, 132, 167
TRS connectors. *See* tip/ring/sleeve (TRS) connectors
tubes, 79–87
  amplifiers powered by, 96, 100, 156
  branding of, 86
  construction of, 79–80
  designations for, 84
  functioning of, 81–84
  life of, 87
  preamps and, 90
  problems with, 85–86
  testers for, 84–85
tweeters
  frames of, 68
  piezo-electric, 71–72
  size of, 42
  testing of, 46

Ultra High Frequency (UHF), 75
UniVox, 111

Vacuum Tube Volt Meter (VTVM), 178
vacuum tubes, 22, 80
valves. *See* tubes
Van Halen, Eddie, 208
variac, 208
Vaughn, Stevie Ray, 208
Velcro strips, 211
velocity sensitivity, 112
Very High Frequency (VHF), 75
Very Large Scale Integrated Circuits (VLSIs), 25
vocals, mics for, 128, 138
voice coil, 45–46, 68, 159, 160, 161–62, 181, 202
Volt-Ohm-Milliammeter (VOM), 178
voltage. *See also* electromotive force (EMF)
  AC and, 37–39
  bias, 97–98
  in circuits, 32, 34–36, 40
  fluctuations in, 153–54, 155, 156
  impedance and, 48–51

input sensitivity, 201
  junction, 94
  measurement of, 179
  of NiCad batteries, 63
  resistors and, 19–21
  signal levels and, 217–18
  in solid-state amp, 99
  testing in tubes, 85
  in transformers, 38–39, 52
  of tubes, 80
voltage-controlled amplifier (VCA), 110
voltage-controlled filter (VCF), 110
voltage-controlled oscillator (VCO) circuit, 110
voltage output, 209
volume controls, 91–93, 95, 126, 128

wall warts, 39, 209
warranties, 184–85
watts, 34
  output power and, 204–5
wax cylinders, 117
weight, 206
Westinghouse, George, 38
Winter, Johnny, 208
wipers
  in guitar, 144, 146
  in resistors, 20–21, 91–92
wire-strippers, 174
wireless data transmission
  in-ear monitoring, 78
  IR diodes in, 23
  problems in, 76–77
  quality and, 77
  radio waves and, 73–75
  systems, 75
wiring
  color codes, 133, 192
  of connectors, 198–200
  extension cords, 154
  gauges, 191
  guide to, 189–91
  guitar, 144–48
  parallel, for speakers, 46–47
  power, 191–93
  resistance in, 36
  series, for speakers, 46–47
  seventy-volt line systems, 52
  in sound systems, 132–33
  tinning, 174, 200
woodwinds, mics for, 137
woofers, size of, 42
words, 105
wow, 120

XLR (Cannon) connectors, 54, 139, 198–99

Yamaha, 111, 112–13

zener diodes, 23
zinc, 32
zip ties, 211